"To the Memory
of my Mother and Father"

# THE STORY OF GALLOWAY

By
John F Robertson

Colour Pictures by
T C B Phin

# INTRODUCTION

In welcoming this reprint of "The Story of Galloway", it might be appropriate first of all to say a few words about its inception and purpose.

"The Story of Galloway" first appeared in weekly serial form in "The Galloway News" during the years 1962-3 and it was immediately published in book form in the autumn of 1963. A second edition appeared the following year and a third in 1971.

This present edition is an exact reprint of the text of the original except for the last chapter which has been rewritten to give a more general account of the changes which have occurred in the present century and bring the story up to date.

"The Story of Galloway" is an attempt to give an account in narrative form of life in Galloway in different stages of its development. With this end in view, therefore, only those aspects of its political, economic and religious history which seriously affected the actual lives and customs of the inhabitants have been dealt with. For example, the impact of the Bruce-Baliol struggle and the influence of the Douglas family, although political in nature, had a profound effect on the ordinary people of the province. Similarly, the troubles which arose during the reformation and covenanting times, although part of church history, disrupted the whole life and economy of Galloway for over a hundred and fifty years. Wherever possible, however, emphasis has been laid on the social life of the people.

I should like to remind readers that this work is essentially a "story" and not a "history", since it allows me greater freedom in my method of narration. In the early chapters of the book — those dealing with prehistoric times and the Dark Ages — where documentary evidence was either non-existent or, at the best, somewhat nebulous, I have taken the liberty of attempting to "dramatise" or relate events as they might have happened, but still within the framework of what is known about the events themselves and the people concerned in them. In the Middle Ages, where factual history and legend become inextricably entwined, I have tried in the course of the narrative to distinguish between the two. From Chapter XV (Town and Trade) onwards it has been possible to refer to historical records and statistics to illustrate the story, and these sources have been acknowledged in the text.

It must be remembered that the geographical position of Galloway, round the corner from the main north-south line and bounded by hills to the north and east and by the sea to the south and west, has been responsible for many peculiarities in the way in which it has developed. It remained fiercely independent when the rest of Scotland was united; the influence of England predominated at many stages of its history; its proximity to Ireland has led to a continuous flow of immigrants for several thousand years; and, despite its central position in the British Isles, Galloway was almost completely unaffected by the Industrial Revolution and its unwelcome side-effects.

Until the middle of the eighteenth century the province remained essentially a rural and somewhat isolated agricultural community. Since then, however, the advent of the railway and the motor car has changed all that. Galloway may be still round the corner geographically, but it is no longer cut off from the rest of Britain; and it is this fact that has had the most influence in shaping the story of Galloway during the present century.

Finally, I should like to take this opportunity of thanking an old friend and colleague of my Galloway days for his contribution to this reprint: Mr.T.C.B.Phin for his attractive colour photographs on the cover.

John F.Robertson

Banff,
August, 1985.

"THE STORY OF GALLOWAY".
Published by Lang Syne Publishers Ltd., 45 Finnieston Street, Glasgow G3 8JU.
Printed by Dave Barr Print, 45 Finnieston Street, Glasgow G3 8JU.

Colour pictures by T.C.B. Phin. Chapter end illustrations by Ken Lochhead whose works are available as individual prints. This is a facsimile of the 1963 edition published by J.H.Maxwell Ltd., Castle Douglas and we would like to thank their successors Scottish and Universal Newspapers and Mr. Robertson for consenting to a new edition. The author has prepared a new introduction, population table and In Conclusion Chapter which brings the Story of Galloway up to date. Photographs from the original edition are not included and the index does not account for new points featured in the final chapter.
First published 1985. Reprinted 1994
ISBN N0. 0946 264 49 X

# CONTENTS


Chapter Title Page

**I—THE STONE AGE** ........................................ **17**

The earliest inhabitants — Fishers and hunters — The earliest farmers.

**II—THE METAL AGES** ........................................ **22**

Bronze brings civilisation nearer — Tribes and villages in the Iron Age.

**III—THE ROMANS IN GALLOWAY** .................... **26**

Natives taken by surprise — The tribes accept the Romans as masters — Conquest of Galloway completed — Roman influence on Galloway.

**IV—ST. NINIAN — FOUNDER OF THE CHURCH IN SCOTLAND** ............................................ **30**

His boyhood at Whithorn — He decides to go to Rome — The religious centre of the Celtic world — A Christian stronghold in a pagan land.

**V—SEVEN CENTURIES OF INVASION** .............. **34**

The tribes build a great wall — The Angles invade from the east — "From the fury of the Northmen deliver us, O Lord!" — Galloway under the rule of the Vikings.

**VI—NORMAN CONQUEST OF GALLOWAY** ......... **40**

First Lord of Galloway — Fergus of Galloway defies the king — "A half-naked horde of savages" — Fergus founds many churches.

**VII—NORMAN SETTLEMENT OF GALLOWAY** ...... **45**

The great Mote of Urr — A century of change completed.

**VIII—ALAN THE GREAT — DEVORGILLA THE GOOD** ........................................................ **49**

Galloway navy in action — The Abbey of the Sweet Heart.

**IX—SOCIAL LIFE IN THE EARLY MIDDLE AGES** **54**

Castle and cottage — The state of agriculture — Galloway justice.

**X—GALLOWAY UNDER ENGLISH CONTROL** ...... **60**

"King Empty Jacket" — The English king in Galloway — English engineering feat.

**XI—THE BRUCES IN GALLOWAY** ....................... **66**

The murder of the Red Comyn — Trapped in the Galloway hills — Edward Bruce, Lord of Galloway.

**XII—THE RISE OF THE DOUGLASES** ................. **73**

The Douglas family tree — The last of the Baliols — Archibald the Grim.

**XIII—THE FALL OF THE DOUGLASES** ................ **80**

Conflict with the Crown — The ruthless earl — The last Lord of Galloway.

**XIV—THE CHURCH IN THE MIDDLE AGES** ........ **88**

Distinguished visitors to the abbey — The monks at work — The flying abbot.

Chapter Title Page

XV—TOWN AND TRADE .................................... 98

The earliest burghs — Trade brings wealth — The state of society — Early town and country planning.

XVI—THE REFORMATION .................................. 107

Its causes and beginnings — Galloway loyal to the queen — The Glenluce forgery — Disposal of Dundrennan and Sweetheart.

XVII—BAN THE BISHOPS .................................... 117

Episcopacy triumphant — Growing power of the parishes — Presbyterianism victorious.

XVIII—THE COVENANT GOES TO WAR ................ 127

The Stewartry War Committee — The covenanters under arms — A split in the covenant ranks — The extremists gain control.

XIX—THE PERSECUTION BEGINS ....................... 138

Restoration of the bishops — Economic ruin of Galloway — The Pentland Rising.

XX—THE COVENANT DEFIANT ......................... 151

The government shows toleration — "The Highland Host" — Bothwell Bridge.

XXI—THE KILLING TIMES .................................. 162

Merciless persecution by the courts — The blood of the martyrs — The seed of the Church.

XXII—FIFTY YEARS OF DEPRESSION ................... 176

Poverty-stricken peasantry — No trade or transport — The Levellers —A state of lawlessness.

XXIII—A CENTURY OF PROGRESS ...................... 187

Improvements in agriculture — Shipping and smuggling — Flourishing industries — The Kirk and the people — Some famous Gallovidians.

XXIV—IN CONCLUSION ........................................ 208

Galloway at the present day.

CHAPTER I

# THE STONE AGE

## THE EARLIEST INHABITANTS

ONE day, about 8,000 years ago, a fleet of tiny coracles might have been seen approaching the coast of Galloway. Far out in the North Channel, where the mighty Atlantic waves sweep round into the Irish Sea and Solway Firth, these frail vessels—nothing more than a frame of basketwork covered with skins—tossed and turned alarmingly as they pursued their erratic course eastwards.

One moment they were but a cluster of tiny specks on the crest of a wave, the next they had descended again into the trough of the waters. Seconds later, just as it seemed certain that they had at last been engulfed by the waves, they would re-appear momentarily, always nearer to the land.

Propelled by a brisk westerly wind, the coracles were driven quickly past the forbidding rocks of the Mull of Galloway, and soon they were gliding smoothly into the sheltered waters of Luce Bay.

The occupants of the coracles now had time to look around them. They paddled in a more leisurely manner, with just sufficient speed to hold a steady course up the west side of the bay. All the time they scanned the shores for a suitable landing place.

To these intrepid explorers the coast of Galloway presented a grim and inhospitable appearance. From the horizon far above to the very edge of the sea stretched a vast impenetrable forest. As the tide was full, no beaches could be seen, and the trees seemed to rise straight out of the waves along the margin of the bay.

Eventually the coracles reached the head of the bay. Inevitably their adventurous voyage had ended. The sailors disembarked in the shallow water and drew their boats up on to the narrow strip of turf.

The first human beings ever to walk on the soil of Galloway had arrived.

For some time before this a colony of Stone Age people had been living at Larne, on the sea-coast of Northern Ireland. About

6,000 B.C. a number of these folk became dissatisfied with their life there and decided to make a move.

One can only guess what motives drove them to risk their lives to the mercy of the sea in such fragile craft. Perhaps the colony at Larne was becoming overcrowded and they sought more living-room. More probably it was simply a "wander-lust," that seemingly irresistible force which has impelled adventurous spirits, during all ages of history, to court the danger and experience the excitement of exploring and conquering new lands.

From their home in Ireland, the Mull of Galloway and the Mull of Kintyre appeared as fingers beckoning on these daring families to brave the twenty-mile crossing and seek a new country. Two groups of Larnians who accepted the challenge succeeded in overcoming all the dangers, and the earliest human settlements in Scotland were founded at Campbeltown and Luce Bay.

It is thus quite possible that those people who landed at Luce Bay were also the first human inhabitants of Scotland.

## FISHERS AND HUNTERS

Life in the Stone Age followed a regular and uncomplicated pattern. It was simply a never-ending search for food. These earliest settlers knew nothing of agriculture and depended for their food on fishing and hunting. But, since their weapons were made only of stone or bone, the pursuit of game or the catching of fish was by no means an easy matter, although there were abundant supplies of both.

At that time the effects of the last Ice Age were still being felt around the coast of Scotland, and seals and whales—often stranded when the tide ebbed—were frequently obtained. Shell-fish, of many different varieties, was their most common fare. The dense forest, which covered the whole country, abounded in game, but the Luce Bay people were fishers rather than hunters and, except for deer, did not eat much meat.

It is probable that their food was eaten raw. Although they had fires, they did not possess utensils to cook anything in, and in any case cooking was probably considered an unnecessary refinement. In fact, the discovery of cooking was possibly made quite unintentionally, when a piece of meat fell accidently into the fire and it was noticed that its flavour was thereby improved.

Their weapons and tools were crude, but many of them, especially those of stone, were quite beautifully made. The colony at Larne was renowned for the quality of its manufacture of flint tools, and some of the migrants to Galloway were undoubtedly experts in this craft. Arrow-heads, knives, borers and scrapers (for dressing animal skins) were cunningly fashioned from flint and fitted with wooden handles. One of the finest remaining examples of these Luce Bay craftsmen is a flint saw-blade with 35 teeth, all regular in size, in a length of 1¾ inches. Bones from large animals or whales were sharpened by flint knives and made into spears and harpoons.

Animal skins, sewn after a fashion with bone needles and strips of leather, provided their only clothing. Since no instruments were available, their hair was un-trimmed and their faces unshaven. Many of them, however, were at considerable pains to enhance their appearance with the aid of necklaces of teeth or shells, bracelets and rings of bone, and no doubt, in due season, garlands of flowers or berries.

The colony gradually increased in numbers and some of them seem to have migrated to the shores of Loch Ryan, near Stranraer. It is equally probable that others made their way along the eastern shores of Luce Bay and possibly settled in other parts of the Solway coast as well.

Unless the Luce Bay colonists died out—and there is no reason to suppose they did—they remained there for the next 4,000 years, and during that time their mode of life remained completely unchanged.

Several hundred years after the migrants from Larne there came a second wave of Stone Age people, again by sea, but this time from England. These latest in-comers, however, were hunters rather than fishermen for they established themselves not on the coast, but further inland.

The great forest which covered Galloway at that time formed an impenetrable barrier to people whose only tools were of stone or bone. On the high ground grew birch and pine trees, and in the river valleys gigantic oaks and elms. In the great oak forest of the Cree valley there were trees whose trunks were 15 feet in girth and 50 feet in length. Everywhere there was a dense undergrowth of hazel, alder and other smaller trees and shrubs. The only means of access to the interior was by the rivers, and it is in the valleys of the Cree and Dee that traces of these Stone Age hunters have been found.

In the depths of the forest lurked animals of many kinds. Red deer, roe deer, reindeer and elk were the most common. More difficult to capture were the wild pig, the giant long-horned ox and the brown bear. Animals of prey included the wolf and the lynx. Like many primitive peoples, these Galloway hunters often killed animals by means of traps—deep pits dug in the ground and camouflaged with grass. Fish was also a regular item on their menu, for the streams and lochs abounded in salmon and trout. For dessert they had, in season, a plentiful supply of fresh fruit, berries and nuts.

It is clear that they were a different race from the Larnians who came to Luce Bay, for these forest-dwellers had no knowledge of the use of flint in tool-making. Instead their weapons were most commonly made from the bones, antlers or horns of animals they killed.

## THE EARLIEST FARMERS

Farming has always been Galloway's principal industry. It is therefore appropriate that it was the introduction of farming which produced the first major change in the course of our history. The earliest farmers appeared in this area about 2,500 B.C. and made their living, as their descendants do to-day, by grazing herds of domesticated sheep and cattle on the Galloway hills.

But before these pastoralists arrived, two important changes had occurred, first in the climate, and then, as a result, in the face of the country. Between 5,000-3,000 B.C. the rainfall increased greatly, the country was lashed by gales of exceptional force, and altogether it became much wetter and colder in Scotland. This spell of severe weather razed hundreds of square miles of forest more efficiently than any humans could have done. All over the high ground trees fell and turned into peat mosses. A second climatic change then took place between 3,000-1,000 B.C. when the weather became very much drier. This allowed the peat mosses and bogs to drain and dry up. Thus was formed the great area of moor and grassland which, even to-day, still stretches from the Clyde to the Borders.

It was on these cleared areas that the earliest farmers built their tiny stone houses and tended their herds of cattle, sheep and goats. The wild goats which can still be seen in various parts of the Galloway hills are no doubt descended from the animals belonging to these Stone Age farmers.

The earliest vestiges of primitive religion date from this period, for the burial customs of these people show some kind of belief in life after death. Important members of the community were buried in chambered cairns, with their weapons and personal belongings alongside their bodies. In the centre of each cairn were a number of chambers, constructed with stone slabs, where the bodies were laid. Entrance to the chambers was by smaller stone-lined passages. The burial chambers and passages were then completely covered with a great mound of earth. Examples of these megalithic tombs have been found at Cairnholy, near Gatehouse, King's Cairn, Water of Deugh, White Cairn, near Bargrennan, and Kilhern, near New Luce. Traces of many more such cairns have been recognised on moors all over Galloway.

The contribution made by these late Stone Age people to the

story of Galloway was a notable one—the introduction of farming. And although the population was not yet great (perhaps no more than a thousand or two) it was at least more widely spread. By the end of the Stone Age there were farming communities living on most of the high ground in Galloway.

KIRKCUDBRIGHT

THE TOWER IS THAT OF THE TOLBOOTH — PRISON FOR A VERY SHORT TIME OF JOHN PAUL JONES, NATIVE OF GALLOWAY AND FIRST COMMANDER OF U.S. NAVY

## CHAPTER II

# THE METAL AGES

### BRONZE BRINGS CIVILISATION NEARER

THERE is no doubt that the most exciting event in the prehistory of Galloway was the introduction of metal. One can imagine the joy with which this discovery was hailed by the primitive inhabitants. For five thousand years the only materials they had to work with were stones, bones or shells. Now they had a metal which could be melted, bent, hammered and shaped into hundreds of useful articles.

No modern housewife ever displayed greater excitement over a new labour saving device than did the Galloway woman of 3,000 years ago when she saw her first bronze cooking pot. Now she could really cook meat properly, by boiling or stewing it, instead of serving it up either half raw or burned to a cinder after grilling it on the point of a stick over the fire. No modern man ever expressed greater delight over the latest electric razor than did his Stone Age ancestor after trying out his new bronze "face-scraper". Now he could trim his hair, shave his whiskers, or even cut his enemy's throat with the greatest despatch.

The invention of bronze, a mixture of copper and tin, made possible the manufacture of a whole range of new or improved tools and weapons. It revolutionised the old way of life and enabled prehistoric Galloway to take its first big step towards civilisation.

Bronze was brought in by tribes of Celtic people who entered South-West Scotland from England about 1,000 B.C. Their earliest settlements were in the eastern part of the Stewartry, but soon they had spread to all the coastal lands and river valleys of Galloway.

These Bronze Age people bestowed yet another benefit, for it was they who first introduced the cultivation of land and the growing of crops in this area. During the Stone Age the level of the sea had dropped by some 25-50 feet, leaving what are called "raised beaches" all around the Solway coast. This land, particularly near the estuaries of rivers, was rich soil and easily worked. There they established their farming communities and raised their crops of rye and barley. It is also noteworthy that they were the first people to domesticate the horse and use it for work.

The burial customs of the Bronze Age were quite different from those of the Stone Age. The earliest Bronze Age peoples buried their dead individually in under-ground stone-lined cists, and with the body they placed an earthenware beaker, or ceremonial drinking vessel, containing liquid. Later in the Age, a food vessel, containing grain, was interred in the tomb. Many of these "food vessel" graves were surmounted by stones engraved with "cup and ring" markings, or spirals, which presumably had some religious significance. Numerous examples of these sculptored stones can be seen all over Galloway. The later Bronze Age people were still more advanced in their funeral rites, for they cremated their dead and deposited the ashes in cinerary urns which were then interred in under-ground cemeteries.

The many Stone Circles and Rocking stones still to be found all over this district were erected during the Bronze Age and indicate the religious beliefs of the people of that time. The Stone Circles were the temples of sun-worshippers, and it is probable that Druids officiated at ceremonies there. (It should be remembered that for every ancient monument that still remains there must have been scores that were destroyed. The large, flat stones from circles, cairns and tombs provided masons with excellent building materials for centuries later).

Finally, comment must be made on the wonderful ornamental work of the Bronze Age. There were craftsmen who specialised in the manufacture of beautifully designed and decorated articles of bronze. Some of their jewellery—rings, pins, brooches, necklaces and bracelets—provide excellent examples of early Celtic Art. It was also during this period that gold, possibly mined in the Leadhills, was first used here in the making of jewellery.

By the end of the Bronze Age the population of Galloway had increased considerably, numbering several thousand, and was high compared with other parts of Scotland. Almost every district in the province was inhabited. It is interesting, however, to note that the greatest concentration of people still seemed to be in the Glenluce-Dunragit area, the site of the original colony.

## TRIBES AND VILLAGES IN THE IRON AGE

Inventions are often regarded as mixed blessings. If they are put to the wrong use they can produce more misery than good. This was true, in a sense, in the case of iron.

When the Iron Age civilisation reached Galloway it brought many benefits in the way of manufactured goods. But it also brought war. And war, or simply the threat of war, had a profound effect on the life and habits of the people.

The Celtic tribes who introduced the use of iron to Galloway arrived not long before the birth of Christ. Some of them came from the east of Scotland; others were migrants from older Iron Age settlements in England. It is possible that they arrived as complete tribes, under chieftains, and not just disorganised groups of individuals, for it was during this period of history that the tribal system first became established in Galloway.

The ever-increasing population, the inevitable inter-tribal jealousy and greed and the greatly improved efficiency of their weapons all combined to make wars more frequent and more deadly. The old inhabitants of Galloway could no longer live in peace on their scattered farms. Instead they had to ally themselves with a neighbouring tribe and move their dwellings to some place which could be more easily defended. Galloway soon became a land of fortified villages built on hill-tops or on artificial islands on lochs.

In every parish there were a number of hill-forts, villages of wooden huts encircled by high fences or stone walls and ditches. During the day the inhabitants cultivated the cleared land on the hill-side and plain, and at night they retired with their flocks to the safety of the fort. On some of the hill-tops there was what is called a "vitrified" fort. These forts were constructed with double stone walls between which was left a space filled with dried timber and brushwood. This inflammable material was then set alight on a windy day, and the fire generated so much heat that the stones partly melted and fused with each other, thus greatly strengthening the walls. Two fine examples of these vitrified forts have been discovered at Stairhaven, near Glenluce, and at Trusty's Hill, near Gatehouse.

The migrating Iron Age Celts brought from Switzerland the practice of building villages, or crannogs, some distance out from the edge of a loch. A number of platforms, composed of gigantic tree trunks and brushwood and weighed down with boulders, were sunk in layers in the loch until an artificial island was formed. On this the tribe then erected their village of wooden huts. In some lochs there were secret under-water causeways, known only to the inhabitants, leading from the village to the mainland. In the construction of a small crannog in Barhapple Loch, near Glenluce, over 3,000 large trees were used. Other known crannogs in Galloway were at Loch Dowalton (drained 1863) and the White Loch at Ravelstone, both near Sorbie; and at Loch Trool, Loch Grennoch, Carlingwark Loch and Milton Loch in the Stewartry.

As iron is considerably harder than bronze the quality of tools, implements and weapons was greatly improved. With iron axes, saws and chisels it was possible to clear forests, build houses, and even make furniture much more quickly and efficiently. Agriculture benefited tremendously when iron could be used in the manufacture of ploughs, scythes and other implements. Carts and chariots, with a horse on each side of a single centre-shaft, came into regular use as soon as iron "tyres" became available for their wheels.

Great progress was made in various arts and crafts during the Iron Age. People became "clothes conscious" for the first time, having learned the art of spinning, dyeing and weaving wool. The introduction of the potter's wheel enabled them to turn out earthenware utensils in a great range of new designs. The deservedly great reputation of the Iron Age craftsman rests chiefly, however, on the quality of their metal work. Two of the finest examples of Late Celtic Art that can be seen today were found in Galloway: one, a bronze chamfrein, or horse's mask, with beautifully designed scrolls and long, curved horns, discovered on the farm of Torrs, near Castle-Douglas; the other, an exquisitely decorated bronze mirror, dug up in a bog near Balmaclellan.

It is interesting to note that the people of the Iron Age amused themselves in much the same way as their descendants do today—at least in one respect. The discovery of a set of dice shows that gambling was already a popular diversion with Galloway folk nearly 2,000 years before the "age of bingo."

Such, then, was the state of civilisation in Galloway about the time of the birth of Christ.

## CHAPTER III

# THE ROMANS IN GALLOWAY

### NATIVES TAKEN BY SURPRISE

IT was a lovely morning in the spring of A.D. 82. The inhabitants of the crannog on Milton Loch at the eastern end of the Stewartry were busy in their fields along the shores of the water, tilling the soil and sowing their grain. In the clearings of the wood and on the higher ground grazed small herds of sheep guarded by the children of the tribe. On the outskirts of each flock the youngsters played happily at their games or watched with fascinated eyes the antics of the many newborn lambs. It was as peaceful a scene as any in Galloway.

Suddenly the quiet of the morning was shattered by shrill cries of alarm. A number of the young men of the tribe, who had been posted as sentries in the outer ring of woods, came running into the clearings, gesticulating wildly towards the east.

With a speed born of long practice the workers collected their tools and quickly drove the cattle and sheep into strongly fenced pens at the edge of the loch. The older men, the women and children speedily embarked in the waiting coracles and tree-trunk canoes and paddled furiously to the island. In the stockade, among the animals, the warriors of the tribe manned the high wooden fences and with their iron spears and swords at the ready awaited the expected attack.

Then the enemy appeared. For some moments the tribesmen stood stock-still at their posts, their mouths agape in bewilderment. Here was something amazing, something they did not understand! What they had expected was a ragged and indisciplined rush by a horde of tribesmen like themselves, dressed in skins and coarse woollens, wielding primitive iron weapons and uttering wild war-cries.

Instead, the enemy advanced silently and with steady tread into the clearing, their breast-plates, shields, helmets and all their mighty display of arms glittering and resplendent in the bright sunshine. Rank after rank emerged from the wood and, at the order of their officers, formed up in the open space. The Romans had come to Galloway.

## THE TRIBES ACCEPT THE ROMANS AS MASTERS

In A.D. 79 the great Roman general Julius Agricola had begun his attempt to conquer Scotland and had pushed as far north as Melrose on the Tweed. The following summer he had penetrated into Annandale and Nithsdale and subdued the tribes there. His campaign of A.D. 81 took him as far as the Forth and Clyde. But before venturing further north he decided to ensure the safety of his left flank by conquering the tribes of the south-west.

Agricola's intelligence service had reported the presence in that area of two important tribes whom they called the Selgovae and the Novantes. The former inhabited the country between the rivers Nith and Dee, and the latter the remainder of Galloway to the west.

The Roman attack on the south-west of Scotland was a combined operation using both land and naval forces. Agricola's army sailed across the Solway from the Cumberland coast and landed at the mouth of the Lochar, a natural port. The Romans cut down trees, constructed a causeway across the Lochar Moss and built a fort on Wardlaw Hill. Continuing up the estuary of the Nith, they then forded the river at Dumfries and pushed their way steadily westwards.

At that point of history no tribes anywhere in Europe could stand up to the might of the advancing Roman legions, and certainly not in open warfare. The Romans and their mercenary soldiers were well equipped, highly trained and probably the best disciplined fighting force the world has ever known.

Their methods in dealing with conquered and occupied territories were, for their time, most enlightened and generally successful. Those tribes who submitted to the Romans were required, first, to pay tribute (usually food for the army) and also to give hostages who would be killed if their tribe failed to comply with the terms of the agreement.

In return the conquered people enjoyed all the benefits that Roman civilisation brought them and, what was more important, their leading men became Roman citizens. Any tribe agreeing to those conditions became allied to the Romans and, if attacked, it could count on the whole weight of Roman power coming to its assistance. For this reason the leaders of many tribes submitted quite willingly to the Romans.

It is fairly certain, therefore, that the tribes of Galloway, having already had time to learn of the Romans' methods from the people in Dumfriesshire, preferred to be friends of the invaders rather than enemies. Thus the Romans were probably accepted, if not exactly welcomed, in Galloway.

## CONQUEST OF GALLOWAY COMPLETED

Having received hostages from the Milton Loch tribe and negotiated the amount of tribute to be paid, the Romans quickly continued on their journey westwards. Marching whenever they could on high ground, the invaders next reached Buittle and accepted the submission of a hill fort there. Other strongholds of the Galloway Iron Age tribes at Castlegower, Sypland, Whinnieliggate, Bombie, Dunrod and Drummore all fell to the Romans, and their inhabitants gave satisfactory assurances of their future good behaviour. On the hill above Drummore, since it commanded the estuary of the Dee, the Romans decided to establish a fort which they called Caerbantorigum.

In the meantime several cohorts had been detached to the north to subdue the important Iron Age settlement on a hill at Halferne. Having accomplished this, the Romans carried on westwards until they discovered a place near Glenlochar where the river Dee (Deva) could be most easily forded. There, as at Drummore, they established a permanent fort.

The Romans next turned their attention to the country of the Novantes to the west of the Dee. Near Gatehouse they built two camps, one at Enrick and the other at a ford over the river Fleet.

Meantime, while their army continued its steady advance westwards, ships of the Roman navy were also playing a part in the conquest of Galloway. Sailing from the Cumberland ports of Ravenglass and Maryport, their vessels made landing at Kirkcudbright (which they named Benutium) and on the Wigtownshire coast near Whithorn, where they set up their main fort (Leucophibia) in the western part of the province. Although no traces remain, it is almost certain that they would also have established garrisons near Luce Bay (Abravanus Sinus) and Loch Ryan (Rerigonius Sinus).

After having completed the conquest of Galloway in the summer of A.D. 82 the Romans then continued to exercise control over the province for the next 300 years. During that time their fortunes varied considerably in battles with the Picts in other parts of Scotland and Northern England, but the Romans appear to have retained their hold on the remote south-west province until their final departure from Britain soon after A.D. 400.

## ROMAN INFLUENCE ON GALLOWAY

Perhaps the greatest benefit the Romans brought was peace, the famous Pax Romana: for in occupied territories they acted as a kind of international police force. Moreover, the Galloway tribes, by submitting to the Romans, gained the most powerful ally that any nation could have. On at least one occasion during their occupation the Romans assisted the Galloway tribes in a battle near Loch Doon against invaders from Ayrshire. Many Galloway tribesmen enlisted in the ranks of the Roman army and saw service in Europe. A Roman historian, writing about A.D. 360, described the Galloway soldiers on the Continent as "fierce" in battle and "a British people who fed on human flesh." Although the King's Own Scottish Borderers have long been renowned for their valour in wars of recent times, they certainly never achieved the reputation their early ancestors enjoyed!

The Romans were the greatest farmers of their time and it was always their policy to encourage and improve agriculture wherever they went. In this way the peoples they conquered were better able to raise the food tribute levied on them for the upkeep of the Roman army. The new methods of farming introduced into Britain turned Southern England into "the granary of Europe." It can be safely assumed that the primitive agriculture of Galloway also benefited greatly from the more scientific ideas of the Romans.

Education undoubtedly began in Galloway during the Roman occupation, for until that time there was no written language in Scotland. Agricola and some later governors ordered the establishment of schools in all the main Roman centres. Although there would not have been many of these schools in Galloway, the sons of tribal chiefs, and of others whose rank entitled them to Roman citizenship, certainly did learn to read and write Latin. Some of them even went to Rome to continue their education there. The leading members of tribes would also have adopted the more civilised manners and customs of the Romans. The manufacture of goods for sale and trade generally were encouraged by the introduction of coinage.

Probably the Romans' greatest contribution to civilisation in Galloway, however, was the introduction of Christianity. In A.D. 314 Roman bishops were appointed to London and York, and ten years later Christianity became the "official" religion of the whole Roman Empire. It was not long then before there were Roman missionaries preaching among the people of Galloway. Their work was soon to have a profound and far-reaching effect, not only on Galloway but on a great part of Scotland. Although almost all of the Roman influences were swept away during the centuries that followed, the lamp of Christianity was to remain alight in South-West Scotland throughout even the blackest years of the Dark Ages.

CHAPTER IV

# ST. NINIAN—FOUNDER OF THE CHURCH IN SCOTLAND

## HIS BOYHOOD AT WHITHORN

THE young boy was a familiar figure to all the sentries at the main gate of the Roman camp at Leucophibia, near Whithorn. Almost every day of the year (it was A.D. 372) they had seen him passing in and out, sometimes alone, with scrolls of parchment under his arm, at other times accompanied by a gang of noisy ten-year-old youngsters.

As he was a likeable young lad, the sentries usually gave him a friendly greeting, but it was noticeable that they treated him with a shade more respect than they showed to the other boys. Young Ninian, or Nennius, as the Romans called him, was rather better dressed than most of his companions and carried himself perhaps just a little more proudly. He was the acknowledged leader in all their games and exploits. This was but natural, since he was not only the son of the chief of a tribe of the Novantes but also the dux of their little school in the camp.

By the age of ten Ninian could speak two languages—Gaelic and Latin—with equal fluency. Along with the sons of the leading citizens and officers he attended classes under a Roman teacher and was already able to read and write in Latin. He was naturally clever and learned his lessons so quickly that his teacher was already prophesying a great future for him.

Many years before this Roman soldiers, who had been posted to Whithorn after service in Italy or the continent, brought with them stories of strange happenings in the province of Judea during the governorship of Pontius Pilate. They related how a certain carpenter, Jesus of Nazareth, by his preaching and miracles, had set the whole of Judea talking, and how this great man had then been arrested and crucified on the orders of the Jewish leaders who feared they might lose their hold on the people.

As the years passed an ever-increasing number of soldiers brought more news of Jesus and his teachings, and also of the formation of Christian churches in all the lands of the eastern Mediterranean, and even in Rome itself. Soon many of the men reaching the camp were active and professing Christians, and their religious beliefs were being eagerly discussed by all the educated Romans and tribesmen.

Finally, not long before Ninian was born, the first consecrated missionaries arrived at Whithorn. Ninian's father was one of the first tribesmen to be converted to Christianity, and when Ninian was born he too was baptised and received into the Church.

## HE DECIDES TO GO TO ROME

As he grew to manhood Ninian continued with his studies until there was nothing more he could learn at Whithorn. He helped in the fields and took his share in the affairs of the tribe. All this time, however his thoughts were turning more and more to Christianity, and he wondered what he could do to bring others into the faith. Then suddenly all his ideas and dreams resolved themselves into one great desire—to be a missionary of Christ among his own people in Galloway.

In A.D. 385, when he was about 23 years old, Ninian set off for Rome. The journey was some 1500 miles in length, and apart from short sea crossings he had to walk every mile of it. Since the whole route lay within the Roman Empire no passports were needed and no frontiers had to be crossed. Nevertheless there was always the danger of attack from thieving tribesmen. Military passes signed by the Romans and letters of introduction to Christian missions no doubt helped him on his way, and Ninian arrived safely in Rome after after a six months' journey on foot across almost half of Europe.

Ninian spent the next ten years in Rome, first in study and then serving as a priest at the headquarters of the Church. In A.D. 395 he was consecrated by the Pope as the first bishop to be appointed to Scotland.

On his return journey Ninian spent about a year at a monastery at Tours in France, where St Martin, once an officer in the Roman army and now the most progressive churchman of his time, was abbot. This great saint had worked out many new ideas on the purpose of monasteries and the duties of monks. In the early days of Christianity monasteries had often been regarded as places of retreat, where monks could spend their time in meditation and prayer or in study. St Martin, however, thought differently. Instead he looked on monasteries rather as centres where monks would be trained as missionaries and would then go out as evangelists among the heathen. As will be seen later, the young Bishop Ninian was greatly influenced by the ideas of the elderly St Martin.

## THE RELIGIOUS CENTRE OF THE CELTIC WORLD

St Ninian landed at the Isle of Whithorn in 397, accompanied by a number of monks, some of whom were masons and craftsmen. On this rocky peninsula he built his first tiny chapel in the land of his fathers, Candida Casa or White House, which he dedicated to St Martin.

Now he was ready to begin his mission, to preach the gospel to the tribes of Galloway. At the same time, inspired by the teachings of the Abbot of Tours, St Ninian had still another ambition which he was determined to achieve. This was to establish in the south-west a monastery to serve as a training school for monks recruited, he hoped, from all over the Celtic world.

The bleak and windswept promontory where Candida Casa stood was quite unsuitable for this purpose. A monastery should be built in some gracious situation, surrounded by rich, arable land on which the monks could raise their food. The ideal site, however, lay not far away, as St Ninian remembered very well, for it was only a short distance from the Roman camp where he had gone to school as a boy. It was a place of hallowed memories for him, and there St Ninian decided to build the first monastery in the British Isles.

While the masons he had brought with him were erecting the simple Abbey Church and the cells for the monks, St Ninian set off on the first of his missionary journeys. To begin with these were confined to Galloway, but later he travelled further afield.

At that time a few days' journey into the interior of Scotland was an even more dangerous undertaking than a year's trip to Rome and back, for the northern Picts and Scots had no love for any who were connected with the Romans. Anywhere north of the Galloway border was hostile country, where life was of no account.

But no physical dangers could deter St Ninian, and he pressed steadily northwards, preaching, converting and establishing communities wherever he went. In the course of his various journeys he reached Glasgow, Stirling, Strathmore, and even penetrated as far as the coastal regions of eastern Scotland.

Throughout his journeys, however, St Ninian's thoughts constantly returned to Whithorn and his beloved monastery, and he would return at intervals to supervise the great work that was going on there. The fame of this monastic school had spread rapidly among the Celtic peoples, and Christians from far and wide, some even from Ireland, made their way to Whithorn for training and inspiration.

Among the students who attended Whithorn were many who were later to become the great fathers of the Celtic Church in Ireland, including St Finnbarr, the teacher of St Columba, and Caranoc, who baptised St Patrick. Pupils who had trained at Whithorn carried the message of Christ to the Picts of the far north, and even to the Shetlands, where there were already churches dedicated to St Ninian before St Columba arrived in Scotland.

## A CHRISTIAN STRONGHOLD IN A PAGAN LAND

St Ninian must have derived special pleasure from the knowledge that so many of his own people in Wigtownshire became converts to the Christian faith. Although nothing remains of their tiny churches, which were later destroyed or built over, some relics of St Ninian's time have been found. At the church at Kirkmadrine, in the parish of Stoneykirk, gravestones were discovered which tell that three Roman priests, who probably accompanied St Ninian to Galloway, were buried there early in the fifth century.

Inevitably there were times when the ageing saint felt in need of a period of rest and desired to withdraw for a little from the endless activity of the busy seminary. On such occasions he was accustomed to retire alone to the shores of the Solway, some three miles west of Whithorn, where he had found a lonely cave in which he could seek peace for private devotion and meditation.

In his later years St Ninian was entitled to feel deeply satisfied with the success of his mission. Not only had be made Whithorn the cultural and religious centre of the Celtic world, but he and his disciples had established Christian churches in many remote parts of Scotland. In addition he had ensured that successors were available to carry on his work after he had gone.

It is perhaps a pity that the glory of Whithorn should have become overshadowed in later ages by that of Iona, in its island setting and with added fame as the burial place of kings. Historians far too frequently applaud the work of St Columba and neglect even to mention the great saint of the Solway. To put their relative values in proper perspective it is only necessary to remember that had it not been for St Ninian there might have been no St Columba: had it not been for Whithorn there might have been no Iona.

St Ninian died at his birthplace on 16th September, 432, aged about 70 years. His body was laid to rest in Candida Casa, but his memory and his work lived on. Despite invasions by successive waves of heathen races, the monastery at Whithorn continued to keep alight the lamp of the Christian faith in a land that was for long almost completely shrouded in the darkness of paganism.

## CHAPTER V

# SEVEN CENTURIES OF INVASION

### THE TRIBES BUILD A GREAT WALL

GALLOWAY was subjected to an almost non-stop invasion during the seven centuries following the departure of the Romans about A.D. 400. Wave after wave of barbaric people—Britons, Irish-Scots, Angles, Norwegians—poured into the province, but none of them ever really conquered it permanently. Instead, most of these foreigners who remained became gradually absorbed into the Gaelic stock. The ancestors of present-day Galwegians thus had the blood of many different races in their veins.

It was this fact which gave rise to the name "Galloway." These tribes were Picts, but different from the Picts of the north. They were Gaels, but not as other Gaels. Because of this they came to be known as "stranger Gaels"—gallgaidhel or Galwydel, from which the word "Galloway" is derived.

The first people to take advantage of the absence of the Romans, who had protected the Galloway tribes for some 300 years, were the Britons of Strathclyde and Ayrshire. No sooner had the Romans gone than these fierce tribesmen swarmed over the Galloway hills and into the fertile valleys, destroying villages and farms and making off with whatever plunder they could seize. Only the inhabitants of the more strongly defended hill forts or crannogs were safe from these raids of the Britons.

The Galloway tribal chieftains met to discuss how they could combat this continual threat from the Britons. Although attack might be the best form of defence, they were not powerful enough to invade the populous and well-guarded lands of Ayrshire.

Then they remembered the defensive methods of their old masters, the Romans. A wall was the answer. If they could build a great dyke along the line of hills to the north and east—as Hadrian and Antonine had done elsewhere—they would be able to sleep more peacefully at night. Even if such a wall could not give complete security, it might hold up the enemy long enough for reinforcements to be rushed to the point of attack.

Plans for the wall were drawn up and dimensions agreed upon. The dyke was eight feet broad at the base, with a deep ditch on the northern side. Stone was used wherever readily available, otherwise a mixture of stone and earth. At regular intervals in the wall forts or watch-towers were constructed, some of them of large dimensions: at least one of these forts, circular in shape, was 192 yards in diameter.

Each tribe was allocated a section for which it was responsible, first in construction and then in defence. When the gigantic task was completed Galloway was cut off from the rest of Scotland by this great dyke, some 80 miles in length.

The wall began at Loch Ryan and, passing by Braid Fell, continued to the northern end of Lochs Maberry and Ochiltree. From there is ran more southwards, following roughly the line of the upper Cree valley. After crossing the northern end of the parish of Minnigaff the wall passed by Talnotrie and Craigencallie, and then on to Dalry. Its course then lay through the districts of Moniaive, Tyron and Penpont until it reached the Nith. On the Dumfriesshire side of the river the wall was continued in a direct line through Lochmaben, and it finished on the Solway Firth near Annan, opposite Bowness, where Hadrian's Wall commenced.

It was about this time too that the Scots from Ireland began their infiltration to Argyll and Galloway, a migration which continued for many centuries. These Irish-Scots, however—a Gaelic-speaking people like the Galwegians—were possibly quite welcome here, since they were bitter enemies of the Britons of Strathclyde.

## THE ANGLES INVADE GALLOWAY FROM THE EAST

Meantime, in the far east ominous events had been taking place. From the plains of Central Russia the Huns, a migratory and warlike people, who lived and even slept on horseback, were sweeping steadily westwards. The races of Eastern Europe—the Goths, Vandals and Franks—fled before their relentless advance. All over Europe people were moving westwards. The unfortunate tribes who lived on the North Sea coast had no option but to take their boats, and the only direction in which they could sail was towards Britain.

In this way, from A.D. 450 onwards, the seaborne tribes of the Jutes, Angles and Saxons began to settle on the east coastline of Britain. The Saxons conquered southern and central England, and the Angles, after an invasion in greater force in 547, soon overcame the whole of the east of Britain between the rivers Humber and Forth. By about 650 the Angles, in search of more living room had reached the Solway coast and had begun the penetration of Galloway.

Another of these continental tribes, the Friesians, may possibly have approached the Solway by ships, for they were a great sea-trading race. They decided to settle on the banks of the Nith at the lowest points where it could be forded and where there was a harbour, and there they established a fortified community which was named Dun Fries—the fort of the Friesians.

By this time many of the heathen Angles had been converted to Christianity by missionaries from the Celtic Church at Iona; by St Aidan, a disciple of St Columba, and by St Cuthbert, who was once a shepherd lad on the Border hills and whose name is commemorated in the town of Kirkcudbright. In 730 King Osric of Northumbria appointed Pecthelm as bishop to the see of Whithorn. Galloway was by then completely under the domination of the Angles.

In 740 an army of northern Picts and Scots from Dalriada, united under King Alpin, broke through the great dyke and invaded Galloway. A combined force of Galwegians and Angles defeated them in a battle in the valley of the Dee, and the invaders were forced to retreat westwards. When riding through Glenapp Alpin was killed in an ambush and his grave was marked by a stone. Laicht Alpin, "Alpin's Grave." The place was thereafter called Gleann Alpin, later modified to Glenapp.

As a reprisal for this raid the Galwegians and Angles invaded Ayrshire and annexed Kyle and Carrick. This marked the beginning of the expansion of Galloway and, as we shall see later, the province was soon to take in all south-west Scotland.

The rule of the Angles, however, was coming to an end. Unknown to them, in the overpopulated creeks and fiords of Scandinavia, other heathen races were massing for the invasion of Britain, just as the Angles themselves had done several hundred years before.

## "FROM THE FURY OF THE NORTHMEN DELIVER US, O LORD!"

The appearance of Viking ships off the Solway coast, sometime about 800, must have struck terror in the hearts of the Galloway tribesmen who first saw them arrive. One can imagine the added apprehension they must have felt when they discovered that some of the ships held as many as 200 stalwart and heavily armed men. Here was an enemy which in stature and weight of arms far excelled any they had ever had to deal with before.

Nor had they ever seen such ships. Some of them were over 80 feet in length, 17 feet in beam and 7 feet in depth. Still more astonishing than their size was the speed at which they cut through the water, leaving a seething, frothy wave behind the rudder oars at their sterns. The lines of their hulls were as graceful and as scientifically designed as those of a modern yacht. Even when their square sails, gaudily striped in red, white and blue, scarcely filled to the gentle breeze, the streamlined vessels still made extraordinary speed, propelled by the power of some 20-30 oars on each side of the ship.

Although the Galwegians had never seen the Vikings before, they no doubt had heard of them. From the Angles they would have learned of the arrival of the Danes—dubh gall, or "dark strangers"—who had attacked and sacked the monastery of Lindisfarne in 793. The wandering Scots of Ireland and Dalriada would also have brought the story of the massacre of the monks and the destruction of Iona in 795 by the tall, fair Norsemen—finn gall, or "white strangers."

And now the dreaded Norsemen had arrived in Galloway, a country greatly weakened by the departure of many of the Angles, who had returned to Northumbria to help to defend it against the Danes.

The monks at Whithorn must have received the news with even greater apprehension, for these heathen invaders seemed to concentrate their greatest fury on monastries, where the most valuable plunder was to be had. Was their beloved Whithorn to suffer the same fate as Iona and Lindisfarne?

At first, however, the Norsemen contented themselves with sporadic raids on the coastline, but later in the ninth century they began to settle in Galloway, as they did in Ireland, the Isle of Man, and northern France.

By some miracle Whithorn was spared: presumably the Galwegians had quickly come to terms with or submitted to their new overlords. In fact some Irish chroniclers of that time suggest that the Galwegians made their peace with the Norsemen by renouncing Christianity and accepting the pagan worship of the Viking gods Odin and Thor and the goddess Freya.

The Norsemen were certainly present in Galloway in considerable numbers before the middle of the ninth century. The exiled Kenneth MacAlpin, with the help of a force of Galwegians and Norsemen, regained his kingdom of Dalriada, beat the northern Picts at the battle of Fortrenn, and conquered the rest of Scotland as far south as the Tweed. When he was crowned king at Scone in 844 Kenneth became the first monarch to rule over an almost united Scotland. Only the Orkneys, Shetlands, Caithness, Sutherland, the Western Isles and Galloway still remained under Norse domination and outwith the Scottish kingdom.

It was in reward for their services to his cause that Kenneth MacAlpin conferred on the men of Galloway the right to march in the van of Scottish armies, a privilege which they were to retain for many centuries.

Relations between Viking-controlled Galloway and the rest of Scotland remained friendly, for Kenneth wisely gave his daughter in marriage to a Norse-Galloway chieftain, Olaf the White. When Kenneth died in 860 Olaf claimed the Scottish throne, and with a combined Norse-Galwegian force he captured Dumbarton and took great booty and many captives back to Galloway.

## GALLOWAY UNDER THE RULE OF THE VIKINGS

Danger was now threatening Galloway from another quarter. In the east the Danes had completed their conquest and occupation of Northumbria and were seeking farther lands to overcome. Under their leader Halfdan they invaded Strathclyde and Cumberland in 875, causing great devastation wherever they went. Carlisle, for example, was so completely destroyed that it remained uninhabited for two centuries later.

During this campaign a force of these dark Vikings made their way into Galloway and defeated a native army at a battle between Castle Douglas and Crossmichael.

In 944 the Danes in Northumbria suffered a temporary set-back when they were defeated by the Angles. The Danish King Ronald fled with his army to Galloway, where he established his headquarters on the slopes of Craig Ronald on the shores of Loch Grennoch. Ronald the Dane must have exercised control over at least a part of Galloway, for English historians of the time refer to him as "Duke of the Galwegians."

The Norsemen, however, were still the principal overlords of the south-west. In 1008 Sigurd the Stout, Earl of Orkney, enjoyed the title of Lord of Galloway. He appointed Earl Malcolm, who was a Norse-Galwegian native of the province, as his resident governor. Malcolm and his successors lived in a "palace" near Whithorn, some say in an early Cruggleton Castle.

Malcolm was succeeded by the mighty Thorfinn the Skullsplitter, one of the most colourful of the great Norse "jarls." He is said to have held nine Scottish earldoms and thus ruled over not only Galloway but also a large part of Scotland and of Ireland. The remainder of Scotland was under the control of Macbeth, but he retained his crown only with the help and agreement of the powerful Earl Thorfinn.

During Thorfinn's reign it became apparent that most of the Norwegians had become converted to Christianity, for it was Thorfinn who established the first bishop's see in the Orkney Islands. Whithorn not only continued to flourish as a monastery, but had for some time been considered as a shrine of the church. It is recorded that Kenneth III was the first Scottish king to make a pilgrimage to Whithorn in 994.

During the 300 years the Norse ruled Galloway they "lived on the land," for they never neglected to collect their tax. Each tenant of land was required to make an annual payment in kind to the Norse overlord. In order to assess the amount payable and also to collect the grain and livestock the governor or his deputy made an annual trip throughout Galloway. In the course of this journey the earl and his retinue were accustomed to receive board and lodging at certain farms which were then referred to as "Bordlands," from which the name "Boreland" is derived. These farms were exempt from the payment of tax because of their annual hospitality to the earls.

On the whole, the Norsemen appeared to have exercised a very benevolent control over Galloway, and they permitted local chiefs—some of whom were even called "kings"—to rule over their own people and to administer their traditional laws. Provided they paid their taxes regularly, the Galwegians were thus allowed a considerable measure of self-government.

In 1057 Malcolm Canmore, son of the murdered Duncan, avenged his father's death by killing Macbeth and taking over the throne of Scotland, When the great Thorfinn died that same year Malcolm made a most astute move by marrying the Norse earl's widow, Ingibiorg, who was a native of Galloway. Through this marriage Malcolm brought many of the Norse controlled districts, including Galloway, under the rule of the Scottish crown.

## CHAPTER VI

# NORMAN CONQUEST OF GALLOWAY

### FIRST LORD OF GALLOWAY

THE inhabitants of Galloway were for long considered to be a wild and independent set of people. This has proved to be the case at many periods in the course of their history. But it was probably never more true than during the Middle Ages.

The barons of Galloway were a particularly bold and bloodthirsty lot—and that in an age when no noble was held to be worth his salt unless he was permanently at war with some of his neighbours.

For nearly five centuries, from about 1100-1600, the great landowners of Galloway and their followers caused more trouble to the Scottish kings than all the rest of Scotland put together.

But this state of continual warfare held up the social and economic progress of Galloway for a very considerable time. The land became neglected and impoverished. Trade and commerce remained at a standstill or even deteriorated. Because of this Galloway was to remain, several hundred years later, a backward and undeveloped district, long after the rest of the Lowlands were beginning to benefit from the agrarian and industrial revolutions.

The first Earl of Galloway to be officially appointed by a Scottish monarch was David, who was later to succeed to the throne in 1124. It was during his term as earl that the word "Galloway" was first used in official documents, when in 1120 he presented a charter to the monks at Selkirk granting them revenues from certain lands in the province. David, however, never took up residence in Galloway during his earldom.

At that period Galloway's boundaries were more widespread than at any time in its history. In addition to the present counties of Kirkcudbright and Wigtown Galloway also included in 1100 the whole of Ayrshire, Renfrewshire, Lanarkshire and stretched as far as the forest of Selkirk to the east.

Now Earl David had been brought up at the English court

and had learned the Norman methods of government. He was in fact an English baron and owned estates in Huntingdon. As an enthusiastic supporter of Norman ideas David was determined to introduce them to Scotland. One of his first actions when he became king was to give the whole of Annandale to a Norman baron, Robert de Brus. Although Norman ideas had been creeping into Scotland since the days of Malcolm Canmore, this marked the beginning of the feudal system in Galloway. By the end of his reign David was to bring almost the whole of Scotland, except for odd corners of Galloway, under control of Norman barons.

Under the feudal system the whole country was held to belong to the king, who could then sublet areas of it to nobles. In return these nobles had to pay rent in kind or in service. For example, Robert de Brus, the first Lord of Annandale, had to pay for his estate there by providing 10 knights (plus their esquires and other followers) to fight when required for King David. In this way the king had a regular standing army he could call on, and at the same time had his kingdom effectively policed—provided the barons remained loyal.

Occasionally the sons of free-men who were favoured and trusted might be given the opportunity of rising through the various ranks of page, esquire, knight and might even—if they did the king some special service—become nobles. The vast majority of native inhabitants, however, remained as serfs, slaves or bondsmen. In return for a miserable hovel to live in, free timber, and a small strip of land to cultivate for themselves, these wretched serfs had to work for their master for several days a week, and also had to be prepared to fight for him when called up for any campaign.

By thus purchasing the loyalty of many Norman nobles, with their private armies, David hoped to have a force strong enough to keep the wild natives in check. His intention clearly was to encircle Galloway, the noted trouble spot, with a ring of loyal Norman barons.

## FERGUS OF GALLOWAY DEFIES THE KING

But in planning this David had not reckoned with the first of the bold, bad barons of Galloway, Fergus. From his stronghold on an artificial island on Loch Fergus, near Kirkcudbright, this native chieftain had been viewing the unopposed Norman conquest of his land with grave misgiving. Yet his position was a difficult one. In the first place he was himself an old friend of David's: he had lived with the king in their younger days in England, and they had been brought up together to Norman ways. In fact Fergus was married to a daughter of the King of England. Secondly, there was the fact that he held extensive lands, not only around Kirkcudbright but also in Wigtownshire, where Cruggleton was his seat, under allegiance to David.

Nevertheless Fergus had no Norman blood in him. He was of Galloway stock, his ancestors having been some of the Norse-Galwegian overlords of the province. Although he had no objection to the introduction of the feudal system, he saw no need to import Norman barons to enforce it, especially when there were local and hereditary landowners like himself available.

Accordingly Fergus allied himself with another Scottish malcontent, the Earl of Moray, and in 1130 they rose with a native force against the king and his Norman supporters. The rebellion was defeated, Moray slain, and Fergus, a good churchman despite his treason, took refuge as a monk in Holyrood Abbey, David's own foundation in Edinburgh.

## GALLOWAY SOLDIERS—"A HALF-NAKED HORDE OF SAVAGES"

Meantime David, having a difference of opinion with the English king, invaded England. The two armies met at the battle of the Standard, near Northallerton, in 1138. As overlord of the province David had enrolled a large force of his Galloway serfs to accompany him.

The Galwegians, although very poorly armed compared with the rest of the Scots, claimed their rightful privilege of being in the van. David was at first reluctant, but in the end he agreed to their demand. At first the Galwegians' ferocity and courage compensated for their lack of arms and armour. They descended on the enemy with terror-striking cries of "Albanach!" but the well-trained English stood their ground and greeted the Galwegians (described by a English historian as "a half-naked horde of savages") with jeers of "Irish!" In the end the English archers began to take their expected toll. The Galloway leaders fell, the rumour was spread that David had been killed, and the Scots army fled.

But, win or lose, the Galloway men usually contrived to leave a battlefield with some kind of booty. On this occasion they had managed to round up a large number of the English female camp-followers who always accompanied armies of those days. The Galwegians were jubilantly driving their captives back home when they were met near Carlisle by the papal legate who was there arranging peace terms. It is a measure of the high regard these wild Galwegians had for the Church that they readily agreed to the churchman's request to release such interesting and unusual prisoners.

Of course in those days the Church was truly the church militant. Only a few years later a rebellion broke out among some of the Irish-Celtic peoples of Wigtownshire, led by a former Bishop of Man. The rebels were met by a local force under the command of the equally militarily-minded Bishop of Whithorn. A battle was fought at Causewayend, between Wigtown and Newton Stewart, and resulted in a victory for the Whithorn Bishop and his flock. Bishops could then wield a weapon as dexterously as a pastoral staff, and the Bishop of Whithorn is credited with winning the battle by felling his opposite number from the Isle of Man with a gigantic battle-axe.

## FERGUS FOUNDS MANY CHURCHES IN GALLOWAY

In 1139 Fergus of Galloway received a free pardon from the king by an astute trick. David was visiting Holyrood Abbey, where Fergus was still in hiding, and the Galloway ex-chieftain, seeing he was not recognised by the king, persuaded the abbot to petition David "to pardon everyone of us every fault committed against your majesty." The king was graciously pleased to agree. "Dear brethren, I forgive you all," he said, "and I commend myself unto your prayers."

After this David received Fergus back into favour and restored him his lands and his title of Governor of Galloway. In gratitude for this Fergus built the Priory of St Mary's Isle, near his home in Kirkcudbright, and gifted it to the Abbey of Holyrood.

David, however, realised the need to keep an eye on such a cunning customer as Fergus—and insisted that the governor of Galloway hand over to Hugh de Moreville some of his lands in Borgue. This Norman baron, who had already been given the former Galloway lands of Cunningham and Lauderdale, was then Constable of Scotland and no doubt had a special commission from the king to ensure that Fergus and his wild Galwegians were kept in order. By 1150 David had removed most of Lanarkshire and Renfrewshire from the earldom of Galloway, and it was not long before the boundaries of the province were whittled down, by further Norman encroachments, to their present limits.

But Fergus seemed incapable of keeping the peace. When David died in 1153 and was succeeded by Malcolm IV, a ten-year-old boy, Fergus again rose in rebellion to prevent further inroads on his lands. The Norman barons supporting the young king defeated Fergus who once more sought sanctuary in Holyrood Abbey where he died in 1161.

The behaviour of Fergus established a pattern which was to be followed by numerous successors as Lords of Galloway: allegiance to the king only when it became completely necessary; defiance whenever they thought they could get away with it. Like many of his successors, too, Fergus did much to help in the development of the Church in Galloway, for he gifted land and money and was largely responsible for the foundation of the Abbeys of Dundrennan, Tongland and Saulseat, as well as of the Priories of Whithorn and St. Mary's Isle.

SWEETHEART ABBEY,
NEAR DUMFRIES

Ken Lochhead 1976

CHAPTER VII

# NORMAN SETTLEMENT OF GALLOWAY

## THE GREAT MOTE OF URR

THE great new "castel" in the Urr Valley was the main topic of conversation in the district for many a year. From all over the countryside folk journeyed to inspect and marvel at this great miracle of engineering. These new Norman lords had many queer ideas, they knew, but this beat them all. Why, an army could shut itself up inside that great fortification and be safe for a year.

Some of the more venturesome visitors even dared to approach close enough to it to measure, by pacing, the length and breadth of the great mound of earth and stones. They discovered that it was some 210 paces long and over 100 paces broad at its widest part. The height to the topmost point of the great wooden walls they reckoned to be at least 100 feet.

Looking up from the base of the mound, they could see only a tall wooden fence, over which the highest turrets of the castle were just visible. But if they had been able to look down on it from above, they would have discovered quite a number of buildings and further fortifications.

On the top of the hills there had been built up a still higher mound, which was called the Mote. And on this highest point—the citadel as it were—stood the castle itself, mightily impressive both because of its slimness and its height. Hundreds of oak trees from the forests around had been felled and used in the construction. Its great height showed that it consisted of several storeys, something unheard of before. And, as if the castle were not already sufficiently impregnable, a wooden fence had been erected on earthen ramparts on the very edge of the mount.

From a narrow gateway in this fence a steep flight of steps led down to the Bailey, or main courtyard, which occupied the whole of the flat top of the hill. Within this area stood a number of buildings of various shapes and sizes, but there was still plenty of room left to exercise men or horses. This courtyard was also surrounded by a high earth rampart on which was built another great wooden palisade, too high to be scaled by even the most agile climber.

To complete the defences the course of the river Urr, which was only a short distance away, had been diverted, so that the whole hill was surrounded by a natural and sometimes fast-flowing moat. Authorised persons had easy access to the main gate by way of a narrow path which wound upwards round the side of the hill.

And what did the local inhabitants think of it? How did the people who lived in this beautiful corner of the fertile valley of the Urr, about six miles from the sea, regard this innovation? Well, since they had been forced to build it, and in doing so had expended much blood, sweat, toil and tears, they might have had good cause to hate it. Nevertheless they were proud of their achievement, for surely it was the finest castle in all Galloway. Indeed it was. And, had they but known it, the Mote of Urr was almost certainly the finest castle of its kind in the whole of Scotland.

During the latter half of the twelfth century Norman castles of this type were being erected all over Galloway, although none other was designed on quite so grand a scale as the Mote of Urr, which covered over five acres of ground. There were thirty of these castles in Kirkcudbrightshire and about a dozen in Wigtownshire. Most of them were situated in fertile river valleys or on the low-lying coastal lands. It is possible that many were built direct on natural hillocks, but usually there had to be some reconstruction by manual labour. None of the others had such a vast bailey as the Urr castle, and in fact a good many had no courtyard at all, the castle standing alone on a small mote.

At this period the castle was always made of wood and usually consisted of several storeys. Narrow slits in the walls served as windows. The castle was occupied by the baron, his family and personal retainers. The bailey generally accommodated numerous smaller buildings consisting of a chapel, a barn, a smithy, stables, and quarters for the servants and garrison.

## A CENTURY OF CHANGE COMPLETED

It was a son and grandson of Fergus of Galloway who were chiefly responsible for having these powerful castles built, and with their construction the Norman feudalisation of Galloway was completed.

When Fergus died in 1161 his lands in Galloway were divided between his two sons, Uchtred being given the estates in Kirkcudbrightshire, Gilbert's share being the properties in Wigtownshire. Both sons resembled their father, but in different ways. Uchtred inherited all his father's virtues, Gilbert all his faults.

Uchtred realised the benefits of the pacification of the country under Norman feudalism, and he brought many more Anglo-Normans into Kirkcudbrightshire. It was during Uchtred's term of office that the first mote and bailey castles were erected in the part of Galloway he controlled. On the other hand Gilbert, no doubt influenced by his contumacious Celtic colleagues of western Galloway, hated the Normans and wished to preserve the ancient independence of the province. Uchtred, like his father, wanted to help in developing the Church in Galloway, for he founded churches at Kirkcudbright, Twynholm, Kelton, Urr and Buittle; and at Lincluden, near Dumfries, he established the first convent for nuns.

After William the Lion's ill-fated invasion of England in 1173, in which the two brothers and their forces played a major part, Gilbert falsely accused his brother of treachery and captured him, after a long chase, at Cave Uchtred, near Portpatrick. Gilbert then had Uchtred blinded, horribly mutilated and finally murdered. During the next ten years Gilbert fought the Norman barons of eastern Galloway, successfully played off the kings of Scotland and England against each other, and generally did what he pleased.

His double-dealing career was ended, however, in 1185, when Uchtred's son Roland, with the approval of both kings and the assistance of many Norman friends from Cumberland, invaded Galloway. Gilbert was defeated and killed, and Roland was appointed Lord of Galloway by William the Lion, the Scottish king.

William, however, remembered how his grandfather David I had clipped Fergus's wings and he too decided to cut the powers of the Lords of Galloway still further. By making Dumfries a royal burgh in 1186 he removed Nithsdale from the control of Galloway. Then, in 1197, William decided that Gilbert's son Duncan deserved some recognition and appointed him Earl of Carrick. By this act William reduced the size of Galloway to its present dimensions—"from the brig end o' Dumfries to the braes o' Glenapp." He also introduced a complication which, as will be seen later, resulted eventually in Bannockburn.

Now Roland owed much to his English Norman friends who had helped him to regain power in Galloway, and so he repaid his debt by giving grants of land to many of them. He introduced a number of his Cumberland allies to the province, settling them in lands in the Colvend, Southwick and Twynholm areas. It was also during his term of office that rebellious Wigtownshire became properly feudalised and that many more Norman castles were erected in Galloway.

Roland was obviously held in high favour in both England and Scotland. He owned land in both countries and therefore owed allegiance to both kings. Only a year after he became Lord of Galloway, on the orders of King John of England, Roland led a force of his Galwegians to quell a rebellion on the border of Wales. The following year, 1187, he was up in the north of Scotland helping the Scots King William to deal with a revolt there. Galwegians were far travelled even in those days!

Roland earned for himself a great name as a soldier, statesman and churchman. That he was a fine soldier is obvious from his military campaigns. His reputation as a statesman is apparent from his appointment, in 1196, as Constable of Scotland. And in Church matters his legacy was the founding of the abbey of Glenluce in 1190.

Roland's death in 1199 came almost at an appropriate time. In the course of a century his grandfather Fergus, his father Uchtred, and he himself had seen Galloway transformed from a backward, almost barbaric state to an up-to-date Norman civilisation. The contribution all three had made in the establishment of a powerful Church had put Galloway to the forefront in ecclesiastical affairs. Finally, despite occasional changes of heart, they had brought the province into closer alliance with the Scottish crown, yet always reserving for the Lord of Galloway the right to take an independent line whenever he thought fit.

THE HARBOUR
KIRKCUDBRIGHT

## CHAPTER VIII

# ALAN THE GREAT – DEVORGILLA THE GOOD

### GALLOWAY NAVY IN ACTION

TWO memorable and unique events occurred during the years when Alan, son of Roland, was Lord of Galloway. The first was that the province then possessed, for the only time in its history, a Navy: and one which was sufficiently powerful to challenge the Norse control of the western seas. The second occurrence of great moment was a brilliant display of aurora borealis, so exceptional that it struck terror to the hearts of Galwegians, in much the same way as the appearance of a mushroom-shaped cloud over the Solway would affect us today.

The Abbot of Glenluce, an enthusiastic if somewhat unscientific observer noted down full details of the performance of the aurora, and his account was fortunately preserved in the Chronicles of Melrose.

For several successive nights in the autumn of the year 1216 the inhabitants of Galloway had witnessed the awe-inspiring spectacle provided by the "northern lights". As the gigantic fingers of light traced their fantastic patterns across the darkened sky, their meaning seemed as full of ill-omen as the writing on the wall had been to Nebuchadnezzar. The women folk huddled together in apprehensive groups and interpreted the signs as a prophecy of doom. To their superstitious minds such a phenomenon could mean only one thing—a disaster of the greatest magnitude. And well might the women of Galloway fear the worst, for, at that very time, several thousand of their men had accompanied the Scottish king, Alexander II in an invasion of England.

After besieging and eventually capturing Carlisle the Scottish army remained there expecting that, since the English king had just died, satisfactory peace terms would be negotiated. Such inactivity, however, did not meet with the approval of the Galloway contingent, who were always on the lookout for plunder, and so they decided to go off on a foraging expedition of their own.

Now the Galwegians of that time had undoubtedly a great

respect for the sanctity of the Church and its properties—but only, it seems, in their native province. Anywhere "abroad" they considered the Church "fair game". On the Cumberland coast of the Solway they captured, and burned to the ground, the Abbey of Holmcultran, laying waste to the country around and taking a great store of booty. The Galwegians then set off for home, driving, as usual, a number of captives with them.

When they were taking a short-cut across the sands of the Solway at low tide, they were caught in quicksands. The sea rushed in on them before they could free themselves and, like Pharaoh's host, they were engulfed by the waves. Over 2,000 of them were reported to have been drowned. Thus the icy waters of the Solway wrought vengeance on the Galloway soldiers for their wanton desecration of Church property. And truly had the heavens foretold their doom!

The Lord of Galloway was summoned by the Scots king to explain this shameful episode. To show his disapproval Alexander dismissed the men of Galloway in disgrace from the Scottish army. He was by no means the first, or last Scots monarch to discover that the Galloway troops could sometimes be more of a nuisance than a help.

The Lord of Galloway, however, seemed to be personally very popular with the monarchs on both sides of the Border. He had inherited lands in England and owed allegiance for them to King John with whom he was, at first, on very friendly terms. Nevertheless, Alan was present, with the other barons of England, at Runnymede in 1215, when they forced King John to sign the Magna Carta. At the same time, despite the misbehaviour of his troops at Holmcultran, Alan continued in favour with the Scottish king who made him Constable and Chancellor of Scotland.

Alan was the founder of the Galloway Navy which fought with great distinction on numerous occasions during his term of office. His fleet had its first engagement in 1207 when he assisted the English king in an invasion of Ireland. For his services in this cause the Lord of Galloway was rewarded with lands in Antrim. After this Alan conducted a series of combined naval and military operations on his own account. In 1212, for example, he again ravaged the coast of Ireland with a fleet of 76 ships.

For several years after 1220, Alan led his navy into action against the Norsemen who still held all the islands off the west coast of Scotland and also the Isle of Man. His raids were so successful that Olaf, Norse King of Man, was forced to flee, leaving Alan in possession of his kingdom. Olaf appealed to King Hakon of Norway to help him to regain his lost lands. When this was reported to Alan he sent a message to Hakon threatening the Norse king with a Galwegian invasion of Norway.

Hakon, however, answered Olaf's appeal by providing him with a fleet of 80 Norwegian ships which assembled at the Orkneys. Reports reached Alan of the approach of the Norsemen, and he mustered the Galloway Navy in full strength—150 ships with troops on board—at the Mull of Galloway, intending to force an action with the Norse ships as they sailed through the Channel. But Olaf, on learning what was in store for him, turned and fled northwards again, and no engagement took place.

It is interesting to speculate as to what further action Alan might have taken: whether he would have fulfilled his threat to carry the war into Norse territory. But, at that point, he died, and nothing more was heard of the Galloway Navy after his time.

Alan died in 1234 and was buried with much ceremony in Dundrennan Abbey which his great grandfather had founded. As Lord of Galloway he had enjoyed a distinguished reputation in both England and Scotland, and English historians of that time referred to him as "Alan the Great" and as "King of Galloway". He was, however, the last in the male line, leaving three daughters to inherit his titles and lands, a fact which was to have unfortunate consequences for Galloway during the next hundred years.

## THE ABBEY OF THE SWEET HEART

During the eighty years following the death of Alan, Galloway came more under the domination of England than at any time in its history. Although there were several rebellions against England's increasing power, by the end of the thirteenth century Galloway was more closely-allied to England than to Scotland. When Edward I paid his visit here in 1300 Galloway was in fact a vassal province of England. Finally, at Bannockburn the Galloway troops, who had so often claimed the right of leading the Scots into battle, were absent.

This situation arose principally because Alan left no direct male heir, and his three daughters married Anglo-Norman barons who were mostly concerned with the need to keep in favour with the English king. Helena, the eldest daughter, married Roger de Quency, Earl of Winchester; and he, in accordance with feudal custom, then succeeded to his father-in-law's titles as Constable and Chancellor of Scotland. The second daughter, Christina, married the Earl of Albemarle. Devorgilla, the youngest, married John de Baliol of Barnard Castle, near Durham. At Alan's death in 1234 his lands were divided among the three daughters.

When Christina died in 1245, the province was divided between her surviving sisters, whose husbands then shared the Lordship of Galloway. Roger de Quency was over-lord of Wigtownshire, with his castle at Cruggleton: John de Baliol was over-lord of Kirkcudbrightshire, with his headquarters at Buittle.

Because of their ancestry, de Baliol and especially de Quency were at first highly unpopular with the Galwegians who regarded them as "foreigners". Several risings against de Quency broke out in Wigtownshire, and he had eventually to seek the protection of the Scottish king. When de Quency died in 1264, the king, realising the need for a strong man to keep the wild west of Galloway in order, appointed Alexander Comyn, Earl of Buchan, as the first Sheriff of Wigtownshire. Comyn was already married to a daughter of de Quency and, on his appointment, he had Wigtown Castle built as the Sheriff's residence.

Meantime, in east Galloway, relations between de Baliol and his subjects appear to have been much more cordial, and both he and his wife were becoming popular and respected. Baliol was one of the wealthiest men of his time, owning great estates in England and France. Devorgilla, in her own right, also possessed lands and castles in England: one of these was Fotheringay, later to be the scene of one of the saddest episodes in Scottish history.

Whatever kind of man Baliol may have been, Devorgilla was certainly one of the most wonderful characters that Galloway has ever produced. She had been educated by the ladies in the court of her grandfather, the Earl of Huntingdon, and she brought back to the most lawless corner of Britain everything that was best in Norman civilisation. She would have been accounted a great lady in any period of history, and, had there been a female order of chivalry, the gentle and gracious Devorgilla would assuredly have been elected its head.

After Baliol's death in 1268, Devorgilla spent the twenty-one years of her widow-hood in a multitude of good works. One can picture the ageing lady sitting in her castle at Buittle, high on a crag overlooking the estuary of the Urr, signing charters for this and that benefaction, and ensuring that the poor and sick were never turned empty away from her door.

Her husband had already instituted a hostel for sixteen poor students at Oxford, providing free accommodation and an allowance of 8d a day for each one. It was his widow, however, who was responsible for building and endowing the magnificent College named after her husband. In the seven centuries since then hundreds, perhaps thousands of Scottish students attending Baliol have remembered with gratitude the name of Devorgilla in the "bidding prayer" regularly offered up in the College Chapel in thanksgiving for its foundation.

In Galloway, Devorgilla was renowned for her benefactions to the Church and to the poor. She founded monasteries for the Black Friars at Wigtown and for the Grey Friars at Dumfries.

These orders, just recently introduced to Scotland, specialised in carrying the gospel to those common people who lived out-with the influence of existing monasteries, and in ministering to the needs of the sick and the poor. Another gift of inestimable value to the burgh of Dumfries was a bridge over the Nith, which enabled the friars and citizens to go about their business without getting soaked every time they forded the river.

The greatest monument she erected to her husband's memory was, appropriately, situated in Galloway. On a lovely site near the estuary of the Nith, in 1273 Devorgilla founded, named and supervised the building of the Abbey of the Sweet Heart. Its very name is an ever-lasting reminder of the beautiful love-story of Devorgilla and John de Baliol.

When her husband died, she had his heart embalmed and enclosed in a casket of silver and ivory, a not uncommon practice in medieval times. Wherever she went the casket accompanied her. Even when she was carried in a litter, attended by a powerful retinue of guards and serving-women, to visit her estates in England, she took the precious relic with her. As she sat at meals the casket always occupied the dead noble's accustomed chair, food was placed before it and later distributed to the poor.

When Devorgilla died at Barnard Castle in 1289, her coffin was carried in a great funeral procession to Sweetheart Abbey. There, before the high altar, in the soil of Galloway which she loved so well, the monks reverently laid Devorgilla to rest, the casket containing the sweet heart of her husband resting on her breast.

Thus ended one of the most moving of all Scottish love-stories: a love-story pure in spirit, purged of all passion, and entirely free from blemish.

## CHAPTER IX

# SOCIAL LIFE IN THE EARLY MIDDLE AGES

### CASTLE AND COTTAGE

THE earliest townships in Galloway sprang up around the Norman castles. Larger baronies would have contained a number of 'ferm-touns'—clusters of cottages belonging to the serfs. These cottages, however, might be more accurately described as mean and miserable hovels, for they provided only very inadequate shelter and certainly no comfort at all. They were made of stone or wood plastered with clay and had thatched roofs. There were no windows, and the smoke from the fire escaped through the door or through a hole in the roof. Unless the householder was useful with his hands it is unlikely that one would have found much furniture in the single room. The serf and his family slept on beds of rushes or straw on the floor. A bare minimum of kitchen utensils sufficed since the whole family ate from the communal pot, using either their fingers or their 'personal' spoons.

Although the baron's great tower appeared so very much more pretentious, it could by no means be described as comfortable either. The castle would no doubt have contained a certain amount of rather rough furniture, and the bareness of the wooden walls was perhaps concealed by a few tapestries woven by the ladies. The floors were usually covered with straw, or perhaps coarse rush mats. For defence reasons the windows were always tiny and few in number, so that the whole place was eternally dull. The bedrooms, however, would have had some extra comforts, such as pillows and mattresses. The inhabitants of the castle all lived and dined in the one great hall, the noble and his family at the head table and the servants 'below the salt'. Perhaps the greatest drawback to life in such a building was the ever-present danger of fire; the castle was constructed entirely of wood, and all its furniture and furnishings were highly inflammable.

The inhabitants of both castle and cottage had, however, one things in common—a positive aversion to the use of water. In the Middle Ages water was considered suitable for cooking, putting out fires or filling the moat, but seldom for washing. Medieval civilisation has been well described as "a thousand years without a bath"!

It is unlikely that either noble or serf lacked food in Galloway of that time. Beef, mutton, venison, pork, fish, fowl were all plentiful, and in good harvests the crops of oats, barley, peas and beans would have been adequate for the needs of the people. Those were the days when a baron of beef was a daily dish on a nobleman's table, and when a roast of pork meant the whole animal.

The quality of the food, however, was another matter. At certain times of the year not even all the peppers and spices brought home by Crusaders from the east could conceal the rancid taste of salted meat which had gone "high." Fish that was at all bad was never eaten, as it was believed to cause leprosy, a very common disease in Scotland at that time. Home-brewed ale was drunk by all classes, and the nobles were able to enjoy French wines shipped in through Kirkcudbright.

The ladies of the castle led a simple life, their chief occupations being spinning, weaving, embroidery, or tapestry work. Occasionally they would take a turn out-of-doors to indulge in the sport of hunting with falcons.

The baron, however, led a busy life. He had to keep himself constantly fit for warfare by exercising with sword or lance and by taking part in friendly jousts with his knights. A good deal of his time was taken up in hunting, looking after his estate and dispensing justice in his court. Occasionally he had to dictate letters to the local priest, who invariably acted as secretary. (In Galloway of that time three languages were in common use. A form of French was spoken by the noble and his family. The noble could probably also converse with his servants in Gaelic, which was the language of the common people. Church services and correspondence were conducted in Latin.) Nobles were often required to make many journeys away from home on business, visiting the castles of their friends or, if in favour dancing attendance on the king.

These might be described as the duties of a baron, but he also knew how to relax and enjoy life. A writer of that period describes the pleasures of a noble as "playing chess, talking to the ladies, eating heartily, drinking merrily, enjoying a good belch, and watching the snow fall."

One can just picture the Great Chamberlain of Scotland, Walter de Berkeley, "relaxing" in this manner in his manificent castle on the Mote of Urr in the year 1190!

## THE STATE OF AGRICULTURE

There was no relaxation, however, for the serf—only work. On several days of the week he had to give his services free to his master. The rest of the week he had to toil at his own affairs if he and his family were to live. Every ferm-toun had attached to it a certain amount of land which was divided among the serfs for their own use. This, along with free timber, was all they received in return for servitude to their masters. Each serf had his own " rig " of arable land where he grew his crops, and he also shared in the communal grazing.

Every estate in Galloway in the Middle Ages had a Milton, where stood a corn-mill driven by a water-wheel. Both the miller and the landowners were entitled to extract a proportion of all grain milled there, and as the serfs were compelled to use this service it was a monopoly which gave frequent cause for complaint. Almost every baron established and built a small wooden church on his land, its site being named the Kirkton or Chapelton, and the priest was maintained by contributions of food from all people on the estate. The baron's own home farm, large and prosperous, since it was worked by the serfs, was situated next to the castle and was invariably called the Mains.

Although their methods and implements were somewhat primitive, agriculture appears to have been in a reasonably good state in Galloway in the early Middle Ages. Ploughing commonly required a team of four oxen to pull a single share plough and four men to control the operation. One man walked with the oxen driving them on; a second held the reins; the third stood on the plough to keep it in the ground; and the fourth held the beam to guide it. The seed, after being broadcast by hand, was then harrowed in by means of a whin or thorn bush tied to the tail of an ox. Crops grown were oats, barley (for brewing), peas and beans.

The beasts which belonged to the serfs and grazed on the common pastures had to be tended by children all the time, as there were no fences. Rootcrops were unknown then and haymaking was practically impossible, except perhaps on the home farm, because of overstocking. Consequently there was little in the way of winter feed for the livestock, most of which had to be killed at Martinmas (11th November) and then salted.

Milk was practically never drunk, being used instead in the making of cheese most commonly, or butter on rare occasions. Breeding had to be arranged so that the cows would come into milk in the spring and summer, when they could be adequately fed. Those beasts that survived the winter, spent in a turf shelter in the lee of a cottage, or perhaps in the cottage itself, were so weak that they had to be lifted bodily to the pasture when the grass grew again in the spring.

Despite all their difficulties the Galloway farmers of the thirteenth century managed extraordinarily well, and before the end of that century they were actually exporting grain from Kirkcud-bright to England and Ireland. The inhabitants of the province were better fed in the early days of the feudal system than they were two or three hundred years later. In fact, no major improvement was to be made in agricultural methods in Galloway until about the eighteenth century.

## GALLOWAY JUSTICE

Until nearly the end of the fourteenth century Galloway retained its own traditional code of laws, and criminal or civil offences were dealt with in accordance with these. Justice was dispensed by the baron, or his bailie or steward, in the " court " of the castle.

Galloway's code of laws, however, was a particularly flexible one, since it was interpreted differently from one barony to another. There were, for example, several peculiar but interesting ways of proving one's innocence, and all were in common use in Galloway from the twelfth to the fourteenth centuries.

Where " trial by ordeal " was an acceptable method the accused could plunge his hand and arm into boiling water or grasp a red-hot bar of iron, and if the skin healed within a specified time then the accused was innocent. If " trial by combat " was permitted the accused person could challenge his accuser to a duel, and if the accused won he was found not guilty. To us these may seem strange ways of " trying " a person's innocence or guilt. But to the theologically minded Galwegians of that time they were perfectly logical means, since they believed that God would never allow the innocent to suffer or to be killed.

Perhaps the oddest method of all of proving one's innocence was that of " trial by compurgation." This form of " trial " stipulated that if the accused could find a certain number of persons (usually twelve) who were prepared to state on oath that they believed him innocent then the accused was allowed to go free.

Some baronies in Galloway had officers described as " sergeants " of the peace " whose duty it was to bring offenders to trial. They were paid by being awarded a proportion of fines imposed on the offenders they arrested. In Galloway of that time the only crime punishable by death was robbery, and the sergeants of the peace had powers to behead a robber instantly if they caught him in the act.

Every noble in Galloway had his own gallow's hill and drowning pit (for female offenders) and there is evidence to suggest that they were both in constant use on many estates. A ruthless baron could hang anyone he wished to get rid of for the most trivial offence. In those days a Galloway landowner generally regarded himself as a law unto himself within the bounds of his own domain.

Nevertheless, whenever it appeared that the local justices were failing to administer the law in the prescribed manner, the king often appointed a sheriff who would in theory have jurisdiction over the courts of the nobles. By 1263 Aymer de Maxwell had already been installed as sheriff of Dumfries, and in the following year Alexander Comyn was appointed the first sheriff of Wigtown. Despite the creation of these offices, however, the crown continued to recognise the right of the Galloway nobles to administer their own code of laws.

In 1244, when a "royal commission" was appointed to inquire into the conduct of courts of justice in Scotland, Galloway was excluded because "it has special laws within it." Then when King Robert the Bruce was attempting to bring the jury system into operation throughout the country in 1324 Galloway was again excepted. Finally, as late as 1384 it was still being admitted in the King's Council and Scottish Parliament that Galloway had special laws of its own

In some respects the ancient law in force in Galloway drew a nicer distinction between "God's law" and "man's law" than do the present laws of either England or Scotland. Whatever the bible may have to say about "an eye for an eye" or "a tooth for a tooth," that was God's law. In thirteenth-century Galloway man's law said that the penalty for depriving another of an eye was half a merke; for a tooth it was twelvepence.

Except for robbery all crimes, even murder, were punishable by fines. These were usually paid in cattle, the most valuable commodity, but after the introduction of coinage to Galloway in the reign of David I a money fine could be added or substituted. The penalty of murder varied, of course, according to the importance of the victim. The following table reproduces several extracts from the scale of fines that were imposed in Galloway for the murder of persons of various ranks:—

A king .............. 1000 cattle
A king's grandson 150 cattle or 400 shillings
An earl .............. 44 cows, 21 pennies and 2 parts of a penny
A serf .............. 16 cows

At that time in certain parts of Galloway bees were carefully protected by law, and anyone interfering with them or stealing honey was liable to particularly heavy punishment. The reason for this was that some areas of Galloway, especially the district around Borgue, were renowned for the quality of their honey, from which was brewed mead, the most popular and most potent alcoholic beverage in the province.

In twelfth-century Galloway taxes were even more unpopular than they are today, for people had then to pay them twice over—once to the lord of Galloway and also to the crown as well. Such taxes were, of course, almost invariably paid in agricultural produce. During the lordship of Roland an appeal to have the payment to the crown abolished was refused. This double taxation was no doubt the cause of the several attempts in Galloway during the twelfth century to break away from and remain independent of the throne. In addition it must be remembered that all ranks of society might be called on at any time to give military service to their masters.

ISLE OF WHITHORN — KNOWN LOCALLY AS 'THE ISLE'. ONCE A BUSY SEA-PORT; AND THE PLACE WHERE ST NINIAN BEGAN HIS MISSIONARY WORK

## CHAPTER X

# GALLOWAY UNDER ENGLISH CONTROL

### "KING EMPTY JACKET"

CONSIDERED from a patriotic point of view, the Galwegians, formerly the great apostles of liberty, did nothing to distinguish themselves in the Scottish War of Independence. They certainly did not support Robert the Bruce; but neither did they give much assistance to the English. Of course, Galloway had no great love for the Bruce family. If the Galwegians supported any Anglo-Norman at all, John Baliol was their man, since he was Devorgilla's son. Then, when Bruce murdered the Red Comyn, a grandson of Devorgilla, in a church in Dumfries, he forfeited his last chance of assistance from Galloway. Then there was also a suspicion—not confined only to Galloway—that Bruce was waging his campaign for his own personal ambition rather than for the sake of freeing Scotland.

Finally, since all the castles in Galloway were very firmly in the hands of English custodians after 1296, there was little chance of a rebellion being successful. Nevertheless, there is evidence that many of the more humble Galwegians were sufficiently patriotic to believe in Bruce's cause, but they were too few in numbers and too poorly armed to do anything really effective.

In 1286, when Alexander III was killed by a fall from his horse, Margaret, the three-year-old Maid of Norway, became queen of Scotland. Six guardians were appointed to rule until she came of age.

On the 20th September that same year a group of nobles met at the Earl of Carrick's castle at Turnberry and refused to accept the Maid of Norway as queen of Scotland. They resolved that Robert Bruce, Lord of Annandale, then 80 years old but with many sons and grandsons, should be appointed king. They claimed that Bruce (sometimes referred to as "the competitor") was the man "who in accordance with hereditary rights and ancient usages ought to occupy the throne." Present at this meeting was a 12-

year-old page, a grandson of the aged Robert Bruce. It was this boy, also named Robert, who was one day to become the first king of a free Scotland.

Now in fairness to the Bruce's claim to the throne a decision taken in 1238 must be recalled. In that year Alexander II, having at that time no heir, asked his leading nobles to nominate a successor to the throne. The choice lay between Robert (then aged 32) and his cousin Devorgilla. It was decided that Bruce's claim was the stronger, and he was selected as heir to the throne. Since then Devorgilla had borne a son, John Baliol, and a daughter, Alianora, who married John Comyn of Badenoch.

Bruce's claim to the throne in 1286 was, however, no longer valid, as the Maid of Norway was in direct descent from Alexander II. Nevertheless the Bruces decided to back up their claim by force of arms, and they were bold enough to carry the war into that part of the country where the greatest opposition might be expected, namely, Galloway, the home of the Baliols.

Bruce and his private army promptly attacked Dumfries Castle, captured it and drove out the royal garrison. Next he marched to the Baliol's own castle of Buittle and forced it to surrender. At the same time his son, the Earl of Carrick, stormed the third royal castle at Wigtown. In the course of these actions a great number of more humble abodes were destroyed, the fields of the peasantry ravaged and their livestock slaughtered or stolen. This whirlwind campaign, although admirable as a sabre-rattling display of force, certainly did not make the Bruce family any more popular with the inhabitants of Galloway.

The death of the Maid of Norway at the Orkneys in 1290, just when she was arriving to take over the throne, provided the Scottish nobles with the biggest headache they had ever experienced. Who was to succeed to the throne? The situation was further complicated by the fact that the Maid had been betrothed to the eldest son of the powerful King Edward I of England. Had that marriage taken place the crowns of England and Scotland would then have been united, and the two countries might have been spared some three hundred years of strife and bloodshed.

There were 13 claimants for the throne, and since many of them were nobles (or of noble family) it was decided to ask an "outsider," the King of England, to adjudicate. Edward was only too glad of the opportunity to use Scotland's predicament to further his own interests in that country. To begin with he demanded that all 13 applicants should swear that they would acknowledge the King of England as their direct overlord, thus making Scotland a vassal state of England. All 13 agreed.

The leet was soon reduced to two—Robert the Bruce (grandson

of the original "competitor") and John Baliol (son of Devorgilla). Historians and constitutional lawyers have argued for centuries as to which had the better claim. Whether the decision taken was legally correct or not, there is no doubt that Edward I was highly delighted to declare that John Baliol, Lord of Galloway, was elected King John I of Scotland.

It was perhaps as well that Devorgilla had died three years earlier. Whatever pride she might have felt at being the mother of the king of Scotland, it is very doubtful if she would have approved of the unseemly haste with which this weak-willed descendant of Alan, Roland and Fergus rushed to surrender his kingdom to the English.

On 17th November, 1292, Baliol was declared king, and three days later he swore allegiance to Edward I, acknowledging that he held the throne of Scotland under the English king. John Baliol was crowned at Scone on 30th November, and on 26th December he did homage to Edward I at Newcastle.

To the disgust of the Scottish nobles King John gave in to all Edward's demands. Baliol was so lacking in authority, even in his own kingdom, that in 1294 he was compelled by his nobles to appoint a council of four bishops, four earls and four barons who were to be responsible for all public affairs. But this attempt to bolster up the power of the Scottish king did not please Edward I and he decided to teach his Scottish vassal a lesson.

In 1296 Edward led a great army across the Border and penetrated to the north of Scotland by way of the east coast. On 10th July of that year at Brechin John Baliol surrendered his throne, his country and his people to the king of England.

Such was the inglorious end to the brief career of John Baliol as king of Scotland. If only it had been any of the previous lords of Galloway who had been elected to the throne Scotland's story would have been very different. Instead King John is remembered in Scottish history by the derisive nicknames of "Toom Tabard" or "King Empty Jacket." After his surrender Baliol lived in England until 1299, and then at his family estates at Bailleul in France, where he died in 1313.

In the autumn of 1296 Henry de Percy was appointed by Edward I as warden of Galloway and custodian of the castles of Wigtown, Cruggleton and Buittle, which then became English fortresses.

## THE ENGLISH KING IN GALLOWAY

The entry of Edward I and the English army into Galloway on 17th July, 1300, must have provided the most magnificent and colourful spectacle ever witnessed in the whole history of the province. As the army filed across Devorgilla's Bridge over the Nith and took the dusty path to Lochrutton they presented the inhabitants of Galloway with their first view of the flower of England's chivalry at the height of its glory.

Heading the procession were some 80 of Edward's most illustrious peers and knights mounted on powerful chargers. Since they might expect to be attacked at any moment they travelled under arms, and their chain-mail armour and helmets gleamed and sparkled in the bright sunshine. Their gaily coloured heraldic devices were everywhere displayed—on their shields, on pennons fixed to their lances, and even embroidered on the silk or satin caparisons of their horses. Following the knights came a splendid array of men-at-arms, nearly 3000 of them, all chosen warriors.

When they encamped at night a complete town sprang up as if by magic. Pavilions and tents, gaily striped in the "colours" of their owners and emblazoned with their insignia, were quickly erected by the well-drilled servants. Fires appeared throughout the camp as the cooks prepared the evening meal, and the calm air was filled with the appetising smell of roasting meat. According to one account Edward's visit to Galloway coincided with a spell of exceptionally fine weather, and one can imagine the barons of England sitting at their meat and wine on those lovely summer evenings, while from afar the rugged peasants of the province gazed with wonder and envy at this scene of splendour and rich living.

King Edward spent about ten days in the seaport of Kirkcudbright, living in the ancient keep at Castledykes, and worshipping regularly in the church of Grey Friars. While in Kirkcudbrightshire the English king set an excellent example to all subsequent summer tourists by spending his money freely and supporting local industries. Being anxious to create a good impression, Edward was careful to pay cash for everything purchased for his army and he even awarded compensation to some people whose crops had been spoiled by the passage of his army.

Edward purchased a great quantity of wheat grown in this area, and as local millers were unable to handle such a large amount he had it exported to Whitehaven and Workington to be ground there and then returned to his army in Scotland. The current prices paid by the English for various provisions indicate that food was quite plentiful and cheap. A whole ox cost 5s to 6s 8d, fat pigs 2s 2d to 3s 9d, barley malt 4s 4d a quarter, wheat flour 7s a quarter, claret £1 10s a hogshead, and vin ordinaire (light wine) less than 1d a gallon.

The English army halted at Twynholm for several days at the beginning of August while Edward waited for a fresh supply of money to be sent him from Lochmaben. By 10th August the English were encamped on the lands of Enrick, near Gatehouse of Fleet, and from there the king had to send to Carlisle for more money, this time for army pay. Knights received 2s a day, esquires 1s, cross-bowmen 3d and archers 2d.

It must unfortunately be recorded that the king's officials disclosed several regrettable irregularities in the conduct of the local tradesmen. Edward fined Henry, the miller at Girthon, the sum of 13s 4d for overcharging at his mill. Still more discreditable, however, was the discovery that the inhabitants of Gatehouse itself were using deficient measures and illegal weights, for which crimes the town was fined 40s.

Gatehouse was the most westerly point of Edward's journey, but detachments of his army were sent as far as Wigtownshire, where they received the allegiance of the McDowall family. In crossing the Cree there was a brief skirmish with native forces and some of the English were killed.

Edward returned to Dumfries via Crossmichael (19th-20th August) and Sweetheart Abbey, where he spent the night of 24th August. During the next two months the English king remained in the vicinity of Dumfries supervising the strengthening of the castle there.

## ENGLISH ENGINEERING FEAT

Although Dumfries Castle, situated just across the Nith, was not in Galloway proper, it might be appropriate to give a brief account of its reconstruction in 1300, since it is a perfect example of the military efficiency and organisation of the English army of that period.

Edward I, with all his military experience, immediately recognised the importance of Dumfries as the strategic key, not only to Galloway but also, by way of Nithsdale, to Ayrshire and Lanarkshire. Accordingly he ordered that Dumfries Castle should be greatly strengthened by rebuilding and by the addition of further fortifications. The work on the site at Castledykes commenced on 5th September and was practically finished by 2nd November, when Edward left Dumfries. It was a wonderful achievement considering their limited resources in the way of tools and transport.

An army of carpenters, smiths, sawyers, masons, foresters, quarrymen, labourers, ditchers and clerks was recruited for the job. At times there were as many as 250 ditchers, over 100 carpenters, and scores of masons and labourers working on the site. In the forests of the Nith Valley and in Cumberland gangs of men were busy felling trees. Some of the woodwork was pre-fabricated in the forest and carried in sections by soldiers or floated up the Nith to Dumfries.

In all ages people have complained about the unnecessarily large numbers of " pen-pushers " and " form-fillers " in our armies. Historians, however, may be thankful that there were so many clerks and accountants in England's army of 1300, for they have left us a comprehensive record of the work on Dumfries Castle; how many tradesmen of different kinds were employed and for how long used, and the names of the craftsmen responsible for each job. Master craftsmen were paid 9d a day, foremen 6d, tradesmen 4d, labourers 2d, and women ditchers 1½d. Among the dozens of accounts for materials used is one showing the expenditure of £4 18s 8d for 4100 nails and 62 bolts purchased in Carlisle.

The improvements turned the castle into a double fortress. The stone keep formed the inner defence, and a deep ditch, a rampart and a palisade, with turreted wooden guard houses at intervals, surrounded the site. Entrance was over a great drawbridge operated by ropes.

One extract from the detailed list of accounts for provisions for the garrison and other detachments around Dumfries is an order placed on 21st November for 1300 quarters of wheat, 1300 quarters of oats, 1300 quarters of malt, 3000 quarters of dried cod, 15,000 herrings, 200 casks of wine, and 20 casks of honey. In addition hundreds of carcases of cattle, sheep and pigs were regularly purchased locally.

The farmers of Dumfries and Galloway must have been delighted to have such a profitable market for their produce, for the English army certainly did not starve. In fact it would appear that they lived very well indeed.

## CHAPTER XI

# THE BRUCES IN GALLOWAY

### THE MURDER OF THE RED COMYN

ROBERT THE BRUCE must surely have been the most reluctant tourist ever to come to Galloway. He did not want to come here, he was not welcome, and he certainly did not enjoy his visit. During the months he spent as an unwilling guest among the Galloway hills Bruce walked daily hand in hand with death. And his survival can only be attributed to some benign providence that watched over him and carried him through dangers which would have brought about the death of any normal human being many times over. The hills of Galloway have been the scenes of many exciting episodes in the course of our history, but none could be more thrilling than those in which Bruce took part in the year 1307.

Robert the Bruce reached the point of no return in his career when he murdered the Red Comyn (a nephew by marriage of King John Baliol) in Greyfriars Church in Dumfries on 10th February 1306. Comyn, formerly a fellow-conspirator, had betrayed Bruce's plans to the English King, and the Scots patriot was out for revenge. It was a great misfortune that their first meeting, after the betrayal became known, should have taken place before the high altar of a church. In a moment of uncontrollable passion Bruce stabbed and killed the treacherous Comyn, an inexcusable act of sacrilege which was to do his cause incalculable harm for some time to come.

After this there could be no turning back. If Bruce's quickness of temper could lead him into folly, it could also enable him to take those split-second, momentous decisions which proved him such a great leader. Bruce realised immediately that it was all or nothing for him now—a coffin or a crown, a kingdom or a grave.

Before news of the murder could reach Dumfries Castle, only a few hundred yards away, Bruce and his men had captured it and turned out the garrison. Leaving a handful of troops to hold it, Bruce and a few followers hastened north. On the road to Glasgow they encountered a handsome young knight who at once sprang from his horse and, on bended knee, did homage to Bruce as to his

King. This was an eventful meeting for them both, for the young knight was Sir James Douglas, who was to be Bruce's inseparable companion for the rest of their lives; he was also to become the founder of "the Douglas line" in Galloway.

Bruce hastened on to Glasgow, gathering more followers on the way, and then to Scone where he was crowned King of Scotland on 27th March, 1306.

The following twelve months were, however, to be the saddest of his whole career. His wife, his daughter and his two sisters were captured and imprisoned by the English; his youngest brother, his brother-in-law and several of his closest friends were beheaded. After being hounded through the Highlands, Bruce himself was forced to flee for refuge to Rathlin Island, off the coast of Northern Ireland, where he spent part of the winter of 1306.

When the king returned to Scotland and landed on the Carrick coast in the early Spring of 1307, he suffered yet another blow on hearing of the fate of his two brothers, Thomas and Alexander. They had disembarked with a small force at Lochryan on 9th February and had been captured by the MacDowalls and their Wigtownshire men. Alexander and Thomas Bruce were taken to Carlisle and hanged, and the MacDowalls were generously rewarded by Edward I.

The only consolation that came Bruce's way was that he was rejoined in Ayrshire by Sir James Douglas and a small body of loyal men. But almost immediately the advance of powerful detachments of English soldiers forced the Scottish patriots to take to the hills, and they went into hiding in the neighbourhood of Glen Trool. The whole area between Loch Trool and Loch Doon was then called the Forest of Buchan (after the Wigtownshire Comyns whose title that was) and the many tree-clad valleys offered some protection for the Scots troops.

## TRAPPED IN THE GALLOWAY HILLS

Their situation was now desperate, for the English net was quickly drawing around Bruce and his tiny force of less than 300 men. Some 700 English archers patrolled the Ayrshire border; a second detachment of 70 horsemen and 200 archers was advancing westwards from Nithsdale; the men of Wigtownshire were out in strength guarding the fords of the Cree; and a force of 300 expert English bowmen was closing in on Glen Trool. The most serious threat of all, however, was provided by John of Lorn and an army of 800 Highlanders, accustomed to mountain warfare, who began quartering the hills from the Ayrshire side. Bruce and his men, outnumbered by ten to one, were completely encircled.

When John of Lorn began using blood-hounds, one of which

had actually belonged to Bruce himself, the king decided to separate from his men to prevent their being tracked down as well as him. Bruce was accompanied by only one retainer, a foster-brother. The two of them killed five of Lorn's scouts, but immediately afterwards they had to take to water to put the hounds off the scent. They spent many hours crawling up an icy mountain stream, never daring to set foot on dry land.

That night they encountered three local men who did not seem to recognise Bruce but who appeared to be friendly. The king's foster-brother, however, who was supposed to be keeping watch, fell asleep and was murdered in cold blood. Bruce awoke only just in time to save himself from his companion's fate and, despite his tiredness, succeeded single-handed in killing all three of his assailants.

Next morning Bruce, now on his own, was wandering in the area of Craigencallie when he came upon a lonely cottage. It was several days since he had eaten and he was prepared to run any risk in order to obtain food. The sole occupant of the cottage was an old widow woman who invited Bruce to come in, saying that all strangers were welcome because of one. When Bruce asked who that one might be, she replied:

"It is just good King Robert Bruce, rightful lord of all this land."

To the great delight of the widow, Bruce revealed his identity. Then the old woman's three sons came in, and their mother made them do obeisance to their king. When Bruce insisted on the woman accepting a reward for her kindness, the widow asked for 'the wee bit hassock o' land between Palnure and Penkill." Her request was, of course, granted and later confirmed by Bruce when he came into his kingdom. The "wee bit hassock"—some five miles long and three miles broad!—was divided among her three sons who were thus the founders of the families of McKie of Larg, Murdoch of Cumloden, and McClurg of Kirrouchtrie.

Almost immediately after this the King rejoined his brother, Edward Bruce, and Sir James Douglas who had about 150 men with them. They had discovered an English force of several hundred camped on Raploch Moss, near Loch Dee. The Scots quietly occupied a hill above the English camp during the night and, at daybreak, they swept down on the enemy. The English, although surprised at first, seemed about to make a stand. But, to their consternation, they then beheld what they thought was another Scots army charging down the slopes of the hill. The English waited no longer, but turned and fled.

The "reserves" which the English had seen coming into action were not, however, human. They were in fact a large herd of wild goats which the Craigencallie widow's three sons had driven into action. It was no doubt the memory of this successful ruse that prompted Robert the Bruce to repeat the trick, in slightly different form, at Bannockburn.

The Scottish King's most important victory in Galloway was achieved in early April in Glen Trool. An English army of nearly 2000 well-trained men, under Aymer de Valence the general in charge of operations in Galloway, marched into the Glen with the intention of routing out the tiny Scottish force of about 200. When Bruce's scouts warned him of the approach of the enemy the Scots quietly took up their positions on the hillside above the precipitous Steps of Trool. Meantime the English, unsuspecting and unused to the ways of mountain warfare, marched into the pass below.

At the given signal the Scots on the heights above hurled great boulders down on the English, completely disorganising them. The rocks were followed by showers of accurately aimed arrows and cross-bow bolts, and finally by a charge with sword and spear. Only a small handful of the English escaped from the massacre.

This victory had far-reaching consequences for Bruce's cause. A number of Galwegians, who had hitherto held back, began to join the Scots army. By the early summer of 1307 the Scots King, now confident that the tide of his affairs had turned, decided to move the scene of his main operations to central and north Scotland. He left his brother, Edward Bruce, to contain the English attacks in Galloway and Carrick.

## EDWARD BRUCE—LORD OF GALLOWAY

The English, however, were by no means prepared to surrender their control of the province after such a brief struggle. As long as Edward I lived—and the dying king was still directing operations from just over the Solway—he would continue to hammer away at the Scots. Thus, when the MacDowalls of Wigtownshire appealed for aid, the English sent another strong army, under Umphraville, into Galloway, sometime in May.

Edward Bruce, having now gathered more recruits as a result of the recent Scottish victories, marched down from the Carsphairn area as soon as he heard of the advance of the English. A battle fought at Craignell in the Glenkens resulted in a victory for the Scots.

While pursuing the fleeing enemy Edward Bruce climbed to the top of a high hill which overlooked the valleys of both the Dee and the Ken. He was so enraptured with the view that opened before him that he exclaimed "This beautiful countryside must be mine!" A small cairn was erected on the spot, and the hill was thereafter named Cairn Edward.

The English then tried to make another stand near the village now called the Bridge of Dee, but they were again defeated. Since Buittle Castle was still firmly held by the enemy, Edward Bruce decided to move westwards to try to subdue the men of Wigtownshire who, under the MacDowalls, continued their allegiance to the English. The armies met on the flat plain at Kirrouchtrie, near Newton Stewart, and once more Bruce's men were victorious, the chief of the MacDowalls being killed in the fray.

During the rest of that summer Edward Bruce over-ran the whole of open Galloway and forced many of the landowners to swear allegiance to his brother. Only one or two of the strongest castles held out against him. Meantime, at Burgh-on-Sands on the Solway, King Edward I of England lay mortally ill. And, on 7th June, the "Hammer of the Scots" died in sight of the country he had been trying for over ten years to subdue.

The following year, when a new English army again invaded Galloway, a lucky break in the weather, combined with Edward Bruce's opportunism as a leader, enabled the Scots to gain their most astonishing victory yet. The battle took place among the hills of Kirkcudbrightshire; the exact location is not known, but it was probably in the area between Nithsdale and the Glenkens.

Hidden by a dense hill mist, the English force, consisting of 1500 archers, was marching in column of route through a narrow valley between the hills. Unknown to them they were being "shadowed", from the grassy hills above, by Edward Bruce and about 50 horsemen. Suddenly the mist cleared, and the Scots found themselves within less than a hundred yards of the enemy.

Bruce instantly ordered his men to spread out and attack, and before the English archers could bring their bows into action the Scots horsemen were among them. The Scots, hacking and stabbing, wheeled in and out among the defenceless bowmen, whose weapons were, of course, completely ineffective at close quarters. Bruce and his horsemen continued the slaughter until their horses were blown, and the few English who survived fled to the safety of Dumfries Castle.

On 29th June, 1308, the final battle of the campaign was fought. Donald of the Isles and Roland (a local land-owner, probably a MacDowall) gathered a combined force of Islesmen and Galwegians and made a final stand somewhere in the valley of the Dee. The Galloway leaders, however, were all killed or captured, and it proved an easy victory for Bruce and his men.

Thus, in just over a year Edward Bruce had gained almost complete military control over Galloway. Thirteen castles had been captured from the English, only Buittle and Dumfries remaining in the enemy hands.

The Scots King now created his brother Lord of Galloway and

made over to him all Baliol's estates, as well as other lands in the province. During his infrequent visits here the new Lord resided in Kirkcudbright Castle. One of Edward Bruce's first acts as overlord, however, was to confirm the charters of all the monasteries, priories and church lands in Galloway and, in fact, he granted further privileges to several of the religious communities.

Nevertheless, despite all their successes, the Bruce family never achieved any great popularity among the Galwegians. Although Edward Bruce was undoubtedly a magnificent leader of men, and resembled in character many of the previous Lords of Galloway, he never really won the hearts of the people here.

During the next five years Edward Bruce took part in many campaigns against the English and his brother's enemies, and also in the Scots' invasion of England in 1313. Yet he does not seem to have been supported by more than a small body of Galwegians. Even at Bannockburn the Galloway contingent was almost negligible in numbers. In fact there were probably more "Galloway nags" present in that battle than there were Galloway men. Tradition has it that Robert the Bruce was mounted on a Galloway nag when he slew Bohun the night before the battle.

That particular breed of horse, peculiar to Galloway, had been evolved over several centuries by crossing ponies brought by the Norwegians with the heavier native horses of the district. It had become a popular mount for lightly-armoured horsemen all over Britain: even Shakespeare referred to its qualities The Galloway nag was much less cumbersome and more easily manoeuvred than a heavily-laden battle-charger, and was therefore ideally suited to the irregular type of warfare then most common in Scotland.

Edward Bruce, again like many of his predecessors, was incapable of settling down and adapting himself to the arts of peace. The year after Bannockburn he was in northern Ireland helping the Ulstermen to fight the English, and in this he was so successful that he was elected and crowned King of Ireland in 1316. Two years later, however, on 5th October, 1318, Edward Bruce, Lord of Galloway, fought the last of many battles when he was killed in a skirmish against the English at Dundalk in Ireland.

A final reference to the Bruce family and their connection with Galloway concerns the King himself who paid his last visit here in 1329. On 16th March of that year Robert I was in the town of Kirkcudbright where he signed a charter addressed to the city of Aberdeen.

Robert the Bruce was then already a dying man, having contracted a year before, some form of incurable disease; it was not leprosy, however, as has sometimes been suggested. Within another three months he was dead.

Although Galloway had never been a friendly land for him, it was perhaps not inappropriate that the great patriot's final journey through his kingdom should take him in sight of those inhospitable hills in which he had struck his first successful blows for Scottish freedom.

GATEHOUSE OF FLEET, ONE OF SCOTLAND'S EARLIEST CENTRES OF INDUSTRY. THE TOWN HAS ASSOCIATIONS WITH BURNS. HERE HE WROTE 'SCOTS WHA HAE'

## CHAPTER XII

# THE RISE OF THE DOUGLASES

### THE DOUGLAS FAMILY TREE

BONNIE GALLOWA', the popular anthem of the province, speaks of "the heroes o' the Douglas line," referring to that branch of the Douglas family which produced the most powerful and best known Lords of Galloway. Whether they were truly heroes, or not, rather depends on the sense in which the word is used. It must be admitted, however, that no other family exercised greater influence on Scottish history in the late middle ages; and certainly no other name was more respected, or feared, in Scotland or England at that time.

Their very name in fact became so intimidating that, for centuries, mothers all over Scotland had only to mention it to quell the most rebellious of their children: "Wheesht, now! If ye're no' good, the Black Douglas will come and get ye!"

As to their personal heroism there is no question, for they were truly heroic figures in a heroic age. But it is doubtful whether the miserable serfs in Galloway regarded their renowned over-lords in the same favourable light as does the author of "Bonnie Gallowa'."

During their reign as Lords of Galloway the Douglases were responsible for the loss of probably several thousand Galwegians who were compelled to follow their banners through Scotland, England and even France. And many of these campaigns were waged, not for national necessity, but simply for the Douglases' personal aggrandisement or for revenge. The permanent absence of so many of the men-folk resulted in the most serious neglect of agriculture ever known in the province and, on various occasions, in actual famine. The stirring and romantic deeds of the Douglas line make grand reading in the history books of today, but they meant barren fields and empty barns to the inhabitants of Galloway in the fifteenth century.

It has frequently been remarked that it is most difficult to sort out the many ramifications of the Douglas family: they were so numerous. There are perhaps three reasons for this. First, the parent tree split, at an early date, into two main branches—the Red and the Black Douglases, the latter being the family directly connected with Galloway. Another difficulty is the fact that the Earldom of Douglas passed, by an almost Gilbertian legal quirk, from the Red branch to the Black. Finally, to add further confusion, of the nine Earls of Douglas three were named Archibald, three William and three James.

The earliest records of the Douglases date from the late twelfth century when the family was given a grant of land at Douglas Water in Lanarkshire. It was not, however, until the time of the Good Sir James that they became prominent in history and concern the present narrative.

It is hoped that the family tree and the ensuing story may help to clarify at least the pedigree of the Black Douglases. The tree does not show the descent of the Red Douglas family which eventually produced Lord Darnley who married Mary Queen of Scots. It was their son, James VI, who united the crowns of England and Scotland.

But before the Douglases appear on the scene in Galloway, it is necessary to dispose of the last of the Bruces and Baliols. After the death of Edward Bruce, the lordship of Galloway devolved upon his son Alexander who, unfortunately, seemed to possess little of his father's high spirit and courage. Edward Baliol (son of King "Empty Jacket") did, however, resemble his father, being even more useless a character, if that were possible. He made several visits to this area, and on one occasion he had to depart hurriedly and ignominiously without his trousers.

## THE LAST OF THE BALIOLS

When Robert the Bruce died his son, David II, was only five years old, and so the Earl of Moray was appointed Regent. He died in 1332. His successor should have been the Good Sir James, but he had been killed fighting against the Moors in Spain when he took Bruce's heart on a Crusade. The Earl of Moray was therefore elected Regent on 2nd August, 1332, and only ten days later he was killed at the battle of Dupplin, near Perth.

Edward Baliol, with an English army, had landed in Fife and gained a sudden victory over the Scots. Although Baliol immediately had himself "crowned" at Scone, he did not feel safe in Scotland, and made his way to the Borders where he was nearer the protection of his English friends.

At Christmas of that year Edward Baliol, his brother Henry and Walter Comyn were staying at Annan. One night they were rudely awakened from their sleep when Archibald Douglas, youngest brother of the Good Sir James, and a small band of followers raided their house. In the ensuing fight Henry Baliol and Comyn were killed. But Edward, preferring discretion to valour, escaped through a window in his night-shirt and scrambled hurriedly on a horse. And, in the frosty sky, the Yule-tide stars twinkled merrily down at the sight of a trouser-less rider on a saddle-less steed thundering rapidly over the Border to the safety of Carlisle.

The English King, however, continued to back his protégé Edward Baliol, and the following year he sent another army north to meet the Scots. At the battle of Halidon Hill, near Berwick, Archibald Douglas, now Regent, was killed along with Alexander Bruce, Lord of Galloway, and William Douglas, eldest son of the Good Sir James.

Edward Baliol, with the support of the English army and a few disaffected Scots nobles, was now nominally King of Scotland. Like his father, his first act was to do homage to Edward III, King of England, whom he acknowledged as over-lord of Scotland. Next he surrendered the whole of the South of Scotland, including the counties of Dumfries and Kirkcudbright, to the English. By this act he involved Scotland in a hundred years of warfare to regain her lost territory on the Border.

Thus, once again, the eastern half of Galloway became part of England. Wigtownshire, however, under Sir Malcolm Fleming, later Earl of Wigtown, remained loyal to the Scottish King, David II, who was still living in safety in France during his minority.

The English King magnanimously granted his useless vassal the Baliol's former lands in Kirkcudbrightshire, and Edward Baliol took up residence at Buittle, the only place in Scotland where he felt safe. It must be admitted that the inhabitants of Kirkcudbrightshire seemed genuinely pleased to have a Baliol and his English followers ruling over them once more. But this may just have been due to the fact that trade with a friendly England was easier, and certainly more lucrative than it was with the less accessible parts of Scotland. Several local families, such as the McDowalls, McCullochs and Maxwells, were very active in their service to the English at this time.

Edward Baliol, however, was incapable of exerting any real authority as "King" of Scotland, and in 1353 whatever hold he had over Galloway was abruptly terminated when William Douglas (later to become the first Earl) invaded the south-west and battered it into submission. As usual, Edward had the help of English forces, and some of their cavalry were stationed for a time on an island in what is now Carlingwark Loch, at Castle-Douglas. Baliol fled before the Scots' advance, and the other Galloway landowners submitted to the Douglas. Never again was Galloway to be subject to English domination.

The final act in the Baliol story, and a typically sordid one, was played out at Roxburgh in January 1356. There Edward Baliol, in return for 500 marks cash down and an annual pension, "sold" the crown and Kingdom of Scotland to the King of England. With this shameful episode the last of the Baliols passed from the story of Galloway. He was no credit to his grandmother, the gracious Devorgilla, or to the great Galloway line from which he was descended.

When David II became King of Scotland in fact as well as in name, in 1357, one of his first acts was to reward his faithful servant William Douglas by making him an Earl. Twelve years later, in 1369, the Douglas family first became officially connected with the province when Archibald, son of the Good Sir James, was created Lord of Galloway and given a charter as superior of all the lands between the Nith and the Cree.

The new Lord of Galloway was not long in adding to his territorial possessions. In 1371, the Flemings, who had been having serious trouble with many of their Wigtownshire neighbours, sold their lands and Earldom to Archibald for £500. Although the transfer of a title in this manner seems most peculiar, it was apparently quite permissible in those days since the King confirmed it by granting Archibald a charter as Earl of Wigtown.

Archibald then appointed a Steward to collect the revenues, hold courts on his behalf and generally administer his estates in east Galloway. This was the origin of the name "The Stewartry of Kirkcudbright". In Wigtown, however, the King's Sheriff continued to dispense justice, and consequently that part of Galloway came to be referred to as the "Shire".

Thus, for the first time since the death of Alan the Great in 1234, the whole of Galloway was re-united under one over-lord.

## ARCHIBALD THE GRIM

Archibald, the first Douglas to become Lord of Galloway, was singularly unfortunate in his nick-name, "the Grim". It was quite unjustified, and no reflection on his personal appearance or nature; for he was in reality a big, handsome, jovial man. In fact it was the English who first called him "the Grim" because of "his terrible countenance in warfare".

The English certainly had plenty of opportunities of observing exactly how he looked and behaved in battle, for Archibald fought against them on many occasions, the first being his appearance on the French side at Poitiers in 1356. It was an English historian who recorded Archibald the Grim's favourite method of fighting. As soon as the battle became fierce Archibald dismounted and, wielding a great two-handed sword, laid about the enemy mercilessly. He seems to have borne a charmed life.

Archibald, however, also appears to have spent much of his time attending to the home affairs of his estates and his country. In his early years as Lord of Galloway he resided in the ancient castle at Loch Fergus, near Kirkcudbright. But his lasting memorial in Galloway is Threave Castle which he had built, between 1370-80, on a small island in the River Dee, about two miles west of Castle-Douglas. This mighty four-storeyed castle is an outstanding example of the tower-houses of that period.

But Archibald had many other duties thrust upon him in addition to those of his Galloway estates. In national affairs he attended parliament and the King's Council regularly and, in 1385, he succeeded in bringing the laws of Galloway more into line with those of Scotland generally; but, at the same time, he ensured that certain of the ancient legal customs should be retained as being more suited to the nature of the province. Then, on at least one occasion, he acted as royal ambassador to France. From time to time he had also to visit estates which he owned in other parts of Scotland: at Bothwell, in Aberdeenshire, Kincardine, Forfar, East Lothian, Selkirk and Annandale. Before he died he had become the greatest land-owner in Scotland. He was Warden of the West Marches and codified the laws pertaining to their security against English raiders.

Despite his many peaceful preoccupations at home, Archibald could never forget his hatred of the English. To him the only decent Englishman was a dead one, and preferably one killed by himself in battle. He was already over sixty years of age when he fought his final battles against the "auld enemy". In 1385 the old warrior accompanied a Franco-Scottish force over the Border to lay waste to vast areas of northern England. And in the years immediately following, Archibald and his men of Galloway made at least two other highly profitable raids into Cumberland and returned with extraordinary wealth in the way of plunder.

An English chronicler gives an interesting description of those hardy Scots who followed the Lord of Galloway in these frequent forays over the Border.

"When they (the Scots) make their invasions into England they march from twenty to four-and-twenty miles without halting, for they are all on horseback except the camp-followers who are on foot. The knights and squires are well mounted on large bay horses, the common people on little Galloways. They bring with them no carriages on account of the mountains they have to pass; neither do they carry with them any provision of bread or wine, for their habits of sobriety are such in time of war that they will live a long time on flesh half sodden, without bread, and drink the river water without wine. They have therefore, no occasion for pots or pans, for they dress the flesh of their cattle in the skins after they have taken them off; and being sure to find plenty of cattle in the country which they invade, they carry none with them . . . .

"Under the flap of the saddle each man carries a broad plate of metal; behind the saddle a little bag of oatmeal. When they have eaten too much of the sodden flesh, and their stomachs appear weak and empty, they place this plate over the fire, mix water with their oatmeal, and when the plate is heated, they put a little of the paste upon it, and make a thin cake like a biscuit, which they eat to warm their stomachs. It is therefore no wonder that they perform a longer day's march than other soldiers . . . ."

Archibald the Grim was not present at Otterburn in 1388 when his kinsman James, 2nd Earl of Douglas was killed. It was the death of this Earl which has been so dramatically, if inaccurately preserved for use in the famous ballad, "The Battle of Otterburn", or "Chevy Chase", to give its English title. By some peculiar form of entail the earldom now developed upon Archibald who thus added to his numerous titles that of 3rd Earl of Douglas.

In 1398 a still higher honour might have been his if he had chosen to accept it. King Robert III then introduced to Scotland the title of "Duke" and created his son Duke of Rothesay and his brother Duke of Albany. Archibald, however, refused the dukedom offered him, and when a herald announced him as "Sir Duke" he quacked derisively in reply, "Sir Drake! Sir Drake!"

Archibald was held in especially high esteem by the Church because of his many benefactions. While he was Lord of Galloway, Sweetheart Abbey appears to have been in a bad way financially and, according to papal records, it was due to Archibald's generosity that the monastery there was enabled to survive and indeed expand. He built a hospital at the Abbey of Holywood near Dumfries and endowed it with lands at Crossmichael and Troqueer. At Bothwell he established the collegiate church in which he was later to be buried.

Archibald, however, did not simply bestow his benefactions blindly, but made sure that they were put to proper use. For example, when he rescued Sweetheart Abbey from virtual bankruptcy, he only did so on condition that the monks there made sweeping changes in their methods of economy and accounting. Similarly, when he heard the scandalous rumours concerning the "irregular conduct" of some of the nuns of the Convent of Lincluden, he acted promptly and closed it down. In its place he built a beautiful collegiate church and endowed it for a provost and twelve canons.

Archibald the Grim, Lord of Galloway and 3rd Earl of Douglas, died at Threave Castle on Christmas Eve, 1400, aged about seventy-five years. While he had all the characteristic love of the Douglases for feuding and fighting, he also possessed many of the qualities of a good statesman. The province of Galloway, the Church, and Scotland had all benefited at various times from his wise counsel. And if his successors, during the next fifty years, had only inherited some of his wisdom and prudence, the history of Scotland might well have been very different, and the condition of Galloway happier and more prosperous.

AUCHENCAIRN, AT THE HEAD OF THE BAY WITH THE SAME NAME AND BACKED BY SCREEL AND BENGAIRN, IS BUILT ON A STEEP BRAE

## CHAPTER XIII

# THE FALL OF THE DOUGLASES

### CONFLICT WITH THE CROWN

ARCHIBALD THE GRIM was succeeded by his eldest son—another Archibald—who thus became the 4th Earl of Douglas and Lord of Galloway. The new earl played an important part in national and international politics but does not seem to have devoted much time to the affairs of Galloway. His chief claim to fame arises from his name appearing in one of Shakespeare's plays and from his appointment as Marshal of France.

This Archibald and many of his supporters were captured by the English at the battle of Homildon Hill in 1402 and taken into the custody of the Percys. According to Shakespeare's " Henry IV " they were then released on promising to assist the Percys, Owen Glendower and other rebels in their uprising against the king of England. Although the rebels were defeated at Shrewsbury in 1403, the 4th Earl of Douglas is greatly commended by both Scots and English historians (and Shakespeare) for his personal bravery in the battle.

Archibald remained a prisoner of the English until 1409, when he broke his parole. In 1412 he visited France with a large force and entered into treaties of mutual assistance with various French nobles. On his return home he was closely associated for about eight years with the Regent the Duke of Albany in the governing of Scotland.

In 1423, however, the King of France asked for his assistance in fighting against the English, and the Earl of Douglas, always ready for a fight, accepted the invitation and sailed for France with an army of 10,000 men, many of them from Galloway.

The Scottish troops were given a tremendous welcome, and the following year the Lord of Galloway was created Duke of Touraine—one of the loveliest provinces of France—and appointed lieutenant-general of the French forces. That summer he and his army made a ceremonial entry into the sun-drenched city of Tours, where the archbishop waited to welcome him at the cathedral door and then installed him as a canon. Wine flowed lavishly in the streets and altogether there was great merrymaking.

The English met the combined Franco-Scottish army at the battle of Verneuil in August, 1424. At first the French refused to take orders from the Douglas, and then when they saw that the battle was going against them they deserted, leaving the Scots to fight alone. Before the engagement commenced the rival commanders had agreed on a fight to the finish. The Earl of Douglas and nearly all of his 10,000 men were slain; only a handful of Scots escaped to return to Scotland with the news.

The fourth earl had married Margaret, daughter of the late Robert III of Scotland. Although their son—yet another Archibald—succeeded to the earldom, it had already been decided by the will of the late earl and the agreement of James I, that the fourth earl's widow should retain the lordship of Galloway.

During the next 15 years the Lady Margaret lived quietly at Threave Castle and administered Galloway wisely and peacefully. As Lady of Galloway she granted charters to many landowners, one of the first in 1426 being to Andrew Agnew as Constable of Lochnaw. It was this Agnew who later became the first of the hereditary sheriffs of Wigtownshire.

Margaret Duchess of Touraine and Lady Galloway outlived three more earls of Douglas—the 5th, 6th and 7th. She heard of the execution of her two teen-age grandsons and saw her granddaughter, the Fair Maid of Galloway, married to the eighth earl. When she died about 1450 she was buried in collegiate church at Lincluden, where her tomb, richly decorated in flamboyant gothic ornament, may still be seen.

Even before his father's death Archibald, the 5th earl of Douglas, had gained much military experience in France, where he commanded a force of several thousand Scots, most of them from the Douglas lands. During the reign of James I, however, the 5th earl seems to have trod delicately and offended nobody, for on the assassination of the king he became lieutenant-general of Scotland and acted as a somewhat indecisive and inefficient regent for two years. He died (from natural causes!) in 1439, and was succeeded by his fourteen-year-old son William.

The sixth earl was a gay young noble, properly cast in the Douglas mould. Since his house was the most powerful in the land he would let everyone know it. He played the part of a young prince and wherever he went he was accompanied by a "tail" of 1000 retainers.

But the wily Sir William Crichton, Chancellor of Scotland, was determined to break the power of individual nobles and regarded the young earl of Douglas, with all his vast estates and resources in money and men, as the greatest potential threat to the peace of the kingdom. Accordingly in 1440 he issued a most cordial invitation to the earl and his young brother David to visit Edinburgh to meet the ten-year-old King James II.

When the two young Douglases sat at a magnificent banquet in Edinburgh Castle a black bull's head was placed before them—the sign of death. They were arrested, subjected to a mock trial and, despite the pleas of the young king, were then beheaded in the courtyard outside. By this shocking deed Crichton not only eliminated a couple of possible troublemakers but also broke up the family's territorial possessions. The earldom passed to the elderly James Douglas (earl of Avondale and a son of Archibald the Grim), but the lordship of Galloway now came to the eleven-year-old Fair Maid of Galloway, who could still rely, however, on the advice of her aged grandmother, the Duchess of Touraine.

The 7th earl of Douglas was undistinguished for anything apart from his size. He was nick-named "the Gross" because of his corpulence, which was so excessive that it actually prevented him from getting about. Chancellor Crichton, however, no doubt considered that this defect in a Douglas was probably a boon to everyone else and a cause for general thanksgiving. James the Gross died in 1443 and his son William, then only 18 years old, succeeded him.

## THE RUTHLESS EARL

Although the Douglas fortunes had suffered a considerable setback, the family had still a few tricks left, and the young William was the first to take them. On inheriting his title he immediately went to Stirling to swear allegiance to the 13-year-old James II. Despite his family connections the 8th earl obviously created a most favourable impression on both the king and his closest adviser and guardian, Sir Alexander Livingstone, for he was promptly appointed lieutenant-general in charge of the royal forces. Earl William was equally quick to demonstrate that he had inherited many of the qualities of his grandfather, Archibald the Grim, by quelling rebellions almost as soon as they had begun by the united Crichton and Red Douglas families.

The 8th earl played his strongest card, however, in 1444, when amid great rejoicings he married his second cousin, the lovely Maid of Galloway. With this astute trick he reunited all the Black Douglas possessions and became by far the greatest landowner in Scotland; in addition to Galloway he also owned vast estates in the counties of Inverness, Moray, Banff, the Lothians, Lanark and Ayr.

The 8th earl now spent most of his time at Threave Castle, administering his Galloway estates efficiently and dealing ruthlessly with all who did not dance to his tune. He gave serious attention to his duties as warden of the marches, and after several incursions by English raiders realised the need to improve the Scottish defences. In 1448 he called a meeting of Border gentlemen at Lincluden. The laws for the defence of the marches, which Archibald the Grim had originally drawn up, were then written down and published the following year as an appendix to the Scottish Acts of Parliament. These laws ordered, among other things, that bale-fires be kept in constant readiness on hill-tops all along the Border and used as a system of warning if raiders appeared from the south.

It was perhaps just to try out the enemy's defence system that in 1449 the Earl of Douglas and his brothers led the men of Galloway in a raid over the Border and wrought tremendous devastation in Cumberland. Unknown to the Scots an equally strong English force under the Percys was at the same time successfully invading the eastern Border country of Scotland. (It may be noted that these operations were taking place during a period of truce between the two countries!) The two private armies met on their return journeys near Gretna, and the Scots, although they suffered appalling losses, were victorious. Prominent in this battle was the first Lord Maxwell, head of a family which was before long to replace the Douglases in power in Galloway.

The same year the Earl of Douglas attended the great tournament and festivities held at Stirling to celebrate the wedding of James II. In those dangerous days every nobleman was expected to be accompanied on his travels by a "tail" of armed retainers — the bigger the tail the more powerful its owner. But when the Douglas turned up at the ceremony with a personal bodyguard of 5000 men there were many eyebrows raised in wonder. Was he just being unduly cautious or gratuitously offensive? Perhaps the canny William was only remembering what had happened to a former earl who had been invited to dine with the same king at Edinburgh Castle.

Whatever national ambitions the eighth earl may have had, he certainly acted as complete master in his own domains, ill-treating his tenants by hanging any who dared to cross him. In 1450 the Douglas was guilty of hanging the laird of Ochiltree on his own gatepost and of various other similar crimes of oppression. When news of these reached the king his growing jealousy of the powerful Douglases swelled to anger, and the Lord of Galloway then deemed it prudent to travel abroad for a time for the good of his health.

The Douglas's holiday trip through France and Italy was conducted on a truly royal scale, and it has been described as a veritable pageant of chivalry. He was accompanied by a train of six knights with their own suites and attendants, fourteen gentlemen of the best families in the country, with their servants, and a body of eighty mounted men-at-arms. The inhabitants of Rome, who were advised of his coming, were reported to have given him a great welcome and " received him very princely within the town."

During the earl's absence his estates in Galloway were administered by his brother John, Lord of Balvenie, whose behaviour and extortions were so tyrannical that the Galwegians complained to the king, and the royal forces invaded Galloway on two occasions. When news of this reached Rome the earl hurried home, apologising for his brother's conduct, and swore allegiance to the king. On giving a solemn promise as to his future good behaviour the Douglas was reinstated in his title and lands.

But the bold earl now considered he had reached the stage when he could defy his monarch with impunity. No sooner had he returned to Galloway than he captured Sir John Herries of Terregles, a close friend of the king, and hanged him. The dead Herries had been supported in his feud against the Douglases by Sir Patrick Maclellan of Bombie, who lived at Raeberry Castle, a cliff-top stronghold on the Solway near Kirkcudbright. In order to justify his subsequent actions the earl then accused Maclellan of murdering one of the Douglas men and stormed Raeberry Castle. Sir Patrick Maclellan was captured and imprisoned in close confinement in Threave Castle.

When King James heard of this he wrote a politely worded letter to the Lord of Galloway requesting him, as a favour, to hand over Maclellan for proper trial in Edinburgh. This letter was delivered at Threave by Sir Patrick Gray, commander of the royal guard. The cunning earl at once guessed the purpose of Gray's mission, and before either negotiations or the letter could be opened he invited the royal messenger to take some refreshment. As the two men sat at dinner the earl contrived to give secret orders for the immediate execution of Maclellan. When the meal was finished Gray presented the king's letter and asked for Maclellan to be handed over. By this time, however, the unfortunate prisoner had lost his head. And not even all the explanations and apologies of the Douglas could soothe the king's displeasure at this defiantly high-handed action.

In fact James II now realised clearly that he could never be master in his kingdom as long as his nobles continually defied him. He had no doubt also heard rumours of a secret alliance between the earls of Douglas, Crawford and Ross to seize complete control of the country. The king therefore devised a plan to force a show-down with his most troublesome noble. He sent a gracious invitation, accompanied by letters of pardon and safe conduct, bidding the Douglas to meet him at Stirling to discuss the matter amicably.

The Earl of Douglas, despite all the assurances as to his safety, set out rather reluctantly for Stirling. There he was cordially welcomed by the king and treated with the greatest friendliness at the royal banquet. After the meal the king and the earl retired together for a private conversation in which James begged Douglas to break his alliance with Crawford and Ross as its existence threatened the peace of the realm. The earl of Douglas haughtily retorted that nothing would induce him to break a solemn agreement which he had pledged with his friends. At this the king drew his dagger and stabbed the Douglas in the neck and body. Sir Patrick Gray and other attendants then rushed in with pole-axes and swords and slashed and hacked at the dead earl, whose body received 26 wounds.

Thus perished on 20th February, 1452, at the hands of his own king, the eighth earl of Douglas, one of the most turbulent and powerful of all the lords of Galloway. The threat he had represented to royal authority may be gauged from the fact that he alone could muster an army of nearly 20,000 men, and the annual revenue from his estates was even greater than the king's. By assassinating the eighth earl in a fit of temper James II probably served his own interests better than he knew at the time. William was, next to Archibald the Grim, by far the most ruthless and efficient of all the Douglases and, had he lived, might well have rewritten much of Scottish history.

## THE LAST LORD OF GALLOWAY

James, the ninth earl, promptly renounced his allegiance to the king and prepared to plunge the country into civil war to avenge his brother's murder. But the king, who was now beginning to get the measure of the Douglases, acted more quickly still. James II personally led an army through the Borders into Galloway, burning crops and laying waste to all the Douglas lands on the way. The royal forces besieged Threave Castle during part of the summer and, after negotiations, the earl decided to capitulate. On 28th August, 1452, before the gate of the castle, he swore allegiance to James II and gave his solemn oath never to enter into any future conspiracy against his monarch.

The ninth earl then sought—and oddly enough the king supported him—and obtained papal dispensation to marry his sister-in-law. (The lady was not consulted; if she had been she would have objected!) By this marriage he gained control over Galloway as well as over all the Douglas lands. During 1453 the earl was temporarily in favour, for he was sent on a mission to the court of the English king. When he was there it is believed he took the opportunity to negotiate secretly for the help of the English in an attempt to overthrow James II.

Before his plans could mature, however, the king again struck first, capturing Douglas properties in the Lothians. The Black Douglas family now had to fight alone, for their former allies deserted them and were either won over by the king or remained neutral. The Earl of Douglas, who had obviously none of his predecessor's courage or ability, fled to England, but his three brothers—Moray, Ormond and Balvenie—tried to raise the men of Galloway for a last stand. In this they were not very successful; for even in the heart of the Douglas country the king now had his supporters, and Sheriff Agnew, Herries of Terregles and Lord Maxwell were able to recruit a strong royalist force in the province itself.

At the battle of Arkinholm, near Langholm, on 1st May, 1455, the king's army inflicted a crushing defeat on the Douglases. Moray was slain on the field, Ormond captured and executed, and Balvenie fled to England to join the earl in exile.

On hearing of this defeat the earl of Douglas immediately transferred his allegiance to Henry VI and made over to the English Threave Castle and his lands in Galloway in return for an annual pension of £500. (His wife, the Fair Maid, was given safe conduct to England the same year. Later she divorced the earl, whom she had always disliked, returned to Scotland and married the earl of Athol.)

When the Scots parliament met a month after the battle the earl of Douglas was attainted and all his estates forfeited to the crown. Some of his lands in Galloway were given, by way of reward for services to the royal cause, to Agnew of Lochnaw and to the Herries and Maxwells, whose families then began to play increasingly important parts in the story of Galloway.

In the autumn of 1455 James II visited the Stewartry to receive the allegiance of the new landowners and to arrange for the administering of the crown estates in Galloway. By that time Threave Castle had been fortified by an English garrison, but it offered only token resistance when the king brought in one of those "new-fangled canons" (**not** Mons Meg!) and to the great delight of the admiring countryfolk began knocking holes in the walls. All the Douglas lands were at last in the royal hands.

The exiled earl and his brother John of Balvenie, in the hope of regaining their fortunes in Scotland, made several raids over the Border, assisted by the English, but none was successful. In one of these affrays in 1463 Balvenie was captured by the Scots and executed. The earl remained in England until his death in 1488. Since all the other members of his family had perished, most of them violently, and he had no heir, he was the last of the Black Douglases.

Such was the inglorious ending of the last of a great family. At the height of their fortunes, under Archibald the Grim or William the eighth earl, the Black Douglases were unquestionably the most powerful family in Scotland of 1350-1450. Their career provided a typical example of the way in which the barons exercised their power in the Middle Ages, and was also a perfect illustration of the merits and defects of the feudal system.

DUNDRENNAN ABBEY FOUNDED IN 1142 FOR THE CISTERCIANS. THESE ARE FINE RUINS, PARTLY NORMAN, IN A SYLVAN SETTING EAST OF KIRKCUDBRIGHT

## CHAPTER XIV

# THE CHURCH IN THE MIDDLE AGES

### DISTINGUISHED VISITORS TO THE ABBEY

IT was a lovely evening in the early summer of the year 1373. A party of dusty travellers, realising the need to give their panting horses a rest, reined in and halted on a ridge which commanded a perfect view of the valley below. Although it was a scene with which they were all familiar, they never failed to admire and find new pleasure in it every time they visited there. The prospect which opened before them had never seemed more beautiful than it did on that perfect summer evening.

The whole landscape was bathed in sunshine, and the stones of the abbey church and its attendant buildings were tinted a warm reddish-brown shade in the rays of the setting sun. On both sides of the grey wall surrounding the monastery stretched lush meadows of emerald green grass. One corner of the great expanse of the monastery grounds, enclosed on all sides by a high wall, was a blaze of gay colour as the massed petals of the apple blossom reflected the sunshine in countless delicate shades of pink and white.

On the steeper slopes of the low hills, which almost completely surrounded the flat base of the valley, there were numerous belts of trees, now in the first green glory of their new leaves. The rim of the gigantic bowl was broken in only one place, in the south-west, where the valley of the Abbey Burn carved its way through the green hills, making a small v-shaped gap through which the travellers could just glimpse the grey waters of the Solway.

The riders resumed their journey, picking their way carefully down the rutted track between an avenue of beech and oak, and entered the valley below. In the calm of the evening the blue wood-smoke spiralled slowly upwards from the thatched roofs of the twenty or thirty mud huts that clustered together about a hundred yards from the gate of the monastery. As the travellers cantered along the dusty path between the houses the village dogs were set abarking, the hens fled squawking from beneath the horses' hoofs, the ragged children stared in frank curiosity, and the few adult heads which poked inquisitively out were quickly withdrawn as soon as the strangers were recognised.

The mounted men drew up before the massive gate, with its guard-house fortifications on each side, and a voice was raised to hail the keeper. A tiny wicket, so neatly built into the main gate that it was almost invisible, opened and a face peered out. After a momentary glance at the strangers the face lit up in a smile of recognition. The wicket closed, the great gates were swung open, and the travellers entered, just in time to see a monk's portly figure propelling itself at quite unaccustomed speed in the direction of the abbot's house to announce the arrival of the very important personages.

While they waited for the abbot to appear the strangers had time to observe the odd behaviour of another monk who was engaged in the trance-like contemplation of a sundial. Suddenly he came to life and scurried off through an archway into the cloisters. Seconds later the chiming of a bell rang out clearly over the still air. It was supper time.

The same bell heralded the approach of the abbot, a genial figure, his hands outstretched and on his face the broad beam of welcome which he reserved for only the most honoured guests. And none was ever more welcome within Dundrennan's walls than Archibald Lord of Galloway, third earl of Douglas, and recently earl of Wigtown. For, although he was as big a rascal as any when it came to political intrigue, Archibald was a devout churchman and a great benefactor to all the ecclesiastical foundations within his domains. Another more immediate point in his favour was that he always paid handsomely in cash whenever he enjoyed the church's hospitality: more than could be said of some nobles.

Since it was supper time the earl expressed a desire to eat with the monks and, while he and the abbot departed in the direction of the cloisters, his two knights were accompanied to the abbot's house, and the lesser attendants accommodated in the guest-house of the lay brethren.

The monks in the refectory rose respectfully as the abbot and his distinguished guest made their way to the high table, where there was laid before them two slices of coarse bread, bits of cheese and mugs of ale. The earl mumbled a prefunctory grace, all the fare demanded, and quickly downed a deep draught of refreshing ale. He was thirsty after spending a hot day supervising the building of his new castle at Threave.

In the refectory the only sound to break the otherwise complete silence came from a monk in the pulpit who read in a droning voice from a large volume of folios entitled " Collationes Patrum." From his rusty knowledge of Latin the earl gathered that it was all about the dangers of gluttony. Small chance of that here, he thought, eyeing the scraps in front of him. At the same time he was comforted by the certain knowledge that he would very soon sit down to a sumptuous feast in the abbot's house, with a flagon of really excellent French wine to wash it down.

At a signal from the abbot the monks arose, began chanting a Latin grace and then, led by the prior, filed slowly out of the refectory. In the dim light of the cloisters the line of monks became a procession of ghostly figures as their white cassocks appeared momentarily in the framework of each open archway. As they entered the church for compline, the last service of the day, the murmur of their chant and the persistent clack of their wooden-soled shoes gradually died away.

The abbot and his guests were all sleeping soundly when the monks were roused at midnight. Lighted by candles, the monks make their way from the dormitory along a corridor above the chapter house wing and down the night stairs into the south transept of the church to celebrate matins, the first of their daily services, after which they retired again to bed. This procedure was repeated at daybreak for lauds. The daily services of the religious monks were in accordance with the injunctions of the psalmist: "At midnight I will arise to give thanks unto thee," and " Seven times a day do I praise thee." At Dundrennan, however, there were eight church services daily, one extra for good measure, and all these were attended and conducted by the " religious " monks. The lay brethren who were at work all day were required to be present at only two of the services, prime and vespers.

Prime, the first important service of the day, at 6 a.m., was attended by all the inhabitants of the monastery, except those sick. The 250 lay brethren occupied the nave and aisles of the church. Since the earl liked to set a good example, he and his attendants were all present, which meant that the abbot had to put in an appearance too.

As the earl looked around him during the service he noted how simple, almost bare, the church seemed compared with some he had seen in France nearly 20 years before then. The crosses on the altars were made of plain wood and the altar cloths of white linen, not silk. There was glass in the leaded windows, but none of it was stained. Nowhere could he see any of the gaudy ornamentation or paintings which had become such a feature of other religious houses. The Cistercians at Dundrennan seemed to have retained their original ideas of simplicity in church design and architecture.

## THE MONKS AT WORK

Immediately after worship a light breakfast was served, and then the work of the day began. The earl, who was genuinely interested in estate management and good husbandry, immediately departed across the meadows with some of the head lay brethren who were responsible for the farm work. Dundrennan had a reputation second to none in Scotland for the high standard of its farming; its wool crop was prodigious; and by unique experiments in breeding its stock of cattle, sheep and horses had become renowned all over the country.

The monastery owned practically all the land along the coast and for several miles inland between Auchencairn and Kirkcudbright. This was their most fertile ground and was therefore chiefly under crops of wheat, barley and oats, or used as grazing for their finest dairy cattle. In addition to these coastal farms Dundrennan also owned lands in the parish of Kirkmabreck, in the Glenkens, and an extensive area around Kirkpatrick Durham and Corsock.

The agricultural work of the monastery was all carried out under the active supervision of over a hundred lay brethren; those who managed the distant properties were detached temporarily from the monastery and lived where they worked. Each farm had its own village or "ferm-toun," in which lived the serfs who provided all the unskilled labour required. These serfs had to give the same service to the monastery lands and enjoyed the same privileges in return as they would have done on a nobleman's estate.

When he visited the stables just outside the monastery the earl was full of admiration for the magnificent bay horses that were produced for his inspection, and considered privately that they were just as well bred as any he had seen in France; he could think of no higher compliment. He purchased two for a very reasonable sum and arranged for them to be sent to Castle Fergus, where he was then residing. Later, after he had been shown some black polled cattle and had compared their massive, well-filled frames with the lean, mangy beasts that were raised on his own farms, he requested and was granted the temporary loan of the monastery's head cattleman to show the farm bailiff at Loch Fergus how to improve his own stock.

The monastery, however, had several other productive ventures in addition to farming. The lay brethren provided the monastery with a plentiful supply of fresh fish and lobsters from the Solway, and unlimited numbers of salmon in season from their stake nets along the coast. The sale of their wool crop during a period of good years had brought in so much ready cash that they had decided to invest it in a couple of seagoing ships, and this venture was proving most profitable. Manned by lay brethren, these vessels made occasional trips to France and Holland, where there was an excellent market for their wool and whence they imported, very cheaply, wines and other luxuries. These ships also carried on a regular trade with the growing number of coastal towns in England and Ireland where they could sell their other farm produce at a handsome profit.

Many of the brethren were excellent craftsmen. All the buildings in the monastery had been erected over a period of nearly 200 years by its inhabitants; and repairs, improvements and additions were always being carried out.

The earl missed the 9 a.m. service (tierce) for which the religious monks were in full dress—white cassock, black hood, scapula and girdle—since mass was being celebrated; but he was present at their daily meeting in the chapter house just afterwards. The chapter house had not long been rebuilt and improved, and he noticed that some of the most beautiful stonework in the whole monastery was incorporated in its design. The monks, over 30 of them, sat on stone benches around the north and south walls, and the abbot presided from his chair in the east wall. A chapter was read from the "rule" of their order, some church business was discussed with the monks concerned, and since there were no offenders to be disciplined the meeting was ended with a prayer by the abbot in which he made appropriate references to their honoured guest.

Before leaving the chapter house the abbot drew the earl's attention to the tombstone of Egidius, a former abbot who had died only a few years earlier. The decorative work and the inscription on the stone were all beautifully carved, but the lettering was incomplete. The artist had not left himself enough space in which to finish off the wording, and the date had also been omitted. The earl was told that this was the last piece of work to be carved by their old master sculptor, Brother James. In his declining years, although his hand had not lost its cunning, the old man's brain had been unable to cope with the nice calculations necessary to ensure that the inscription could be fitted into the space available. And so this beautifully sculptured monument, which can still be seen in the chapter house today, nearly six hundred years after it was carved, is just as much a memorial to the humble Brother James and hundreds of other monks like him whose saintly lives are recorded for posterity in the stones of these ancient buildings.

The earl then inspected some of the activities of the religious monks. In the cloisters he found some of them conducting classes for about a dozen young boys who were under training as novices. Upstairs in the scriptorium a number of monks were engaged in copying the bible, sermons and other religious works. From the locutorium came the sound of voices from several monks who had retired there for one of the few periods of conversation officially allowed them. The earl then visited the infirmary, where there were a number of bedridden aged and infirm monks who were spending their last days in greater comfort than they had ever known. The visitor gave the infirmarian a sum of money to provide wine for these deserving cases. The earl was surprised, however, to find there several other monks who looked young and perfectly healthy. These patients, he learned, were only resting for an hour or two after having been "bled," an operation performed on every fit monk several times a year.

After washing their hands at the lavater, a stone basin situated against the wall just outside the refectory door, the monks then filed in for the main meal of the day at about 11.30 a.m. The visitors dined with them, and the earl was very gratified to note that meat was being served. The present abbot, a broad-minded man, had increased the number of days on which meat was permitted to two a week, except of course during seasons of fasting. At one time the Cistercians had been vegetarians, but in later years a certain latitude was being allowed in the strictness of their diet. And the occasion of the earl's visit was further marked by a service of wine to all the monks at the guest's request and expense. When the meal was over the monks once more departed, singing, to the church for their midday service, known as sext. As each day was reckoned to begin at 6 a.m. noon was the sixth hour, and 3 p.m., the time of their next worship, was nones or the ninth hour.

In the afternoon the earl visited the apiary and the orchard and found the bees already busy among the apple blossom. The beekeeping brother, who presided over some twenty hives, was delighted when the distinguished visitor complimented him on the industry of his charges. He informed the earl, however, that the most popular honey was the heather honey they obtained from scores of hives on the hills of their inland farms.

In the orchard the head gardener proudly displayed his latest acquisition, a young apple tree in blossom for the first time. He had obtained it at Wigtown, he said, from the Black Friars, who had by some extraordinary stroke of luck—for they really knew nothing about fruit propagation—developed this remarkably fine apple called the "Galloway Pippin." . . . As the old man rambled on the earl noticed that at intervals in the wider avenues between the trees and along the sides of the walls there were heaps of faggots and branches of trees. They looked as if they were rows of small bonfires waiting to be kindled. And that was exactly what they were, the gardener explained: Dundrennan's secret weapon for defence against the late frosts of May. A number of the brethren took turns to mount guard over the orchard during the danger nights when the blossom was out. If a frost came on the bonfires were lit, and other monks were called out to keep them stoked and control their burning. The heat, and particularly the smoke rising from the small fires, had proved remarkably effective against even the hardest May frost.

Shortly before 6 p.m. a buzz of activity began to spread throughout the precincts of the monastery which had been so quiet all day. The lay brethren who had been at work outside the walls came trooping home through the open gateway, and the cries of the children and the barking of dogs greeted the return of the serfs to their homes and families in the village.

A queue of ragged humans began to form up outside the main gate: aged, crippled, deformed, diseased, helpless creatures who would have starved to death long since had it not been for the monastery. Inside the gate the almoner and his assistants prepared to dole out the food which was set aside every day to be given to the poor. And the poor waited patiently, for they knew, with the typical fatalism of their kind, that their turn would come inevitably. Each received his wooden bowl of food and, ravenous though he may have been, he had to stand silently for a moment while the monk blessed him; food for a broken body, food for a broken soul.

The bell chimed, the gates were closed. Into the Abbey Church of Dundrennan they filed slowly and reverently, a great concourse and variety of men—dignitaries of the church, devout monks, laymen, skilled craftsmen, labourers, men-at-arms, squires, knights, a temporal lord—to bend the knee and do equal homage to their one eternal Lord. Then came the triumphant sound of over three hundred voices raised in their evening hymn of praise and thanksgiving.

## THE FLYING ABBOT

During the Middle Ages Galloway was as well served with religious houses as any part of Scotland. There were the three great Cistercian monasteries at Dundrennan, Sweetheart and Glenluce; but in these monks were cloistered, that is, shut in, and did not really make any direct religious contact with the local inhabitants. Nevertheless their presence undoubtedly exercised a beneficial influence on the people of the province.

The layout of the buildings and the way of life at Sweetheart and Glenluce closely resembled that of Dundrennan. Glenluce, however had at least two unique features which are worthy of mention.

The Cistercian monks from Melrose who first colonised Glenluce in 1191 chose a really beautiful situation for their monastery. Built on the widest and most fertile part of the lower valley of the River Luce, it was sheltered by hills on all sides. The builders used the local whinstone in its construction, and although it may lack some of the beauty of the freestone found at Dundrennan and Sweetheart, it merged perfectly into the landscape in a way that would have won the commendation of our modern town and country planning pundits.

James IV, who frequently visited the abbey, must have been one of the first to admire what was perhaps the most attractive feature of its design—the chapter house. Although it was not particularly large, it was a gem of medieval church architecture, with its ribbed vaulted roof rising from a central pier, two beautiful wide-arched windows and a glazed-type floor. The chapter house has been restored and is still greatly admired by visitors to Glenluce.

Perhaps more unusual for that time, however, was the piped water supply, another feature which can still be inspected today. The pipes, manufactured by the Glenluce monks themselves, were made of fire-clay and were specially jointed so that they fitted tightly into each other. Laid only two feet below the surface (there was no heavy traffic in those days), the pipes carried the water from the springs to the kitchen, wash-room and infirmary. At intervals in the pipeline stone-built inspection chambers were constructed so that a rapid check could be made in case of any failure in the supply. Altogether it is a unique example of medieval plumbing.

In addition to the Cistercian monasteries, however, there were several other religious communities whose duty it was to minister directly to the local people.

First there were three important groups of friars who, unlike the cloistered monks of monasteries, had the whole province for their parish. At Dumfries and Kirkcudbright were established colonies of Grey Friars, and at Wigtown a house of Black Friars. Bound by a vow of absolute poverty, these dedicated men were mendicants who travelled from place to place, preaching and teaching in the open, tending the sick and aged in their homes and carrying the gospel message into every remote corner of Galloway. During the Middle Ages friars attained a great record of Christian service.

Each village or estate of importance had its own place of worship, a tiny church—at first wooden, then later stone-built—and the priests in charge of these were generally supplied by the priories of Saulseat, Whithorn and Tongland.

The monastery of Seaulseat, in the parish of Inch near Stranraer, was founded by Fergus in 1148, and Malachy, an Irish Cistercian monk, supervised its establishment. It was soon given the name of "the monastery of the green lake" because of the prolific growth of spore-like vegetation which gave its water a greenish tint. Only a few years after its foundation the monastery was handed over to the Premonstratensian monks, and it was probably the mother house of this order in Scotland. It continued to function until the Reformation, but it was rather overshadowed by its more famous neighbours at Whithorn and Glenluce. No trace of Saulseat Abbey now remains.

Soon after the foundation of Saulseat Bishop Christian decided that the priory at Whithorn would benefit from an infusion of new blood. Accordingly he imported several monks from Saulseat and established the Premonstratensian order at Whithorn. In this way he preserved St Ninian's missionary ideals, because the Premonstratensian monks were not cloistered, but usually lived and worked away from their parent church. Besides serving the cathedral church of the diocese at Whithorn, these monks, along with their brethren at Saulseat and Tongland, took charge of village churches all over Galloway.

About 1200 a new church was built at Whithorn on the site and partly on top of St Ninian's original priory. It was the age of pilgrimages, and Whithorn soon became a sacred shrine visited annually by thousands of people from all over Scotland, England and Ireland. They came to view the relics and tomb of St Ninian and to worship at the oldest established church in the British Isles. The pilgrims were from all walks of life: poor peasants, whose pilgrimage represented a life-time's savings and months of weary walking; kings and queens of Scotland, including Robert the Bruce, James III, James IV, and James V. On one occasion James IV, being unusually penitent, actually walked the whole way from Edinburgh to Whithorn, and he had to have his shoes resoled at Penpont at a cost of 1s 4d.

James IV was Whithorn's most regular pilgrim. He visited there almost every year of his reign (1488-1513)—sometimes twice a year—and, thanks to the accounts of his treasurer, who noted every item of daily expenditure, we still have a detailed record of his activities in this area. He frequently lodged at the various friaries and abbeys in Galloway. During one such visit we learn that the king lost 18s at a game of skittles played with the abbot and neighbouring barons at Glenluce Abbey.

Abbot John Damien of Tongland, an Italian by birth, was a particular friend of the king and one of the most colourful personalities in the Church of that time. Brought up in the Italy of early Renaissance, he must have been stimulated by the scientific discoveries of Galileo and others of that time and desired to surpass even their great achievements. Damien claimed to be on the point of discovering the elixir of youth and to be able to transmute base metals to gold. James IV, who dabbled in science as he did in most things, took this unusual churchman under his patronage. Abbot John was a man of many talents, for we know that he once won six crowns from the king at cards when James was staying at Tongland.

The abbot's chief ambition, however, was to fly, and in due course he believed he had invented a method. A demonstration flight in the presence of the king and his nobles was arranged to take place at Stirling Castle. The flying abbot, wearing a pair of great wings covered with birds' feathers, launched himself from the ramparts of the castle over the sheer cliff face. Two or three seconds later he hit the ground below. By great good fortune, however, he landed right in the midst of a large head of juicy dung. This soft if insalubrious cushion broke his fall so effectively that the hardy pioneer of Scottish aviation escaped with nothing worse than a pair of broken legs.

Summing up on a more serious note, however, we must remember that during the Middle Ages the Church was the greatest power of good in the land. Although the ancient Church was now succumbing to evil and corrupt influences, it had preserved and fostered learning and had maintained the unbroken tradition of Christianity—without religious controversies—for hundreds of years in Galloway.

## CHAPTER XV

# TOWN AND TRADE

### THE EARLIEST BURGHS

MANY of the Scottish burghs which grew up during the Middle Ages followed a similar pattern. There were several features common to most of them: a castle, a religious community, a tolbooth, a market cross and, if on the coast, a harbour. The usual reason for the growth of such towns was trade. Large villages—for none of them were over 1000 in population—whose inhabitants wished to take advantage of the wealth to be derived from trading, might be elevated to the status of burghs, royal burghs or burghs of barony. Each burgh was usually required to pay an annual sum of money, either a fixed amount or a proportion of the customs it collected, to the king or the superior baron, in return for its charter. This was an arrangement, however, which brought financial benefit to the new towns but not to the person who granted the charter. In fact the presentation was often made by way of award for services rendered by the people of the village. The earliest burghs in Galloway developed in much the same way as other Scottish towns of the period.

There is some doubt as to which is the oldest burgh in Galloway. It is likely that some of the earliest charters were lost, and it is certainly known that many of Wigtown's most ancient records were eaten by rats. As far as we know, Kirkcudbright was the first to become a royal burgh, in 1455, when James II presented a charter to the citizens of the town as a reward for their help in the siege of Threave Castle. Two years later, in 1457, Wigtown also received a royal charter. But as this one refers to and confirms the terms of a previous charter it seems probable that Wigtown had been a royal burgh for some time before then. Both towns certainly had a long history prior to 1450, and were probably burghs of barony some centuries before this date. Whithorn, as will be seen later, was able to produce a charter dated 1325 and may perhaps have been the oldest burgh of them all.

Kirkcudbright must have been founded, at least as a village, about the time of Fergus in the twelfth century, and was undoubtedly a community when the friars settled there a little later.

When Edward I visited the town in 1300 and lived in the "new" castle at Castledykes, he found that Kirkcudbright was already a busy seaport and market town for the area. James IV stayed there on at least two occasions, and in 1510 he presented a second royal charter granting Castledykes and various lands to the town.

Wigtown probably came into being when the first sheriff was appointed in 1264 and the royal castle was built. It was a burgh soon after that, for the list of provosts of the town dates from 1330. Later it also became a thriving seaport, serving the whole of western Galloway.

It is possible, however, that during most of the Middle Ages Whithorn may have been the largest and, in some ways, the busiest burgh in the province. The pilgrim traffic made it the most cosmopolitan town in the south of Scotland, and there is evidence that Whithorn made plenty of money from this early "tourist trade." When the Act of 1581 made pilgrimages of this kind illegal Whithorn quickly degenerated in importance and soon became the quiet, sleepy town it is today.

Stranraer, now the largest town in Galloway, was not founded as a burgh until comparatively late in the history of the province. At the end of the Middle Ages there were two villages close together on the shores of Lochryan—the Chapel and Stranrawer. In 1596 they were combined and became a burgh of barony called Stranraer. James VI created it a royal burgh in 1617. New Galloway, which today has the distinction of being the smallest royal burgh in Scotland, received its royal charter from Charles I. Minnigaff, situated at a ford over the Cree, was an important village in the thirteenth century. Large fairs and markets were held there, and if references in early documents are to be believed it was a burgh at one time.

## TRADE BRINGS WEALTH

What advantages did these villages derive from their new status as burghs? And how did these benefit Galloway as a whole?

In the first place the royal charters gave the new burghs freedom to trade within certain specified areas. This actually meant rigorous protection and a virtual monopoly to any burgh concerned, since it could impose customs duties on all goods passing through it either by land or sea. Moreover, each royal burgh was also protected by law against unauthorised trading by outsiders, who could be heavily punished.

The trading area granted to Kirkcudbright stretched from the Nith to the Cree, and Wigtown enjoyed a similar monopoly between the Cree and the Ayrshire border. As there were no roads in Galloway then, and since land transport was fraught with many dangers, the sea became the safest and cheapest trade route to and from the province. Thus Kirkcudbright and Wigtown flourished as trading ports, they derived great revenue for themselves, and they made possible the flow of imports and exports to and from the landward area of Galloway.

The charters of the two royal burghs specified the fair days (about six a year) and the market days (once a week in winter and twice weekly in summer and autumn). Kirkcudbright and Wigtown were thus not only seaports but important market towns as well. The people from the surrounding countryside brought their produce there to sell and at the same time bought goods imported by sea. "Fair trading" was an essential feature of all business transactions: no private dealing was officially allowed. When a ship arrived in port its cargo had to be disposed of openly, and all merchants had to be given a chance to buy. Similarly, no dealings were permitted on market days until the official bell was rung to declare that business could begin.

The common good funds of the burgh benefited from the customs duties imposed on all goods brought to market. These duties were paid at the Tolbooth, which later came to be used for other purposes as well. Both Kirkcudbright and Wigtown farmed out the collection of customs to the private individual, who offered the highest bid for the privilege. In the same way, to save accounting, the Crown, instead of collecting its share of the burgh's variable revenues, settled for a fixed sum to be paid annually. Wigtown, for example, paid £20 a year to the Crown; and as this sum was the same as that then paid by Dumfries the Galloway town must have been a really busy place.

The burghs had several other forms of revenue permitted by their charters. Kirkcudbright and Wigtown both held the fishing rights in their respective rivers, highly valuable because of the salmon. This right was usually leased to a private individual, often a member of the town council, for there was no end of graft in those days. Each town had another monopoly in its grain mill, which had to be used by all the townspeople and thus produced a steady income. Rent was again paid to the town by all who farmed—and this meant nearly everyone—on the burgh lands. Finally, a heavy down-payment had to be made by all who were admitted to the roll of burgesses, the small number of citizens who were allowed to elect or be elected for the town council.

Burghs were naturally very jealous of their trading rights, and a quarrel about these between Wigtown and Whithorn in 1510 gives an example of the litigation of that time. By an early charter the priory at Whithorn had a modified right to trade, but only in goods carried in their own ships. About 1490 Whithorn, then at the height of its power, petitioned for trading rights similar to those of

Wigtown, but this was refused. The priory town next took the law into its own hands and began diverting Wigtown-bound boats to the Isle of Whithorn. The ensuing action was taken to the High Court, where it was argued for the next 20 years, legal processes then being no quicker than at any other time. Because its charter (1325) was older than any that Wigtown could produce, Whithorn was eventually granted certain privileges in trading, but the Reformation put an end to the burgh's prosperity, and it did not long enjoy the benefits of extra trade.

We are accustomed to think of clothes rationing, inflation and currency restrictions as evils specifically associated with the twentieth century. It is interesting, therefore, to note that these were also economic problems in fifteenth-century Scotland. At that time various Acts were passed restricting the amount of Scots currency a merchant could spend in English or overseas markets; there was a limit to the amount of material to be used in making a dress; craftsmen were required to work longer hours and until 4 p.m. on Saturdays; and excessive spending on unnecessary "frills" was generally discouraged.

These economic crises arose from a permanent shortage of gold and silver in Scotland and the consequent debasement of the coinage. Ideally a pound weight of silver ought to have been made into 240 pennies, and in the days of David I it was in fact customary to mint 252 pennies from each pound—the odd twelve going towards the cost of minting and the Crown. But because of the ever-increasing need for more coins in circulation and the shortage of silver, debasement—and as a result of inflation—continued in Scotland for several centuries, and at a much faster rate than in England. By 1400 the pound of silver was worth 528 pennies; in 1451 it was worth 1152 pennies, and by the end of that century 1680 pennies. This restricted and debased currency was a considerable handicap to Scottish merchants in conducting their business abroad. Further debasement continued until there was practically no silver at all in Scotland's " black pennies " and at the Union of the Crowns in 1603 twelve pounds Scots were equivalent in value to one English pound. This is a point which should be appreciated and remembered in order to understand the frequent references in the following centuries to "pounds Scots" and "pounds sterling."

## THE STATE OF SOCIETY

The growth of the royal burghs produced a new class of society —the merchants. Before this, the people of Galloway, apart from the clergy, might have been divided into two groups: those who owned land, and those who did not. Now, in the new towns the merchants formed a "middle class." They were not land, but property-owners. A merchant's property consisted of his house, shop (a part of his house), merchandise, and perhaps a share in a ship trading from Kirkcudbright or Wigtown. Since there were no banks and no really secure method of safe-guarding money, many of the wealthy traders preferred to convert their cash into "gear".

The merchants were undoubtedly men of considerable intelligence and ability and they soon came to be regarded as the "aristocrats" of the towns. In each of the Galloway burghs they formed themselves into a merchant guild, presided over by a dean, and drew up rules governing the conduct of their businesses. These corporate bodies soon came to control almost completely the affairs of the towns.

Another class of people then became prominent in the life of the burghs, namely the tradesmen: butchers, bakers, candle-makers, saddlers, smiths, wrights, carpenters, and many more. For a long time, however, the tradesmen, although a cut above the peasants and bondsmen, exercised little influence in the towns and were rather looked down on by the merchants. It was the lifelong ambition of many tradesmen to become merchants, but it was only on rare occasions that this happened. In due course the tradesmen became more prosperous and more influential, especially when they banded together, as in Kirkcudbright, and formed a body of Incorporated Trades.

In their earliest days the town councils of Kirkcudbright, Wigtown and Whithorn consisted entirely of merchants, since they were the only citizens entitled to vote. Although there is evidence that they used their official positions to further their own business interests, the merchants undoubtedly did great work in advancing the prosperity of their towns generally. Later in the middle ages tradesmen were also admitted as burgesses and gained representation on the town councils.

It is interesting to note that in the later middle ages towns played a greater part in the government of Scotland than they do now. The three Galloway towns not only sent commissioners to the Convention of Royal Burghs but each was also represented in the Scottish parliament. In fact the Three Estates which then formed parliament—clergy, nobles and burgesses—probably formed a better cross-section of the population than any governing body of today.

The burghs could be called on at any time to produce men for military service, and all burgesses were required by law to be proficient in archery and later in the use of fire-arms. James I condemned his subjects for wasting too much of their leisure time in playing football and ordered them to practise archery after the church service every Sunday. In 1587 James VI presented a "Siller

Gun" to Kirkcudbright, to be shot for each year by the Incorporated Trades in order "to encourage them in the use of firearms".

During the later middle ages criminal offenders were dealt with by four courts—the burghs', the barons', the sheriffs' and the Kings, High Courts of Justiciary. No records remain from the sheriffs' and barons' courts which administered justice in the landward areas, but hanging and drowning were undoubtedly frequent punishments, especially for robbery, the most heinous offence of all. The burghs, however, sometimes considered that their power to hold courts was a doubtful and expensive privilege. There are many cases on record in which criminals escaped hanging because of the heavy cost, to a town, of carrying out the sentence. Imprisonment of offenders in small burghs was also often inconvenient and expensive, and banishment came to be a common form of punishment in some towns. Kirkcudbright, situated on one bank of a river over which there was no bridge or ford, found this the easiest way of disposing of their undesirable citizens.

Persons of rank accused of some offence usually appeared before the "King's ayres"—the medieval equivalent of the present-day High Court—which visited Kirkcudbright and Wigtown from time to time. The sentences meted out by this court were often absurdly light in view of the gravity of some of the crimes, and the criminal was sometimes let off altogether if he could find someone to stand surety for his good behaviour in future.

In 1538 Cuthbert Cunnyngham, provost of Whithorn, stole 1,000 merks from the bedroom of one of the canons at the priory. (It was common in those days when there were no banks to place money and valuable documents in religious houses for safe-keeping.) When Provost Cunnyngham was found guilty at the King's ayre he was ordered to restore the money, but was not otherwise punished as he had found a guarantor as to his future conduct.

Patrick Agnew of Lochnaw, hereditary sheriff of Wigtownshire seems to have been an unmitigated rascal despite his title, for he appeared before the King's court on no less than four occasions in as many years. In 1509 he was fined only five merks for taking a bribe to acquit a murderer. Four years later he was convicted on three charges: two of them were for oppression of tenants and neighbours (total fine, ten merks) and a third for stealing four cows (bound over). The records of the King's courts held in Galloway at that time, sometimes with James IV himself on the bench, tell one long story of killings, affrays, oppressions and thefts by "country gentlemen" like Sheriff Agnew, most of whom were either acquitted or bound over in surety.

Piracy was an occupational hazard for the early merchants who often accompanied their cargoes or ships on voyages overseas. In

1522 Duncan McGowan, a young trader of Whithorn, was captured by pirates and released only after payment of a heavy ransom. The same Duncan, who became provost of Whithorn in 1547, was then divorced from his wife and had to sue her for the return of property which belonged to him. By the final divorce settlement McGowan had to pay his ex-wife £60 (Scots) and 10 bolls of meal annually.

## EARLY TOWN AND COUNTRY PLANNING

The middle ages saw an important change in the use of building materials, from wood to stone and lime. The chief reason for this was not so much the superiority of stone as the shortage of wood in lowland areas.

During the fifteenth and sixteenth centuries many fine stone-built tower-houses were erected throughout Galloway; and these small castles probably achieved quite a satisfactory compromise between the needs of defence and the desire for more domestic comfort. Several good examples of this style of architecture can still be seen: in the Stewartry at Cardoness and Carsluith Castles and Drumcoltran Tower; and in Wigtownshire at the castles of Dunskey, Lochnaw and Park at Glenluce, the last-named being post Reformation and probably built with stones from the abbey near-by. Some of the peasants were also by then beginning to use stone in the construction of their one-roomed cottages. Gaps left in the walls served as windows which remained open in summer and were "steeked" with straw or turf in the winter. The roofs were still of turf or thatch.

In the towns a new pattern of domestic architecture was gradually being established, and it was again the wealthy merchants who were responsible for most of the improvements. At first the houses were built of stone on the ground floor and wood above that; later they were all stone and lime. By the beginning of the sixteenth century the main streets in the three Galloway burghs consisted of terraces of stone-built tenements with numerous closes or pends leading off the thoroughfare. These closes were a particular feature of the High Street of Kirkcudbright, then the only street in the town. The large number of early sixteenth century deeds of conveyance still extant shows that in Whithorn there must have been many desirable tenements which invariably fetched good prices when sold.

It is rather surprising, however, to discover that town planning is not, as one might suppose, a twentieth century innovation, but was in fact in operation as early as the sixteenth century. In 1549 a burgess of Wigtown, William Hannay, who wanted to add another storey to his house and also to embellish it with battlements, applied for and received permission from the Crown to carry out the necessary alterations "in the maist honest and substantious manner he plesis."

The third Kirkcudbright Castle, built by Provost Maclellan in 1582 probably with stones from the Greyfriars' monastery only fifty yards away, was a fine example of the architecture of that period. The second street to be opened up in the burgh took its name from this castle which is still in a good state of preservation. With such a palatial family residence already available, it was only appropriate that founder Maclellan's eldest son should later be honoured with the title of the first Lord Kirkcudbright.

By the seventeenth century it was becoming fashionable for "county" families to have town houses in the royal burghs and, this produced some handsome new buildings. Two excellent examples of this type of architecture are Broughton House and Auchengool House in Kirkcudbright. The families of county land-owners, who had previously suffered from a somewhat isolated existence, were now able to enjoy all the excitement of the social round in a town, without having to go to Edinburgh for it.

The royal burghs of Galloway, with their four levels of society —land-owners, merchants, tradesmen and labourers—had now become firmly established as the administrative and economic centres in the life of the province.

The state of agriculture in Galloway showed hardly any improvement throughout the middle-ages, except on the monastery farms. The peasants lived under the same miserable conditions of servitude as they had done for several hundred years. Methods of farming and implements were still primitive, and the winter-feeding of stock was still the problem it had always been. The land remained undrained and unfenced, and crops of oats and barley were poor. Except in a few isolated cases in which the abbeys granted longer leases to a few privileged farmers. the peasant's tenure was on a year to year basis and consequently no one made any effort to improve the land.

Because of the increased export trade, however, some farmers made a great effort to try to build up their stocks of cattle and sheep. There is evidence of greater production and export from Galloway of both hides and wool. The native sheep were then small and white-faced, and they yielded a crop of wool which was then reputed to be of very good quality. Some of the wool was now manufactured locally, but the bulk of the crop was exported or sent to Dumfries where a well-known broad-cloth was produced.

During the middle-ages the rearing of geese had become popular in many parts of Scotland. Records show that they were commonly-used then in the settlement of rent, still paid mostly in kind, and thousands of geese were raised in Galloway during this period.

The rivers of the province yielded two important products. The Dee, Cree and Bladnoch, as well as other smaller streams, provided great numbers of salmon both for home consumption and export. Near Crossmichael, on the Dee, there was a whole series of large traps which produced vast quantities of eels, then a popular delicacy, especially in England.

As there were no roads in those days, only dusty foot-paths, wheeled transport was rarely used. Produce was taken on sledges or in wicker-work panniers on pack-horses.

The biggest change in rural areas, however, was in the appearance of the countryside. Although considerable forests still remained among the hills, the lowlands of Galloway had become almost completely denuded of trees. For hundreds of years previous to this, wood had been the only form of building material and fuel in the inhabited parts of the country. As the trees were removed many kinds of wild animals, such as wolves and wild boars—hitherto quite plentiful—were more easily killed and soon died out.

Eventually it became apparent that the situation was serious, not only because of the removal of the trees but also because they were never being replaced. In the sixteenth century the Scottish Parliament, realising the grave consequences to the country of a shortage of timber, passed three Acts designed to restore the wealth of Scotland's woodlands. The first, in 1535, required every landowner to plant three acres of trees for every £100 worth of land he possessed. There were two later Acts, in the reigns of James V and James VI: the first ordered each tenant of land to plant one tree for every merk of his rental; and the second Act, intended to protect the recently afforested areas, imposed the death penalty for anyone who damaged or cut down growing trees.

Those of us who today derive so much pleasure from the beautiful trees of the Galloway countryside might remember with gratitude the policy of tree conservation first introduced by a far-seeing Scottish parliament over four hundred years ago.

## CHAPTER XVI

# THE REFORMATION

## ITS CAUSES AND BEGINNINGS

ON fine summer evenings in the years 1530-40 small groups of people might have been seen making their way furtively into the woods that overlooked the placid waters of Loch Ken, on the small estate of Airds in the parish of Parton. The leader of this group, however, would have had some difficulty in concealing his movements, for he was over six and a half feet in height and of immense girth. This was Alexander Gordon of Airds. Throughout the Stewartry he was renowned for his strength and, since he could use it to good purpose when roused, he was nicknamed "Sannie Rough". He lived to the great age of 101 years and in his later life came to be known as "the Patriarch".

Gordon and his followers met secretly to read translations of the Bible, especially the New Testament, in English. Such a proceeding was illegal and punishable, for at that time the only knowledge of the Bible permitted and available to people was the official version read in Latin and expounded by priests in the church services. Gordon's bible-study group aroused great interest and, despite the danger, people from all over Galloway came to take part in it, including members of prominent families such as the Maxwells and Stewarts of Garlies.

Most people already realised that corruption had gradually pervaded many of the establishments of the Church. Now, as a result of their studies and discussions, the members of Gordon's group found that their hitherto unquestioning belief in the doctrines of their ancient religion was severely shaken. They found no warrant in the teachings of the New Testament for many of the practices of the Church which they had followed blindly for years. Nevertheless there was never any intention in their minds of everthrowing the established Church; reform within the Church was all that was needed. Thus was the seed of the Reformation first planted in Galloway by Alexander Gordon and his followers in the woods of the Glenkens.

It was another Galloway man, Robert, fifth Lord Maxwell, who was responsible for an action which perhaps did more than anything else to convince the common people all over Scotland of the need for Reformation. The Maxwells, who owned lands in Dumfriesshire, Kirkcudbrightshire and Wigtownshire, had replaced the Douglases as the most powerful family in Galloway. The fifth Lord Maxwell was captured at Solway Moss in 1542 and taken prisoner to England. When James V died immediately after the battle the new monarch was the infant Mary Queen of Scots, and, with the prospects of a long regency ahead, the thoughts of some of the Scottish Protestant nobles turned towards England. They remembered with envy how Henry VIII had carved up and distributed the Church lands among those nobles who had helped him in the Reformation in England. The English king now wished to negotiate a marriage between his young son Edward VI and the infant Mary, provided that Scotland accepted the reformed faith. In this way the two kingdoms would be united and an English king would rule Scotland. Some of the Scottish nobles who had been captured at Solway Moss, including Maxwell, were released immediately on agreeing to accept Henry VIII as Lord Superior of Scotland and on promising to assist the English king in his plans for uniting the kingdoms. One wonders, of course, what it was that made these Scottish nobles act as they did: whether it was a genuine desire for religious reformation, or whether it was simply the prospect of enriching themselves at the expense of the Church.

Whatever his motives may have been, Lord Maxwell, as soon as he was released and returned to Scotland in 1543, introduced a Bill in the Scottish Parliament making it lawful to read the scriptures translated into the English or Scottish languages. Despite opposition from die-hard churchmen the Bill was passed, and all over Scotland folk were able to read or hear the teachings of Christ and his apostles, told to them for the first time in their own language.

But Henry VIII's plans for Scotland did not materialise as he had hoped. Although many of the Scottish nobles and a large number of commoners would have willingly accepted the reformed religion, they were not prepared to allow Scottish independence to be surrendered to an English king. In the "Rough Wooing" the English armies ravaged the Borders and laid waste to towns and abbeys, but did not compel the Scots to submit. Galloway fortunately escaped this devastation, except for one occasion in 1547 when an English force captured Dumfries and raided the Stewartry. The invaders besieged the town of Kirkcudbright but, to the eternal glory of the royal burgh, its citizens resisted so effectively that the enemy were forced to retreat. As they retired the English drove off some 2,000 sheep, 200 cattle and 50 horses, but when they were pursued by a host of angry natives the enemy had to leave behind most of their booty.

Meantime the flames of the Reformation were being further fanned by the publication of pamphlets and the presentation of plays like "The Three Estates" which exposed and satirised the evils of the Church. They drew attention, among other things, to the wide-spread abuse of the office of Commendator. This was an ingenious ruse whereby a layman was given this title and put in charge (in place of an abbot) of a monastery, so that he could draw the revenues accruing from the givings of the people and the produce or rent of the Church lands. Several kings and many noblemen had provided for their numerous children, legitimate or illegitimate, in this way. It was recalled how James IV had his 11 year old illegitimate son appointed Archbishop of St. Andrews, and how five of James V's illegitimate offspring were put in control of Kelso and Melrose Abbeys and five important priories. Adam Blackadder was promoted to be Abbot of Dundrennan to make way for one of the king's young sons at Coldingham Priory. Some of the nobles regarded the Commendator-ship of an abbey as a family concern, and of the 20 abbeys represented in the Reformation Parliament 14 were in the hands of laymen.

But this practice was by no means the worst of the many evils of the Church. Sincere churchmen were now fully conscious of the need for improvement, and Provincial Councils met in 1549, 1552 and 1559 in a last minute effort to correct the abuses which had brought the Church into disrepute. The recommendations made publicly by these councils indicate clearly just what those abuses were. The Council of 1549 condemned "the corruption of morals and the profane lewdness of life in churchmen of almost all ranks". Statutes were passed against "incontinent, intemperate and negligent clergy", accusing them of using the revenues of the church to endow their illegitimate children, ordering that priests must be examined in their ability to read and expound the Scriptures, and requiring priests and bishops to preach at least four times a year. All these and many others, however, remained only paper recommendations; they were never put into force. In the eyes of the people the old Church was dead: it had signed its own death warrant, not so much by its dogma—which few understood or cared about—as by its conduct.

The Reformation General Assembly and the Scottish Parliament of 1560 abolished the authority of the Pope, forbade the saying of Mass, and by approving the Confession of Faith established the doctrines of the presbyterian Church of Scotland " whose only Head is Jesus Christ our Lord."

## GALLOWAY LOYAL TO THE QUEEN

In 1562 John Knox attended the induction in Dumfries of Robert Pont as the first "moderator", or superintendent, of the "presbytery" which comprised the whole of Dumfries and Galloway. Ministers of the reformed church were then appointed to the parishes in this area, and matters concerning church visitation and education arranged.

The following year Mary Queen of Scots visited Terregles, the home of Sir John Maxwell, brother of Robert, sixth Lord Maxwell. This was to prove an eventful meeting, for Sir John was undoubtedly captivated by the charm and beauty of his young Queen and was thereafter her devoted servant. Later that year Sir John Maxwell and Gordon of Lochinvar, who had hitherto been keen reformers, quarrelled with Knox over his rough treatment of the Queen; as a result they withdrew their support from Knox and, with their clans, pledged their unswerving loyalty to the Queen.

In 1565 Mary and her husband Lord Darnley arrived in Dumfries with an army of about 3,000 in order to quell an incipient rebellion of presbyterian nobles who were determined to get rid of the Queen and her so-called papist "King". The rebels, although smaller in numbers, might have risked a battle, but when the Maxwells and Gordons revealed their support for the royal cause the nobles retreated quietly to Carlisle. Mary and Darnley now enjoyed the hospitality of the Maxwells for a time and, before they returned to Edinburgh, the Queen rewarded Sir John Maxwell of Terregles for his loyalty by creating him Lord Herries.

It is interesting to note that although the Reformation was as popular in Galloway as anywhere else, the majority of Gallovidians remained loyal to the throne. The greater part of the Stewartry was controlled by the Maxwells and Gordons, and in Wigtownshire the most powerful family was the Kennedies who had always been close friends of the Queen, even when she was a young girl in France, before her return to Scotland.

Thus, when Queen Mary escaped from Loch Leven and assembled her forces for a last desperate stand at Langside, on 13th May, 1568, many of the most powerful Galloway land-owners, accompanied by their best fighting men, rushed to support her cause. There were the Lords Herries and Maxwell, Gordons, McClellans of Bombie, Sheriff Agnew of Lochnaw, the Kennedys under the Earl of Cassilis, Vaus of Barnbarroch, Baillie of Dunragit, the McCullochs, and the Commendators of Dundrennan, Glenluce and Saulseat. Only the Stewarts of Garlies, the Dunbars and the McKies followed the Regent.

After the defeat of her army at Langside Mary fled the field, accompanied by the ever-faithful Lord Herries and a guard of

Maxwells, and set off for Galloway. Her journey to Dundrennan has been described in different ways. According to one account Queen Mary travelled via the Glenkens, halted at Barstobrick (where Queenshill is said to be called after her) and crossed the Dee at Tongland, pausing to drink from a well there and enjoying the humble hospitality of a poor woman. The other version maintains that the Queen came via Nithsdale and rested at the Herries home at Terregles. Both stories agree, however, that Mary Queen of Scots spent her last night on Scottish soil at Dundrennan, or in some house nearby, and that she embarked for her voyage across the Solway at Port Mary, near the mouth of the Abbey burn.

On disembarking at Maryport the Queen was taken to Carlisle from where, on 20th May, she wrote an affectionate yet dignified letter to the Earl of Cassilis promising that she would return to Scotland in August to carry on the struggle to obtain her rights. But she was never to leave England again. On 8th February 1587 the final curtain was rung down on the tragedy of Mary Queen of Scots when she was beheaded at Fotheringay, the castle which had once belonged to Devorgilla, Lady of Galloway.

## THE GLENLUCE FORGERY

The Galloway nobles at the time of the Reformation were undoubtedly just as unmitigated rogues as were their ancestors centuries before them. Whatever qualities they may have possessed in the way of loyalty either to the cause of the Reformation or to that of the queen, their first loyalty was definitely to themselves. And, as we shall see, the Maxwells, Kennedys, Gordons and others all emerged from that period of history with increased wealth and power. Moreover, they had clearly no moral scruples as to how they enriched themselves or whom they robbed in the process.

In this, it must be said, they were probably no worse than their colleagues in other parts of Scotland. Most of the land-owners considered that once they had helped John Knox to establish the reformed church they had done all that was necessary. The ambitious schemes of the Reformation leaders for developing the church and providing free education at schools and universities were, in the nobles' view, needless extravagances. Knox had intended that his plans would be financed by the vast revenues of the ancient church. The nobles, however, refused to sanction the necessary legislation to make this possible, and for a very good reason: most of the church property and land had already been or was in the process of being transferred to the hands of the nobles themselves. The only source of income the new Church of Scotland enjoyed was the tiends and offerings from the small number of churches which were not ruled by some monastic house.

Thus, in Galloway, the abbeys and priories remained intact for a long time, and their occupants, monks and prelates, continued to dwell there in idleness, comfort and even luxury until they died. Their way of life was unaltered, except that if they did do any work before the Reformation the majority of them did none after it. In fairness, however, it must be recorded that a number of the monks made every effort to keep the Roman faith alive by conducting services in secret for their sympathisers. And although the majority of Gallovidians welcomed and supported the reformed church, there were still areas where Roman catholicism at least existed, if it did not exactly flourish.

The Kennedies of Wigtownshire were first in the race to acquire church property. This family in fact gained a notorious reputation, nationally as well as locally, for their greed; and the occasion when they roasted the Commendator of Crossraguel in Ayrshire to make him hand over the abbey lands is frequently quoted as an example of the methods used by some nobles to gain their ends.

In 1548 a petition was sent to the Pope asking him to appoint a son of the earl of Cassilis as commendator of Saulseat Abbey. The Pope refused this request and instead promoted John Johnston, who had been a monk at Saulseat, as abbot. Johnston proved to be one of the few abbots who remained true to their ancient faith, and he was charged, on at least one occasion, with celebrating Mass. Although he was kidnapped by the Kennedies and tortured at Dunskey Castle. he refused to yield to his captors' demands and continued as abbot at Saulseat until his death in 1598.

The Kennedies spent many years trying to obtain the lands of Glenluce Abbey, and their efforts in this direction gave rise to a particularly gruesome tale, believed for centuries to be historically correct. This story, now proved to be quite false, has been repeated in nearly all the histories of Galloway up to date. Briefly it is this: When the abbot of Glenluce died in 1560 the earl of Cassilis bribed one of the monks to forge a charter, in the dead abbot's handwriting, making over the abbey lands to the Kennedies. Then, in order to prevent any possible betrayal, the earl hired a man named Carnochan to murder the monk who had forged the deed. Finally, to make doubly sure, Cassilis had one of his kinsmen accuse and hang Carnochan for the killing of the monk. That this story should have been acepted for centuries is not really surprising: the reputation of the Kennedies was such that they were believed capable of any atrocity.

The true account, however, reveals that it was the Gordons of Lochinvar, not the Kennedies, who were the real villains of the tale. Lochinvar's interest in Glenluce was first apparent in 1524 when the bishop of Galloway was accompanied on an official visitation by a detachment of Gordons who committed so many thefts and did so much damage that the whole thing was obviously deliberate and savoured of intimidation. But Abbot Walter Malim was not afraid of either his bishop or Gordon and promptly retaliated by sending in a colossal bill for damages and finally taking Lochinvar to court for payment.

By the 1540's the Kennedies had obtained feus of most of the abbey lands in Wigtownshire, much to the annoyance of the Gordons who had not been so successful. When the rival claims were taken to arbitration in 1546 and 1555 a compromise was reached by which each claimant was given a lease of part of the property, the Kennedies getting by far the larger share. The cunning Abbot Walter was obviously playing off one side against the other and thereby reserving some measure of power for himself.

In 1555 Walter died and was succeeded as abbot by another churchman, James Gordon, a brother of Lochinvar. Being bound by previous deeds Abbot James was obliged, in 1559, to renew the feu charter giving Cassilis and his heirs control of the bulk of the abbey estates. Before he had time to do anything to help his brother, the abbot died suddenly and quite unexpectedly, in 1560. Since the earl of Cassilis happened to be in France at that time, Lochinvar took advantage of his absence by acting quickly. He immediately seized and garrisoned Glenluce, and most of its inhabitants fled.

Among the monks who remained was one Michael Learmonth who had been responsible for drawing up many of the legal documents of the abbey. Lochinvar explained to him the proposed forgery, and Learmonth agreed to co-operate, "in order to prevent bloodshed" as he said later. First they obtained an old charter form which had been made out by Learmonth but which had never been signed or sealed. Lochinvar and the monk then used their penknives to erase various parts of the writing. The blank spaces were filled in and the signatures forged by Learmonth, so that the whole document now read as a great feu charter conveying all the land of Glenluce to Lochinvar. The monk later described how the seal was obtained from another old deed and affixed to the forged charter: "the laird held the faice of the sele to ane wet claith and pat the bak of it to the fyir and I took it fra the tak and put it to the greit charter." A touch of corroborative detail was finally added by making a fake entry in the loose-leaf register of deeds belonging to a solicitor in Glenluce who was formerly clerk of the abbey court, but had recently and conveniently died. This forged charter in favour of Lochinvar, was "signed" on 31st January 1558 and thus ante-dated by a year the genuine one granted to Cassilis.

When the earl of Cassilis returned from France in 1561 and discovered what had happened, he first obtained from Learmonth a confession which described every detail of the forgery. The earl then referred the whole case to the Privy Council and the Court of Session. On 4th November 1561 the lords of those councils, meeting at Holyrood house, decreed that the Kennedies were to retain the superiority of the greater part of the Glenluce lands in Wigtownshire, while the Gordons and their friends kept possession of the estates in Wigtownshire and the Glenkens which they had formerly leased from the abbey. Their lordships concluded their finding by expressing the pious hope that the two parties would in future live in "perfyte lufe, amitie, kyndness and Cristean nychbourheid".

## DISPOSAL OF DUNDRENNAN AND SWEETHEART

The transfer to the nobles of the other church properties in Galloway was accomplished with much less trouble. From 1524 the lands of Whithorn Priory and Cruggleton were held by members of the Fleming family, either as abbots or commendators. Lord Fleming of Cruggleton, Chamberlain of Scotland was commendator of Whithorn in 1567, but two years later the estates there fell into the hands of the earl of Moray and his heirs. In 1560 Stewart of Garlies received the possessions of the priory at Wigtown, including the valuable fishings on the river Bladnoch. Although the families already mentioned were the principal beneficiaries in Wigtownshire, many others—such as the Agnews, McCullochs, Vauxes, McCrackens, McKies, McGowans, Kilpatricks etc.—participated in a lesser degree in the shareout of the church properties.

The same thing was happening in the Stewartry, but there the power of the Maxwells was sufficiently strong to prevent other claimants from muscling in. Adam Blackadder, a conscientious churchman and politician, was the last abbot of Dundrennan from 1541 until his death in 1567 after which the Maxwells stepped in and had Edward Maxwell, son of Lord Herries, appointed as commendator. Thus, practically all the land between Gelston and Kirkcudbright, as well as ground in the parishes of Kirkmabreck, Kirkpatrick-Durham and other parts of the county, passed into the possession of members of the Maxwell family.

By the time Edward Maxwell died, in 1598, James VI had, by the Act of Annexation, the disposal of all church lands. In most cases he confirmed the sitting tenants or "owners" in their titles, provided they were loyal; other times he bestowed the lands on royal favourites. Since the Maxwells were then out of favour, because of their papist beliefs, the king erected Dundrennan to a temporal lordship and presented the lands and titles to John Murray, keeper of the privy purse, receiving in return the sum of

£40 a year. Even after James VI moved to England, Murray continued to enjoy royal favour, for he was later given the lands of Lincluden and Holywood, and finally, in 1624, created earl of Annandale. By 1645, however, a large part of the Dundrennan lands had returned to the Maxwell family, in the person of Robert Maxwell of Orchardton.

Sweetheart Abbey, and its immediate neighbourhood, was the last stronghold of Roman Catholicism in Galloway, and the persons responsible for this were the Maxwells and Gilbert Brown, the last abbot. Despite all they had previously done in furthering the cause of protestantism, the Lords Maxwell and Herries soon returned to their old religion. From 1560—when Lord Herries was ordered but refused to destroy Sweetheart Abbey—until the Jacobite rebellions, almost two centuries later, the Maxwells were concerned in nearly every Roman Catholic plot that was hatched.

Gilbert Brown, whose family owned Carsluith Castle, was appointed abbot of Sweetheart in 1550 and held the title until his death in 1612. No man in the whole of Scotland of that time worked harder to keep the ancient faith alive. He had to flee the country on numerous occasions but he always returned and, under the protection of Lord Herries of Terregles, he frequently resided quite openly at the abbey and preached and administered the sacraments of the Roman church in Galloway and Nithsdale.

On Christmas Eve in the year 1585 Gilbert Brown, the Maxwell family and many others of their faith assembled in Lincluden Church to celebrate Mass in the ancient manner. After this Brown had to leave the country for a time, although the Maxwells did not appear to come to any immediate harm. But as soon as Mary Queen of Scots was executed in 1587 James VI visited Dumfries and Galloway to investigate the activities of the Lords Maxwell and Herries in support of the proscribed religion, and as a result Maxwell was exiled. He went straight to Spain where he tried to persuade King Philip to disembark his troops from the Spanish Armada in Kirkcudbright Bay and then to attack England from Galloway. Early in 1588 Maxwell himself landed at Kirkcudbright and mustered his men to support the Spanish, if and when they arrived. After the defeat of the Armada Maxwell was captured and taken prisoner to Edinburgh. Although seventeen of his fellow-conspirators were hung, the ring-leader Maxwell, who always seemed to enjoy special consideration from the king, was released and pardoned.

In 1602 Gilbert Brown, still residing at the abbey, was engaged in a famous theological controversy with John Welsh, son-in-law of John Knox, and the same year Lord Herries was warned by the privy council, under threat of exile, not to harbour the recusant priest. Brown was again arrested and deported, but he returned once more and continued his ministry until his final apprehension in 1609 by Archbishop Spottiswood of Glasgow. He was eventually allowed to depart to France—unfortunately with all the abbey records—and he died there in 1612. (It is interesting to contrast the comparative leniency shown to the Maxwells and Gilbert Brown with the treatment meted out by the episcopalians to the presbyterians in the following century.) The lands of the abbey, which had remained more or less intact, were granted in 1624 to Sir John Spottiswood who later became Lord Newabbey, as a senator of the Supreme Court.

The ninth Lord Maxwell was imprisoned for his papist beliefs in 1607 but he escaped and, after an exciting chase by the government troops, he hid for a time in a cave on Clawbelly Hill at Kirkgunzeon, near Dalbeattie. From there he fled to France, but on returning to this country he was executed in 1613. Five years later, however, the Maxwell lands were restored to his younger brother, Robert, who was created the earl of Nithsdale, a family which was later to provide noted leaders in the Jacobite cause.

The doctrines and discipline of the ancient church had been discredited, its decadent feudalism had been overthrown and its vast wealth dissipated. The new Church of Scotland had no money, but it did have integrity and authority. Its power, however, was no longer wielded by popes and prelates, but by the democratic bodies of ministers and laymen who constituted the courts of the church. And it was the growing influence of the Church of Scotland which resulted in the common folk playing an increasingly important role in the story of Galloway during the century ahead.

KIPPFORD, ON THE SOLWAY COAST, NOW A BUSY YACHTING CENTRE, WAS IN THE 19TH CENTURY A FLOURISHING SCHOONER PORT KNOWN AS "SCAUR"

## CHAPTER XVII

# BAN THE BISHOPS

### EPISCOPACY TRIUMPHANT

THE bishops were the chief bone of contention during the early seventeenth century, and they came to be detested more heartily in Galloway than in any other part of the country. These prelates earned the hatred of the great majority of Scots people for three reasons.

In the first place the bishops not only represented an episcopal and autocratic form of church government, loathed by all true presbyterians, but also threatened, in the eyes of many, a return to Roman Catholicism. Secondly, the bishops, through parliament and the privy council, soon attained great political power which they always seemed to use to strengthen their own position and to weaken the importance of the kirk sessions. Finally, the private lives of many of the bishops were by no means all that they should have been, and this gave rise to much ribald comment and the composition of numerous rude lampoons satirising their behaviour. One of the more polite of these verses describes the pleasures and preoccupations of the bishops as follows::

St Androes loves a cup of wine;
  Wine Glasgow, with an whoore;
Rosse company; play Galloway;
  Brechin not to be poore.

In this comment Bishop Cowper of Galloway came off lightly, since the reference to " play " was merely a comment on his love for the game of golf and the fact that some folk considered he spent too much of his time on Musselburgh links. Even allowing for prejudiced exaggeration, there is evidence that the personal conduct of many of the bishops left much to be desired.

It took the " ban-the-bishops " movement forty years to gain its object. That they were ultimately triumphant was a tremendous achievement for the ministers and elders of the Kirk, and one which demonstrated for the first time in Scottish history the force of public opinion in determining a major state issue. The majority of the common people solidly supported their presbytery representatives, who continually risked their personal safety in defying the crown, the privy council, the law courts and the bishops. The eventual victory of the commoners over the crown marked the decline in the power of the king and his nobles and proved conclusively the growing influence of the parishes and presbyteries in the control of the country.

James VI was responsible for introducing bishops to the Church of Scotland when, in 1597, he managed to have an Act passed permitting bishops to be appointed and to be allowed to sit in parliament. The Church had agreed most reluctantly to this, provided that such " bishops " were elected annually by and were responsible to the General Assembly and that they should not discharge any episcopal duties; they would in fact be " commissioners," and not bishops at all. This compromise did not suit the king's plans, and in 1600 he used his royal powers, in defiance of the Church, to appoint four bishops to sit in parliament. When he became king of England as well, James determined to bring the Scottish Church into line with the Church of England and refused to allow the General Assembly to meet for several years.

Nine Scottish presbyteries defied the king and sent commissioners to an " unofficial " Assembly at Aberdeen in 1605, one of the leading ministers being John Welsh, formerly of Kirkcudbright and son-in-law of John Knox. Six of the ministers, including Welsh, were arrested and tried for treason by a judge and jury who had been carefully instructed by the king's representative as to what the verdict should be. The ministers were, of course, found guilty, sentenced first to death and then to banishment for life. John Welsh lived in exile in France until 1622, when he returned to England and died in London, after being refused permission by James to return to Scotland.

The king quickly followed up this set-back to the presbyterians by a statute, in 1606, which restored to bishops their episcopal rights and revenues and gave them seats in parliament. The bishopric of Galloway, with its cathedral at Whithorn, was presented to Gavin Hamilton. The minister of Penninghame was appointed archdeacon, and the other members of the bishop's chapter were the parsons of Crossmichael, Twynholm, Kirkcudbright, Dalry and Borgue. Although the bishopric was not worth much to begin with, its income was soon increased, and Galloway became second in importance to the archbishoprics of Glasgow and St Andrews. At the final suppression of episcopacy in 1689 the annual revenue of the bishop of Galloway was £5,634 15s (Scots), and he had other emoluments as well.

In 1609 the bishops were given judicial powers when the king created Courts of High Commission to try and punish anyone committing religious irregularities. These courts had complete jurisdiction over all ranks and classes of society, and there could be no appeal against their decisions. The earls of Cassilis and Wigtown and Bishop Hamilton were Galloway representatives on the first of these courts.

In the following year a weak-willed General Assembly held at Glasgow confirmed the bishops in their powers and declared the king to be " the supreme governor and head of the Church." What would John Knox have had to say to this—or Andrew Melville, who had once called the king to his face " God's sillie vassal "? The archbishop of Glasgow and the bishops of Galloway and Brechin then went to London and were consecrated by the archbishop of Canterbury in accordance with the English episcopal form so that they could ordain their brethren in Scotland in a similar manner.

Bishop Hamilton died in 1614 and was succeeded by William Cowper, a Perth minister, who had hitherto been regarded as a staunch presbyterian and was therefore all the more severely criticised for accepting preferment. Cowper was a favourite with James (a somewhat doubtful recommendation!) and was also appointed dean of the Chapel Royal at Holyroodhouse. It was a common complaint among Gallovidians that their bishop devoted more time to this appointment (since it was nearer his favourite golf links) than he did to his diocese. Nevertheless his name is commemorated within his bishopric in Cowper Cairn, a hill near Glen Trool, where he liked to retire for meditation. He was also responsible for at least one praiseworthy action as dean of the Chapel Royal when he persuaded the king not to decorate the chapel with golden statues of the apostles.

Despite his early presbyterian beliefs, Bishop Cowper was very much in favour of introducing a liturgical form of service and was one of the chief supporters, in 1618, of the Five Articles of Perth—kneeling at communion, private baptism and sacrament, catchechising and blessing of children by bishops, and the observance of church festivals—most of which were regarded by Gallovidians as sheer papistry. The three Galloway commissioners to the Assembly, the ministers of Tongland, Glenluce and Leswalt, voted against the articles, as instructed by their presbyteries, and were then severely reprimanded by Bishop Cowper. When the articles were later ratified by the Scottish parliament in 1621 the earls of Nithsdale and Wigtown, Lord Garlies and the members for Dumfries and Wigtown all voted in support; the member for Kirkcudbright burgh, David Arnot, voted against them.

Cowper was succeeded in 1619 by Andrew Lamb, who had

been bishop of Brechin for thirteen years. The new bishop was also a royal favourite and was therefore an enthusiastic supporter of episcopacy in its most extreme form. Bishop Lamb gained a notorious reputation for his intolerance of presbyterianism and for his cruelty as a member of the Court of High Commission. His actions did much to stiffen the presbyterian resistance in Galloway.

While all this was going on most of the land-owners were walking warily, leaving most of the skirmishing to the churchmen; if anything, the more important barons seemed in favour of episcopacy. James had let it be known that he had still honours to bestow on those who supported him. Sir Alexander Stewart was created Lord Garlies in 1607 and was further favoured in 1623 with the title of the earl of Galloway. Robert, ninth Lord Maxwell, was restored to his title and possessions and, despite his Roman Catholicism, was made the earl of Nithsdale. Sir Robert Maclellan of Bombie (a court favourite) and Sir Robert Gordon of Earlston, heir to Lochinvar, each received several charters from the king. The latter was also given a grant of the barony of Galloway in Nova Scotia in 1621; an award which was of no benefit to him or his heirs, but was of some historical interest.

It was this same Sir Robert Gordon who showed just how easy it was in those days for a Galloway laird literally "to get away with murder," and various other crimes as well. The Kenmure family records read:

"On the 13th December, 1613, Sir Robert Gordon obtained a remission under the Great Seal for the slaughter of Richard Irving and for burning the houses of Gratneyhill, Wamphray, Lockerbie, Reidhall and Lanriggs, confining contrary to law sundry gentlemen, murder of James Gordon, his servant, adultery with Janet McAdam, deforcing the king's messenger who summoned him for these crimes, and obliging him to eat and swallow his warrant!"

## GROWING POWER OF THE PARISHES

But while episcopacy was gaining a stranglehold on the higher courts of the Church down at ground level various important events were quietly taking place: movements which were very soon to undermine the whole fabric of the religious hierarchy the Stewart kings were trying to establish. New forces were already springing up and thriving in conditions which ironically had been created by the government and even by the kings themselves.

There was one thing that James VI and I had been scared to do, and that was to interfere with the lower courts of the Church. The kirk sessions and presbyteries, composed of ministers and elders, still remained intact, and many of them were prepared to hold on to their newly won democratic rights at all costs—even by defying bishops and king, if necessary. The kirk sessions were well supported in many cases by the smaller land-owners who were the heritors of the parish churches. The parish was now replacing the barony as the basic administrative unit, and the heritors and kirk session, working together, were taking over many of the functions of the old feudal barons.

Various Acts of Parliament and of the Privy Council helped this new trend to develop and made each parish a more self-contained unit. Ministers were used as local, unpaid civil servants, acted as registrars of births, marriages and deaths and served the central government in a variety of other ways. Parishes were now responsible for looking after their own poor, and kirk sessions often dealt with civil as well as religious offences. By an Act of the Privy Council in 1616 a school had to be established in every parish at the expense of the parishioners. This was confirmed by another Act in 1633 which authorised a local land tax to meet the cost of education. The purpose of the schools (which were supposed to be regularly inspected by the bishops) was clearly stated: not only were they responsible for religious education, but they were also specifically charged with the teaching of English and the abolition of the Irish and Gaelic languages.

All over south-west Scotland a new generation of common people, many of whom had now learned to read, was being raised. Their reading, however, was confined almost exclusively to the bible and their spoken language, especially when they were passionately aroused, was biblical in style. The folk of Galloway and Ayrshire soon came to identify themselves with the Israelite heroes of the Old Testament, and they regarded the episcopalians as Philistines, Amalekites or any of the other enemies of the chosen race. This kind of thinking profoundly influenced their behaviour and gradually inspired them with great strength of purpose in their crusade against episcopacy.

George Rutherford, whose brother Samuel was the noted minister of Anwoth, commenced his duties as schoolmaster in Kirkcudbright at Candlemas 1630. The agreement between Rutherford and the town council, who employed him, gives details of his appointment. Rutherford had a free house and an annual salary of £80 (Scots); and in addition he received a quarterly payment from each pupil at the following rates: 8s from town children and 20s from landward scholars. The schoolmaster was also obliged " to reid in the kirk the prayers, publicklie, morning and evening to raise the psalmes in the kirk, publicklie, and to wryte in the kirk session, their actes, as he shall be requyred," for which services he was paid 20 merks annually. The appointment of

George Rutherford, a notorious presbyterian and "non-conformist," indicates that the people of Kirkcudbright obviously shared his religious opinions. There must have been a good many more like him throughout Galloway, and these dominies were bound to exert considerable influence on both pupils and parents.

It was at about this time that the royal burghs were at the height of their power, both locally and nationally. By law the whole of Scotland's trade with England or overseas could be conducted only by the merchant burgesses of royal burghs. As a result Kirkcudbright and Wigtown were wealthier and more powerful than at any other period of their history. A new charter of 1633 put the affairs of Kirkcudbright in the hands of a council consisting of a provost, two bailies, a treasurer and thirteen councillors, and gave the royal burgh an almost complete monopoly of trade in the Stewartry. That same year New Galloway received its charter as a royal burgh. Stranraer had already been granted its first charter as a royal burgh in 1617, but it was not until later in the century that it became important, chiefly because of jealous opposition from Wigtown. The royal burghs sent members to parliament, and, as we have seen, they exercised great independence in voting In addition there were then in Galloway a number of burghs of barony, most of which are now villages, such as Minnigaff, Dalry, Milton of Urr, and at least one, East Preston (near Kirkbean) which has now entirely disappeared.

The power of the Church was greatly strengthened by a series of Acts between 1625-33 which provided financial security to the individual churches and their ministers. Charles I, whose rule was an extraordinary mixture of sense and stupidity, was largely responsible for initiating these benefits. The measures made provision for the regular payment to the Church of tiends or tithes. One-tenth of the crops or the increase of stock had to be given, in kind or in equivalent money, by the heritors (land-owners) to their local churches. The minimum stipend was also fixed by an Act of 1633 at £44 8s 11d (sterling) or approximately £530 (Scots) per annum. For the first time since the establishment of the Church of Scotland some seventy years before the parish churches were self-supporting and their ministers financially secure.

Thus, by about 1633, the parishes and burghs of the south-west had become much better prepared for the next stage in the conflict between episcopacy and presbyterianism, and a number of notable Galloway personalities were lining up for the fray on opposite sides.

## PRESBYTERIANISM VICTORIOUS

Charles I visited Edinburgh in 1633 in order to be crowned

king of Scotland. At the coronation service the staunch presbyterians in the congregation were horrified at the sight of an altar, candles, embroidered tapestry and, worst of all, a crucifix. And when they then saw the bishops bend the knee before this "symbol of idolatry" their indignation knew no bounds. But, although they seethed with anger inwardly, the congregation remained on its best behaviour and did nothing to mar the royal occasion. The only awkward moment occurred when the archbishop of Glasgow refused to take part in the ceremony because of the "idolatrous trappings," but this was quickly smoothed over when John Maxwell, bishop of Ross, stepped into his place.

John Maxwell was the son of a landowner in the Stewartry parish of Kirkbean. He was an ardent high churchman and, being also a favourite of the king, was selected for early preferment. Only that year Maxwell had been appointed bishop of Ross and a privy councillor, and he was no doubt delighted to be at his monarch's side at such an important ceremony.

Charles marked the occasion by a lavish distribution of coronation honours, many of which might never have been given if the king had known how quickly some of the recipients were to turn against him. Among those honoured were Sir John Gordon, who became Viscount Kenmure and Lord Lochinvar, and Sir Robert Maclellan of Bombie, who was created Lord Kirkcudbright.

Charles was more firmly determined than even his father had been to make the Scottish Church toe the episcopal line, and he ordered that the Courts of High Commission should be revived and that they should proceed relentlessly against all who opposed the official policy. These courts were given the widest possible powers to deal with "all that are scandalous in life, doctrine or religion . . . contemners of church discipline, blasphemers, cursers or swearers."

The court which functioned in Galloway included as members the new bishop (Thomas Sydserff, promoted from Brechin in 1634), the earl of Galloway, Lord Kirkcudbright, two provosts and three ministers. It quickly gained such a notorious reputation for its severity that the earl of Galloway and Lord Kirkcudbright refused to have anything more to do with it and, as many of the warrants appear to have been signed by the bishop alone, the other members of the court were equally lukewarm in their support. Scores of Gallovidians were fined or imprisoned without the benefit of defence or the necessity for proof for trivial offences, some of the victims being among the most respected members of the community.

Robert Glendinning, aged 79, was removed from his living as minister at Kirkcudbright because he refused to allow one of the bishop's delegates to occupy his pulpit. He was sentenced to imprisonment, and the magistrates of Kirkcudbright were ordered to lock him up in the tolbooth. The magistrates, however, refused. Bishop Sydeserff, with a warrant signed only by himself and no other member of the court, then ordered that the aged minister and the magistrates of Kirkcudbright should all be jailed at Wigtown. William Dalgleish, minister of Kirkmabreck, was also deposed from his charge for nonconformity. Next, because the parishioners and principal heritor refused to accept the bishop's nominee as minister, Alexander Gordon of Earlston was banished from his home. In 1636 Samuel Rutherford, minister of Anwoth, having been hauled before the court, refused to recognise the right of either bishop or court to try him for his religious principles, and he was also deposed and banished to Aberdeen. The same year his brother George, schoolmaster at Kirkcudbright, was ordered to resign his post because of his nonconformist beliefs.

Sydeserff of Galloway and Maxwell of Ross, as the two most high church bishops, were chiefly responsible for drawing up the book of canons in 1636. This was a collection of prescribed services and was accompanied by detailed instructions on church discipline: no church business was to be discussed except in the bishops' courts, no minister or elder was allowed to criticise the bishops or their actions, family worship and private prayers and bible readings were forbidden, and so on. The following year "Laud's Liturgy"—the English prayerbook—was produced and ordered to be brought into use in Scottish churches. Every Scot knows the reception this received when it was first read in St Giles', Edinburgh, on 23rd July, 1637, and Jenny Geddes started the riot by hurling her stool at the minister. Sydeserff ordered two copies of the new prayerbook for every church in Galloway, but nobody used it.

That autumn Bishop Sydeserff, who seemed to have incurred the wrath of presbyterians even outside of his bishopric, was attacked in the streets of Edinburgh. He was stripped nearly naked by an angry mob who were seeking proof of the report that he wore a golden crucifix under his clothes, and was only rescued by a group of well-known presbyterian nobles who managed to persuade the crowd to leave him alone. Soon after this Sydeserff was pelted with mud and stones in the High Street of Stirling by a crowd of angry women who scorned him as "Papist loon! Jesuit traitor!"

On 28th February, 1638, the National Covenant was first signed in Greyfriars, Edinburgh, and later that year a copy of it came down to every church in Galloway where it was enthusiastically received. The copy signed at Borgue on 22nd April is still in existence.

The General Assembly of the Church of Scotland which met at Glasgow during November-December, 1638, was attended by all the leading ministers and elders, and the following were some of the commissioners from Galloway to this notable conference: ministers from the Stewartry included Samuel Rutherford of Anwoth, William Dalgliesh of Kirkmabreck, and John Maclellan of Kirkcudbright; and from the elders were Alexander Gordon of Earlston, Provost Glendinning of Kirkcudbright, and Robert Gordon of New Galloway. Wigtownshire ministers were represented by John Livingstone of Stranraer, Andrew Anderson of Kirkinner, Andrew Lauder of Whithorn, James Blair of Port Montgomery (Portpatrick); and the elders by Andrew Agnew of Lochnaw, Alexander McGhie of Whithorn, James Glover of Stranraer, and Sir Robert Adair of Kilhilt. The earls of Galloway, Cassilis and Wigtown were also present.

By abolishing the bishops the Articles of Perth, the book of canons and the prayerbook this assembly brought about what has sometimes been called "the Second Reformation" in Scotland. Some of the less offensive bishops were allowed to continue as ordinary ministers, but others like Sydeserff and Maxwell were publicly humiliated before being excommunicated. Both were offered an opportunity to defend themselves against the accusations, but they refused.

The charges against Bishop Sydeserff of Galloway detailed all he had done to further episcopacy and concluded by stating that "he had embraced excommuicated papists and proferred more love to them than to Puritans; that he had condemned the exercise of family prayer; and that he was an open profaner of the Sabbath by buying horses on that day and doing other secular affairs. All of which having been proven against him, he was deposed and ex-communicated." Bishop Maxwell's offences were even more serious, for he was condemned as "a bower at the altar, a wearer of the cap and rochet, a deposer of godly ministers, an admitter of fornicators to the communion, a companion to papists, a usual player of cards on the Sabbath, and once on communion day."

This Assembly, besides overthrowing the episcopal order, did much good constructive work, some of which was to be of lasting benefit to Galloway. It altered the ecclesiastical boundaries in the south-west and increased the power of the presbyteries by making them more compact and more easily administered. The River Urr became the dividing line between the presbyteries of Dumfries and Kirkcudbright, and Kirkmabreck and Minnigaff combined with the eight parishes in the east of the shire to form the Presbytery of Wigtown. The Presbytery of Stranraer embraced the nine westerly parishes of Wigtownshire and two from the south of Ayrshire.

The folk of Carsphairn had good cause to be grateful for a decision of this assembly and to Lord Cassilis who presented their case. They had themselves managed to build a place of worship at Carsphairn—" which church lyes in a very desolate wilderness, containing 500 communicants " (one wonders where!), but they had no means of raising the annual stipend for a regular minister. The Assembly decreed that a collection be taken in all churches south of the River Tay and that the money thus raised be used to endow the church at Carsphairn—surely the first church extension charge!

The Glasgow Assembly of 1638 was undoubtedly one of the most important in the history of the Church of Scotland, for it established once and for all the form of government of that Church. Its actions, however, were to have immediate and serious consequences for the whole country. The presybterians had acted in absolute defiance of the king, and the inevitable result of this was war. Moreover, many people were to discover in due course that the church discipline wielded by the presbyteries and kirk sessions was to prove, if more democratic, every bit as rigorous as any that they had experienced before. As an English Puritan John Milton briefly put it, " the new presbyter is but the old priest writ large."

BALCARY FISHERY AND HESTAN ISLAND. THIS PART OF THE SOLWAY COAST IS STUDDED WITH SALMON STAKENET POLES SAND-LOCKED AT LOW TIDE

CHAPTER XVIII

# THE COVENANT GOES TO WAR

## THE STEWARTRY WAR COMMITTEE

THE war-time restrictions which were imposed on the whole of Britain in 1939 were nothing new to Gallovidians. They had experienced it all exactly three hundred years previously. Conscription, rationing, compulsory national savings, post-war credits, price control and the requisitioning of goods were all in force in Galloway in 1639. Moreover there was an enterprising local War Committee, armed with dictatorial powers, to ensure that all the rules and regulations imposed by the covenant leaders in Edinburgh were rigidly enforced in the Stewartry.

By the spring of 1639 war had clearly become inevitable. The Committee of Estates had ordered the raising of levies in all parts of Scotland, and nowhere in the country was the response more enthusiastic than in Galloway. The Lords Cassilis and Kirkcudbright immediately raised regiments in the Shire and Stewartry respectively, and younger members of the nobility, landowners and staunch presbyterian peasants flocked to their standards. In addition, a number of officers and mercenaries with experience of service on the continent enrolled in the Galloway contingents. In May of that year the town council of Kirkcudbright quickly put the royal burgh on a war footing by decreeing that no one was to leave the town without their permission and that all citizens were to hold themselves in readiness with arms.

After Charles I had been intimidated by a show of force by a covenant army of 25,000 there followed a year of uneasy armed truce, a kind of cold war. This respite, however, benefited the covenanters more than the royalists, for it gave the Committee of Estates time to mobilise the whole of the country's resources for war.

Since the ancient feudal method of raising an army was no longer practicable, war committees were appointed in every county. And if all these local bodies were as enthusiastic and efficient as the Stewartry one, then presbyterianism had certainly evolved perhaps the most effective war organisation ever created in Scotland.

The Kirkcudbrightshire War Committee received its orders from the estates, or parliament, in Edinburgh, transmitted them to every parish in the Stewartry and ensured that they were obeyed. Twenty-four representatives of county land-owners, large and small, including Lord Kirkcudbright and Viscount Kenmure, were members of this body.

The minutes of all the meetings of the Stewartry War Committee held between 27 June 1640 and 2 January 1641 are still in existence and provide us with a fascinating and detailed account of its organisation and procedure. During that period the committee met thirty-seven times, that is oftener than once a week, and at six different centres—Kirkcudbright (19 meetings); Cullenoch, later called Clauchanpluck and now Laurieston (5 meetings); Dumfries (5); Milntown or Haugh of Urr (4); New Galloway (2); Threave Castle (2). From the minutes it is clear that the committee transacted an extraordinary amount of business and, from the travelling they had to do on horse-back and with no proper roads, it was obviously a full-time job for its members.

To begin with the committee ordered the raising of a troop of 80 horsemen and 200 foot-soldiers, commanded by Lord Kirkcudbright as colonel of the South Regiment and, at first, four captains to assist him. All beggars and unemployed men were to be immediately apprehended and enlisted. Some 30 commissioners were appointed — at least one to every parish — to ensure that all estates and burghs produced the recruits levied on them. The commissioners were then given powers to conscript men when they were not forthcoming voluntarily, and, as a result, the Stewartry detachment was soon doubled in numbers. Each horseman was equipped with a steel helmet, sword, a pair of pistols and a lance; the foot-soldiers were armed with muskets, swords and pikes.

Not all of the commissioners so appointed, however, had a stomach for the job. The commissioners for Kirkbean, Troqueer, Irongray, Colvend, Southwick, Cavens, Lochrutton, New Abbey and Terregles were all cited to appear before the Committee of Estates in Edinburgh to answer for their neglect in carrying out their duties. No doubt the majority of these "back-sliders" had sincere religious or conscientious objections to the Covenant. Nevertheless is is significant that they all came from the east of the Stewartry, where the power of the Maxwell and Herries families, who had declared for the king, was still great, and their tenants probably had to follow their example.

The first order from Edinburgh dealing with compulsory money raising required all persons who held money in cash to lend it to the government under pain of confiscation and punishment. As was the case in all the regulations, informers were encouraged to report any who failed to declare their wealth by being awarded half of the money or goods thus forfeited. The Stewartry committee were quick to enforce this instruction and almost immediately 59 local people, including the provost of Kirkcudbright and two bailies, had to appear before them to explain why their savings had not been surrendered.

At the same time all persons who owned any gold or silver work were ordered to hand it over to the committee in return for a post-war credit for its value at the following rates:—60s per oz of Scots silver, 62s per oz of English silver, and £38 per oz for gold. Once again the local citizens displayed considerable reluctance in parting with their valuables. The day after the order had been proclaimed in every church and advertised by " tuck of drum " throughout each burgh three commissioners sat down at the tolbooth of Kirkcudbright from 10 a.m. to 2 p.m. to accept the expected bullion. But that day not a single ounce was forthcoming. Soon, however, the silver spoons came trickling in, slowly at first, and then in great quantities. The minute book records the receipt of several stone weight of silver surrendered by county farmers and land-owners.

The absolute ruthlessness with which the War Committee enforced these regulations was demonstrated by their dismissal of two compassionate appeals made to them. Grizel Gordon, wife of the late minister of Urr, was compelled to give up all her silver possessions, most of which had been presented by parishioners to her husband; and, despite her sentimental pleas, Marion McLellan, also a widow, had even to surrender her bairns' christening presents.

Land-owners were required to contribute cash to the amount of one-tenth plus one-twentieth of all rents they received, or of the valuation of any land they retained for themselves. Moreover, if they were late in paying they were charged one-third extra. Tenants also had to hand over one-tenth of the valuation of the land they rented. (The valuation of the burgh of Kirkcudbright was at that time £3,300). Various protests and appeals were made by individuals against the amount of their valuation, but the official ruling was that all such appeals were to be turned down.

The severest penalties were meted out to non-covenanters, mostly Maxwells and their tenants from the east of the county, whose crops and moveable goods were confiscated; and later their lands and rents were also seized. It was in this connection that the committee displayed its only sign of charity, for it ordered parish ministers to make provision for the relief of the wives and children of those dispossessed of their lands for this offence.

Runaways, or deserters, had to be reported to committee, and a long list of these is given in the minute book. Some of them, however, appear to have been eventually excused national service for health reasons on producing the seventeenth century equivalent of a medical certificate. Anyone harbouring deserters was liable to a fine; William Gordon of Nether Corsock, for example, was fined £100, the maximum penalty, for this crime.

Some of the less scrupulous merchants soon began to take advantage of the shortage of clothing and footwear and set up a black market in these commodities. This was quickly countered by the imposition of rigid price control according to the size and quality of the goods. Powers of compulsory purchase, at the controlled price were given to commissioners and, if they were not able to pay cash, they were to credit the merchant with the cost, which would be refunded to him after the war.

Threave Castle, occupied by a small garrison of royalist Maxwells, then surrendered to the covenanters, and the committee delegated the laird of Balmaghie to supervise its destruction. This amounted to the removal of the roof, windows, doors, battlements and outer bastions, thus rendering it uninhabitable and undefendable. At the same meeting William McLellan of Barscobe was given permission to purchase stones from the castle for building purposes on his own estate.

Thus was the Stewartry mobilised for war under the banners of the Covenant. Despite the lack of modern means of communication, and with no established civil service, the Stewartry War Committee of 1640 was nevertheless a wonderfully efficient organisation.

## THE COVENANTERS UNDER ARMS

One of the most prominent covenanting divines of this period was John Livingstone, the well-loved minister of Stranraer. He seems to have enjoyed the confidence not only of his own parishioners but also of the covenant leaders and the Scots parliament and he represented them on several missions to England and the continent.

It was fortunate for historians that Livingstone was in the habit of making written records of many of the activities he was concerned in, and these have provided us with an account of some of the important events of that time. In addition, his writings have left us some fascinating glimpses of the character of this amiable but somewhat eccentric parson.

Livingstone's long and detailed description of his courtship of the lady who eventually became his wife is both moving and entertaining. He seems to have considered her marriageable from the very beginning, but, he says: "I knew her for nine months before I could get direction from God anent the business." But, despite this divine reassurance, Livingstone still seems to have some doubts "anent the business," for he proceeded no further with it in the meantime. Then one day as he was walking home from church with the lady he entertained her by way of conversation with a summary of an important sermon which he had shortly to preach. And when he asked her opinion of it he was obviously delighted with her comments and convinced that he had found the ideal wife, for, he remarks: "I found her conference so judicious and spiritual that I took that for an answer to my prayer."

Although Livingstone had at last made up his mind, he still allowed a decent interval to elapse before he put the vital question to the lady, and when he eventually did so he begged her to think about it for a week or two—presumably in case an immediate answer might be in the negative. Then, when he considered that the appropriate moment had arrived, he proceeded with the final stage of his courtship.

"Being alone with her and desiring her answer, I went to prayer and urged her to pray too, which she did; and I got abundant clearness that it was the Lord's mind that I should marry her. It was about a month after before I got marriage affection to her, and I got it not until I obtained it by prayer. But thereafter I had great difficulty to moderate it."

Whatever he may mean by that, comment is surely superfluous, except perhaps only to regret that his wife has not left us her own account of this unusual wooing!

Livingstone was a notable covenant leader from the beginning, and in 1638 he was despatched to London with copies of the National Covenant to obtain signatures of Scotsmen there. When news of his mission reached the king Charles immediately ordered the arrest of Livingstone, who was forced to flee north. But Livingstone's connection with Galloway dated back to 1626 when he was the guest of the Kenmure family and became especially friendly with the staunchly presbyterian Gordons of Earlstoun. He was then offered, but refused, a call to the church of Anwoth, an appointment which the noted Samuel Rutherford accepted instead.

In 1640, as chaplain to the Earl of Cassilis' Wigtownshire Regiment, Livingstone accompanied the Scottish army of 22,000 across the Border into England. In the battle at Newburn a number of Galloway men under Sir Patrick McKie of Larg displayed exceptional bravery by attacking so ferociously that they threw the English into complete confusion and thus ensured victory for the Scots. Unfortunately, the most notable casualty on the covenant side was Sir Patrick McKie's son, who was one of the Scottish standard-bearers. Young McKie, single-handed, had just captured the English general's colours and was triumphantly flourishing them aloft when he was mistaken for one of the enemy and was killed by a Scottish soldier.

On returning from this campaign Livingstone reported to the presbytery of Stranraer on his experiences while chaplain with the covenant army. From his account it is evident that the military officers must have been considerably plagued by the vast horde of parsons who accompanied the army and invariably insisted on meddling in all its affairs. Livingstone, however, was concerned more with the religious than the military exercises of the troops and he remarks " that after we came to a quarter at night there was nothing to be heard through the whole army, but the singing of psalms, prayer and reading of scripture by the soldiers in their several huts." Nevertheless, although " our tents resounded at dawn and sunset with psalms and prayers," Livingstone admits that, as time went on, " we declined more and more in worship and dependence on God."

Back in Stranraer, Livingstone was shocked to discover that his parish was the only one in the Shire that had not raised its contribution of money for the army. At a service on Saturday he appealed for funds, and on the following day the collection for this cause amounted to £45 sterling, that is £540 Scots. The large amount thus collected in only one day reflects great credit on both Livingstone and his congregation, for Stranraer was then only a small parish and by no means prosperous.

In 1642-3 a considerable number of Galloway troops crossed over into Ireland with a covenant army which had been sent there to prevent Irish Catholics from coming over to England to assist Charles. The presbyterian church in Ireland must then have become quite strong for there are frequent references about that time to the exchange of pulpits between ministers in south-west Scotland and those in Northern Ireland. John Livingstone of Stranraer enjoyed great popularity as a preacher in Antrim, where he seems to have been a regular visitor.

The royalist uprising in Scotland, led by the Marquis of Montrose, had repercussions in Galloway. In 1644 Lord Kirkcudbright was appointed steward of Kirkcudbrightshire when Robert Maxwell, the earl of Nithsdale, was excommunicated and had his estates confiscated because of his adherence to the royalist cause. Lord Herries and his lands suffered a similar fate.

Montrose's early successes in the north in the autumn of 1644 caused Kirkcudbright Town Council to overhaul their state of readiness for war. First they purchased another 25 muskets and bandoliers, increased their " drills " to twice weekly, absentees being fined 6s, and raised the fines on those who failed to turn up for watch duty to 30s. Then in December they added to their present stock of ammunition a further 3 cwt of gunpowder, 30 lb of ball and 6 cwt of match. In May 1645, when Montrose's whirlwind campaign had left the covenanters gasping, the Kirkcudbright council, " taking to their consideration that great danger may befall the town in these dangerous and troublesome times," increased the permanent town guard from six to ten, " three at the Muckle Yett, three at the Moat, twa at the Wynd futt and twa check " (reliefs).

In July, when the town was called on to send its contingent to join the covenant army, there was no money left to equip their soldiers with provisions and pay. The town council, however, did have £180 in cash which they owed to a certain merchant of Edinburgh, and this helped them out of their difficulty, for it was solemnly resolved, in the words of their minute, " that the said soum be presentilie employed for out-reiking of the said souldiers."

The burgh troops took their stand along with the rest of the Kirkcudbright Regiment, under Lord Kirkcudbright as colonel, at Philiphaugh, near Selkirk, in September 1645. According to all accounts this regiment, recruited from all over Galloway, gave a brave display and was awarded the sum of 15,000 merks for " its valuable services in the battle."

## A SPLIT IN THE COVENANT RANKS

It was only six years after the signing of the National Covenant when its supporters began the interminable squabbling which was to be so typical of their behaviour during the following half-century. The trouble began, as might be expected, in Galloway, whose inhabitants had been traditionally and almost continually " agin the government " for some six centuries. It did not matter whether the point at issue was religious or political, there was always a large number of stubborn, almost fanatical Gallovidians, who were prepared to sacrifice everything they possessed, and indeed often their lives, in defence of their beliefs.

By 1644 some of the more deeply religious presbyterians, especially in the Kirkcudbright and Stranraer areas, had formed the habit of meeting during the evening in private houses for the purpose of reading the scriptures and joining in prayer—just as their protestant predecessors had done in the Glenkens a century before. But when these meetings were reported to the General Assembly that year vicious attacks on this practice were made by many ministers. Samuel Rutherford (late of Anwoth), John Livingstone (Stranraer) and John Maclellan (Kirkcudbright) were bitterly condemned by many of their brethren for actively encouraging such meetings. When Maclellan suggested that the Assembly was making a mountain out of a mole-hill the meeting broke into a disorderly uproar, and the Kirkcudbright minister's plea for a sensible discussion of the subject was howled down. The Assembly then proceeded to pass an Act ordaining "that family worship would be performed by those of one family only, and not different families; that reading prayers is lawful only where none of the family can express themselves extempore; and that none be permitted to explain the scriptures but ministers approved of by the presbytery."

The lords of the covenant had spoken, and there was little sign of tolerance in their hearts. It was just about that time that John Milton delivered his famous dictum about presbyterianism: "The new presbyter is just but the old priest writ large." It seemed to be justified! The historical records of Scotland from 1644-1688 reveal little trace of Christian charity in the beliefs of the various religious bodies, whether presbyterian, episcopalian, or any of the numerous splinter groups. And if the extreme zealots of Galloway were sometimes fanatical in their beliefs they were only following the example of the leaders of the church.

It was at this time that the General Assembly of the Church of Scotland instituted what was probably the biggest witch-hunt ever known in Britain. The areas of central Scotland were the first to be affected; Galloway's turn came later. By the direct order of the Assembly scores of poor women whose only fault was that they were a little eccentric in their behaviour were brought to trial by presbyteries, tortured until they confessed and then burned.

The folk of Galloway were also to the forefront during the next decade in many of the political divisions which split the country. The first of these occurred as soon as Charles I was made prisoner in England in 1647, when some of the more moderate covenanters, under the Duke of Hamilton, tried to support the king and effect his release. But the plans of the "Engagers," as they were called, were quickly foiled; first, when their army was defeated by Cromwell's men at Preston; and, finally, when the covenanters of Galloway and Ayrshire marched on Edinburgh with 6000 men to demand no more negotiating with the king. This was known as "the Whigamore Raid," and it was from these Whigs of the south-west that the great political party derived its name.

Nevertheless, it is to the credit of the Scottish people that covenanters of all degrees were united in a strenuous effort to prevent the execution of Charles. One of the Scottish commissioners who went to London to plead with Cromwell and the other parliamentary leaders to spare the king's life was William Glendinning, provost of Kirkcudbright, then a prominent figure in the Committee of Estates.

The covenanters, angered by the attitude of the English parliamentarians and the beheading of the king, then decided to enter into negoiations with Charles II, in exile. Deputations from the Estates visited first the Hague and then Breda to lay before Charles the conditions on which they were prepared to accept him as king. Two of the commissioners at these meetings were the earl of Cassalis and the indefatigable John Livingstone of Stranraer. The latter was convinced that the king was insincere in his promises and that he was simply using the Scots for his own ends. Livingstone was also fully aware of the young monarch's dissolute habits and stated quite bluntly that he was reluctant to treat with him unless Charles was prepared to mend his ways and give proof of repentance. In a sermon at Breda the fearless Livingstone told Charles to his face exactly what he thought of him and how the king would have to behave if he was to win the support of the Scottish covenanters.

When Charles returned to Scotland in 1650 he had first of all to sign a declaration in which he acknowledged the sins of his father and his own depraved habits, and then he had to submit himself to an endless series of lectures and sermons from the most bigoted of the covenanting divines. Charles II never forgave the Scottish presbyterians for subjecting him to these indignities. Although his conduct no doubt deserved their condemnation, the king's attitude to the covenanters between 1660-1685 might have been much more tolerant if he had been spared this public humiliation.

The covenant army which fought for Charles II against Cromwell at Dunbar on 3rd September 1650 contained over 1000 men from Galloway, a large number of whom were among the 3000 killed and 9000 captured. Another 700 troops were levied from the province immediately after this defeat. The covenant armies were proving a sore drain on the menfolk of Galloway.

## THE EXTREMISTS GAIN CONTROL

It was after this defeat that the split in the covenanting ranks began to assume serious proportions. The struggle for control among the various groups was soon in full swing, and the lead was again given by the ministers and land-owners of the south-west.

Some of the moderates in parliament, in an attempt to improve relations with Charles II, passed certain Acts pardoning the "malignants," or royalists, and increasing the personal power of the king. The General Assembly confirmed this resolution (its supporters being therefore termed "Resolutionists"), but only by a small majority. A vigorous protest against the resolution (known as "Protesters") who had no time for the king and wished to see the royalist influence in parliament weakened rather than strengthened. The people of Galloway for the most part supported the protest, and the list of protesters included Lord Kirkcudbright, Samuel Rutherford, John Livingstone, John Maclellan and numerous other prominent ministers and land-owners.

But the split was not yet complete. In addition to the resolutionists and protesters a third party suddenly emerged in Galloway. Its supporters were given the detested name of "Cavaliers" because they stood for the king alone, independent of the Scottish parliament and church. This party included Lord Galloway, Viscount Kenmure and Sir Patrick Agnew, the hereditary sheriff. Even families were divided over this issue, for Sir Patrick's son Andrew was not a cavalier like his father, but a resolutionist.

According to English parliamentary records, "Regiments from Kirkcudbright, Galloway and Dumfries" suffered heavy casualties at the battle of Worcester in 1651, fighting for the king. Most of these would have been resolutionists and cavaliers, for there is some evidence that many of the protesters were no longer willing to fight for the king.

After Worcester the English parliamentarians, under Cromwell as Lord Protector, became complete masters of the whole of Britain. English judges were appointed in all parts of Scotland, and with the backing of strong English garrisons they administered justice very fairly. Colonel Matthew Alured replaced Sir Patrick Agnew as sheriff of Galloway. Heavy fines were imposed on many of the royalist supporters, Lord Galloway, for example, having to pay £4000.

But Viscount Kenmure and one or two other cavaliers refused to accept defeat and raised a force in Galloway composed chiefly of all the vagabonds and riff-raff of the countryside. His principal recruiting gimmick was known as "Kenmure's Drum," a perpetually filled barrel of brandy, which was always carried at the head of his troops. Cromwell, however, quickly replied to Kenmure's defiance by sending a force to burn down Kenmure Castle and the House of Freugh, and the rebellious Glenkens noble had to take to the hills.

Cromwell also knew how to handle the covenanters; he stood no nonsense from them. He encouraged all the presbyterian ministers to carry out their normal religious and parish duties, but he refused to allow them any political power. To ensure this he banned all meetings of the General Assembly.

The protesters or extreme covenanters, however, seemed to enjoy special favour, partly because they were anti-royalist, but also because of the good impression made on Cromwell by the renowned John Livingstone, who was no more afraid of the Lord Protector than he had been of the king. Once, in 1654, when he was conducting a service before Cromwell and his generals, Livingstone had the temerity to pray for King Charles. The generals were horrified and wanted the minister to be arrested at once. But Cromwell, who realised what a genuine character Livingstone was, brushed their demand aside with a quiet remark: "Let him alone; he is a good man."

During the remaining five years of the Protectorate the ministers of the extreme covenanting sect gained a tremendous hold over the common people, especially in Galloway and Ayrshire. Although they had no political power, these ministers exercised a rigid control over their parishes, with the approval and support of the English authorities. A number of them came to regard themselves as divinely inspired and the chosen instruments of the Lord. To increase the awe in which they were already held some even changed the natural tone of their voices and ranted and thundered with all the fanatical fervour of the prophets of old. The influence that many of these extremist ministers thus gained over their congregations was to have far-reaching consequences in Galloway in the following 30 years.

## CHAPTER XIX

# THE PERSECUTION BEGINS

### RESTORATION OF THE BISHOPS

NO attempt was made in the previous chapter to whitewash the characters of the extremist covenanters. Many of them were doubtless gentle, tolerant and sincere Christians, bearing no hatred even towards those who were persecuting them. But it is equally certain that the majority of the covenanters of Galloway were a contumacious, bigoted and fanatical people. They were completely intolerant of any whose religious beliefs differed in the slightest degree from theirs.

Eventually the covenanters' aims became fiercely political as well as religious, for it was their avowed intention to have the Solemn League and Covenant of 1643 rigidly enforced and presbyterianism made the official form of religion in England and Ireland, as well as in Scotland. Indeed, in the 1680s the more defiant covenanters were actually advocating and inciting their followers to wholesale civil war, political assassination and even republicanism. It may be argued on their behalf, however, that they had been driven to these desperate extremes by the sheer brutality of the persecution to which they had been subjected.

No attempt will be made in this and the following chapter to minimise the diabolical atrocities which were perpetrated on the covenanters in Galloway and the south-west. Neither the government nor the bishops can escape blame for these. Nor can Charles II, despite the rough treatment he had received from the presbyterian divines ten years before, be absolved from his share of the responsibility, for he was determined to eradicate presbyterianism completely. The king's ministers, the lords of the privy council in Scotland, were not only ready to carry out to the letter their master's wishes in this respect, but also frequently initiated more cruelly effective methods of bringing the presbyterians to heel; and so they are by no means guiltless either.

The chief villain in high places, however, was undoubtedly that arch-traitor to presbyterianism, Archbishop James Sharp, himself a former covenanter until ambition gave him dreams of power. He it was who was responsible for introducing and enforcing some of the most oppressive and barbaric of all the measures taken against the covenanters.

Then there is a long list of those government officers who were more directly concerned in the crimes committed in the south-west and whose names are execrated in Galloway even to this day: Graham of Claverhouse, Grierson of Lag, Sir James Turner and Sir William Bannatyne, to mention only a few of the more notorious persecutors. Of them it has been said by way of exculpation that they were only carrying out orders. Nevertheless, they often interpreted their orders in such a savage manner that their names to many Gallovidians have become synonymous with sheer brutality and sadism.

At the Restoration of Charles II in 1660 most Gallovidians, except for a small minority of royalists, were covenanters of one kind or another. Yet many of them were probably quite pleased to see the return of the monarchy, if only because it meant freedom from the dictatorship of Cromwell and the English parliament. And now they waited with intense interest to discover what changes the new regime might bring. Many were optimistic. After all, they argued, it was the presbyterians who had brought Charles back from exile, crowned him (on their own terms, of course), and many of them had fought bravely for him at Dunbar and Worcester. Moreover, the king was a Stuart, a descendant of an ancient and honourable Scottish family and would surely deal kindly with the land of his forefathers.

The "resolutionists," those covenanters who had supported the king, were quite well represented among the more important land-owners in Galloway, and many of them in a wave of enthusiasm over the restoration of the monarchy had become wholehearted royalists. They were even prepared to agree to the return of the bishops, especially if episcopacy could be combined, as before, with the presbyterian system of government in the lower courts of the church.

The vast majority of Gallovidians, however, still remained "protesters," left-wing covenanters, and they could not help viewing the situation with some suspicion and not a little apprehension. And their fears were soon proved to be well founded.

The first Scottish parliament after the Restoration met in January 1661. It might well be termed "the Drunken Parliament" since so many of its members were in an almost permanent state of intoxication during its early stages. In this respect they were following the example set by the new Royal Commissioner, Lord Middleton, a former puritan who had kicked over the traces. It is recorded that Middleton was so drunk on several occasions that he was incapable of presiding over parliament, and the sittings had to be adjourned. After almost a decade of stringent austerity under the sanctimonious puritan-presbyterian regime many members were ready for a party and they indulged in conviviality on a truly colossal scale. Bonfires blazing in the streets and fountains running with wine encouraged the citizens of Edinburgh to join in welcoming the restoration of their king and the re-opening of parliament in Scotland.

Despite their initial preoccupation with spirituous matters, however, this parliament soon got down to spiritual affairs and set about the dissolution of presbyterianism. It rescinded the Solemn League and Covenant and, by revoking all Acts passed since 1640, it swept away all the legislation that had authorised the presbyterian form of church government.

In April of that year the Synod of Galloway met to draw up a petition begging parliament not to re-introduce episcopacy. The earl of Galloway, as a member of the privy council, broke into their deliberations and, in the name of the king, dissolved the meeting. But the members of the synod refused to disperse until the moderator had closed the session with prayer. The covenanters of Galloway were the first to realise that the fight was now on and demonstrated that they were prepared to stand up for their presbyterian rights.

Parliament then required all its members to sign an oath of allegiance acknowledging the king's supremacy over " all persons and in all causes." Two members, the earl of Cassilis and the Laird of Kilbirnie, held that the king's jurisdiction should be limited to civic affairs only and should not apply to the church. Accordingly they refused to take the oath and made their way quickly homewards before trouble might befall them.

In July 1661 parliament adjourned, and the government of Scotland was left in the hands of the privy council, with full powers to enact any legislation they wanted. With possible troublemakers now safely out of the way during the parliamentary recess, the council set about restoring the episcopacy. In the autumn James Sharp, former presbyterian minister of Crail, who had used his position as spokesman for the church to ingratiate himself with the king, came back from London with the royal command that bishops were to be appointed to all the former dioceses. Sharp managed to obtain the key job for himself as archbishop of St Andrews, primate of all Scotland.

Once again it was the covenanters of Galloway who took the lead in protesting against the re-introduction of the bishops. In January 1662 the presbytery of Kirkcudbright commissioned John Duncan, minister of Rerrick, and James Buglass of Crossmichael to present a petition to the privy council. The following extract from it indicates the reasonable and moderate nature of the petition: "And particularly we humbly beg that we may have liberty, with freedom and safety, to express our minds against the re-introduction of prelacy upon this church and kingdom; in doing whereof we resolve in the Lord to walk close by the rules of scripture, of Christian prudence, sobriety and moderation; in all our actions testifying our real affection, faithfulness and loyalty to the king's most excellent majesty; the preservation of whose royal person is the thing in this world that is, and ever shall be, dearest unto us, next unto the flourishing of the kingdom of Jesus Christ." The petition was, of course, ignored by the privy council.

The parliament of 1662 confirmed the bishops in their appointments and re-invested them with all their former powers and dignities. Sharp was now not only head of the church but also the most influential member of the privy council, wielding immense authority in civil as well as religious affairs.

Now that they had created bishops the next step was to persuade the presbyterian ministers of the church to accept them. To achieve this parliament passed an Act requiring every parish minister to have his appointment confirmed by the bishop of his diocese within the next four months. This was a subtle move, since it forced the clergy not only to accept the bishops but also to acknowledge their superiority. In most parts of Scotland the ministers submitted tamely to this ruling, but in Galloway they deliberately ignored it, and trouble lay ahead.

## ECONOMIC RUIN OF GALLOWAY

The years 1662-1666 witnessed the economic ruin of Galloway. During that period some 550 covenanters in the province, rich and poor, paid almost £140,000 to the government by way of fines. Even with that colossal sum the records are by no means complete, and the final total was almost certainly much larger still. Moreover, this does not take into account the cost of feeding the troops billeted on the people, nor does it include the widespread depredations of occupying forces or the wilful damage done to crops, stock and property.

Trade in Galloway was brought completely to a standstill. Kirkcudbright and Wigtown harbours, once prosperous ports, were virtually closed for the next 20 years, as there was nothing available for export—no wool, grain or hides; nor had anyone ready cash to pay for imports, or even products to barter. This was the final crippling blow to the economy of Galloway, which had never had a chance to recover from the exorbitant demands of the

Committees during the covenant wars, followed by the exceptionally heavy taxation during Cromwell's rule.

The Scottish parliament of 1662 passed an Act of Indemnity to those covenanters who had made terms with the English during the occupation; but it considered, however, that many of the presbyterians in the south-west had submitted rather too complacently to the puritans and that they should be made to pay heavily for their pardon. In Dumfriesshire land-owners, farmers and merchants were fined £164,200; in the Stewartry 92 similarly unfortunate people had to pay a total of £51,400, and in the Shire 64 covenanters were relieved of £45,560. The highest fine levied was £4,800 and the lowest about £200. The names of all the well-known presbyterian families appear time and again on the list: the Agnews, Kennedys, McCullochs, McGhies, Maclellans, and Gordons, each contributed many thousands of pounds in fines. The Act was ironically officially known as "The King's Free Pardon."

The privy council now directed its attention to those ministers who had ignored the order to have their appointments confirmed by their bishops: that meant all of them in Galloway. In Glasgow, at a notorious meeting of the council referred to ever since as "The Drunken Meeting" because only one member, Sir James Lockhart of Lee, was sober during the proceedings, an Act was passed against all ministers who had failed to carry out their orders in this respect, "charging and commanding them to remove themselves, wives, bairns, servants, goods and gear from their respective manses and out of the bounds of the presbytery" within four weeks. Throughout Scotland some 350 ministers were expelled from their charges by this Act, simply because they refused to acknowledge the superiority of the bishops.

The ministers of Galloway, however, did not take this lying down. They quitted their manses and forfeited their stipends, but most of them deliberately refused to leave even parishes let alone presbyteries. Sheltered, sustained and encouraged by their ever-loyal parishioners, these faithful ministers rededicated themselves to their calling with still greater zeal than ever before. Hardship and adversity only strengthened their heroic determination to remain true to their presbyterian faith.

As soon as Gabriel Semple, minister of Kirkpatrick-Durham, was driven from his church he was given hospitality by Neilson, laird of Corsock. Semple conducted services in Corsock House until his audiences became too large, then in the garden, and finally in the open fields. This was the first field meeting or conventicle to be held and it set an example which was soon to be followed by other covenanters all over the country. Thomas

Wylie of Kirkcudbright was probably the first to celebrate communion in the open air, and he did so knowing that soldiers were already on their way from Edinburgh with orders from the privy council to arrest him for his activities had already brought him into trouble with that all-powerful body. So many people, not only from his own congregation but from many miles around as well, desired to receive the sacrament for the last time from this respected and beloved minister that he had to hold services on three successive days. Before long, all over Galloway, with no attempt at concealment, similar services were being conducted in the open by the dismissed presbyterian ministers and were being attended by hundreds of their enthusiastic and devoted followers.

Once they had succeeded in emptying the parish kirks of their former incumbents the bishops were then obliged, if only to save face, to fill the vacancies; and with no trained episcopal clergy to call on this was a problem. The bishops overcame the difficulty, however, by recruiting some 300 young men from the more strongly episcopalian areas of the north and east and appointing them as curates to the vacant charges. They were, of course, totally unqualified for the ministry, often uneducated, invariably inexperienced, and wholly unsuited for taking charge of a parish.

One north of Scotland farmer cursed both the scruples of the presbyterians and the plans of the bishops for having brought about this action, for he said that it was now impossible to obtain herds and ploughboys, since all the lads had gone to be curates. Another writer of the time described these young curates as " the poorest creatures ever known as ministers in Scotland, illiterate, juvenile, drunken, and openly vicious." Their only qualities, at least from the bishops' point of view, were their servility and obsequiousness; they certainly would have done what they were told.

With ministers like these in charge of nearly all the parish kirks in Galloway, it is little wonder that their congregations refused to hear them. If the new episcopal curates had been at all comparable in learning and moral character with the old covenanting divines they might have gained some support from the more moderate presbyterians. As it was, the majority of congregations boycotted their parish churches and were to be found instead at some open-air conventicle where they could get the more stimulating theological fare that they were accustomed to.

The introduction of the curates caused at least two riots to break out, at Kirkcudbright and Irongray. The privy council took a serious view of these disturbances and sent a powerful commission, which included the earls of Linlithgow, Galloway and Annandale, to investigate them. They were accompanied by a strong body of troops, the first use of military force against the covenanters.

At Kirkcudbright the commission's inquiries disclosed what they regarded as an alarming state of affairs. Although most of the rioting had been done by a horde of angry women, a number of influential local men had also been present, including Lord Kirkcudbright and John Carson, a former provost. In the view of the commission these two were the chief culprits, for they had made no attempt to stop the riot and were known to be strongly opposed to the appointment of the curate. Both were taken prisoner to Edinburgh, as was John Ewart, who had refused to accept the office of provost and was therefore also blamed for failing to take action against the rioters. In fact the commission discovered that the burgh had no magistrates at all, because no one was willing to take the responsibility of enforcing civil and religious laws with which he did not agree. Kirkcudbright was ordered to elect a provost and bailies immediately, and the town council were compelled to give a bond for the future good behaviour of the townspeople. Five women were arrested for their part in the riot, taken to Edinburgh and punished with imprisonment. Lord Kirkcudbright appears to have escaped punishment, but John Carson was fined 8000 merks, and John Ewart was banished from the kingdom.

At Irongray the commission discovered that a similar disturbance had occurred over the placing of the new curate. On the day appointed for the induction, a local farmer, William Arnott of Littlepark, took up his stance in the doorway of the kirk and, with sword in hand, dared anyone to proceed with the ceremony. "Let me see who will place a minister here this day!" he shouted defiantly to the great delight and approval of his fellow-parishioners who supported him to a man. Arnott was also carted off to Edinburgh and fined 5000 merks.

The prompt and vigorous action taken by the privy council in dealing with these riots showed the covenanters that the government was now prepared to use all its civil and military resources to enforce the will of the bishops on the church. The sword was unsheathed, and the covenanters knew they could expect no quarter.

The bishops, however, had yet another problem on their hands. They had managed to fill the vacant pulpits with curates; now they had to find some way of filling the pews. In Galloway the new episcopalian ministers were preaching to empty kirks.

In 1663 parliament passed an Act designed to ensure regular attendance at the parish churches on Sundays. By this law everyone who was absent from church without due cause was liable for each offence to have a fourth of his money or moveable goods confiscated and to suffer imprisonment as well. The bishops and curates were then entrusted with the task of seeing that this order was obeyed, and the privy council made troops available to them to help in enforcing the law.

During the next three years government troops under the command of Sir James Turner were stationed all over Galloway. Small detachments of soldiers were billeted on people in every village, hamlet and town and, with no proper supervision by responsible officers, they did as they pleased and generally terrorised the countryside.

The curates were required to co-operate with the troops and provided them weekly with the names of those who did not attend the Sunday services. If the curates were lax in this respect the soldiers interrupted services and called the roll themselves. The troops were also ordered to raid the numerous conventicles which were being regularly conducted by the displaced ministers; but in this they were not always so successful, because the covenanters had become cunning and now held their meetings secretly and in remote valleys in the hills. Many a bairn was baptised and many a wedding solemnised twice over, once by the curate in the parish kirk, and a second time at a more solemn and satisfying ceremony in some hidden corner of the moors.

All persons failing to attend church or found present at a conventicle were immediately fined by the soldiers. There was no trial, no opportunity for defence, no plea in mitigation and no appeal against the sentence. If the offender could not pay his fine at once his goods—furnishings, stock and crops—were seized and sold, or he had troops quartered on him to eat him out of house and home. On numerous occasions the fines were far larger than they should have been, so that the soldiers could pocket something for themselves. And since their commander, Sir James Turner, was later court-martialled and found guilty of the illegal extortion in the south-west of fines to the amount of £30,000 it was only to be expected that his men would have followed his example.

The following list shows the fines imposed by the troops on poor families in the Stewartry only between 1663-1666;—

| | £ | S. | D. |
|---|---|---|---|
| 1. In the parish of Carsphairn 49 families have suffered the loss of kirk fines | 4,864 | 17 | 4 |
| 2. In the parish of Dalry, 43 families | 9,577 | 6 | 8 |
| 3. In Balmaclellan parish, 49 families | 6,430 | 10 | 4 |
| 4. In the parish of Balmaghie, 9 families | 425 | 11 | 8 |
| 5. In Tongland parish, out of two or three poor families | 166 | 12 | 8 |
| 6. In Twynholm parish, from some poor persons | 81 | 4 | 0 |
| 7. In Borgue parish, out of 20 families | 2,062 | 17 | 4 |
| 8. In Girthon Parish, out of 9 poor families | 525 | 10 | 4 |
| 9. In Anwoth parish, from some poor families | 773 | 6 | 4 |
| 10. In Kirkpatrick-Durham parish, out of 34 inconsiderable families | 2,235 | 16 | 0 |

| | | | |
|---|---|---|---|
| 11. In Kirkmabreck parish, some few families | 563 | 6 | 0 |
| 12. In Minnigaff, 3 families | 600 | 0 | 0 |
| 13. In Kirkcudbright, 18 families | 2,580 | 0 | 0 |
| 14. In Lochrutton parish, out of 37 poor families, notwithstanding they had no curate | 2,080 | 0 | 0 |
| 15. In Troqueer parish, 12 poor families | 756 | 10 | 0 |
| 16. In Kells parish | 466 | 13 | 4 |
| 17. In Crossmichael parish | 1,666 | 13 | 4 |
| 18. In Parton parish, from 24 families | 2,838 | 9 | 4 |
| 19. In Irongray parish, 42 families | 3,362 | 18 | 8 |
| Total | £41,982 | 12 | 0 |

In Dumfriesshire the fines exacted amounted to £51,575 13s 4d; no records exist in Wigtownshire.

But this vast sum, grim as it is, still fails to describe the full extent of the misery inflicted on the people. Covenanters arrested at conventicles even had the clothes taken from their backs because they no longer possessed any other gear to seize. Women and children were molested and made to suffer all manner of indignities at the hands of the soldiers. The more defiant had their homes burned down and hundreds were homeless, living in the woods or in turf and stone shelters they built on the moors.

Archbishop Sharp, however, was still not satisfied that the measures were severe enough, and went to London to persuade Charles II to re-introduce the Courts of High Commission which would be used to punish those people of higher rank whom the soldiers failed to deal with. Presided over by the bishops, these courts were the most vicious instruments of quasi-legal tyranny —for one cannot say justice—that ever existed in Scotland. Hundreds of covenanters were fined, imprisoned, whipped through the town, or deported to the colonies, without even the semblance of a fair trial. Scores of Galloway land-owners left their homes and property and fled to Ulster to avoid having to appear before these dreaded courts. Gordon of Earlston was sentenced to perpetual exile—with the alternative of imprisonment plus a fine of £10,000—because he opposed the appointment of a curate in his church and attended conventicles.

This form of persecution, however, continued for only just over a year. Once again many of the lay members of the courts sickened of the work they had to do and refused to attend them. In the end Archbishop Leighton of Glasgow also decided he had had enough of it and to his eternal credit told the king that he would resign his appointment unless the courts were suspended immediately. They were; and no one, except possibly Sharp, was sorry to see them ended.

By 1666 the covenanters of Galloway were a broken people

economically. But spiritually those that remained were as determined as ever to continue their fight for religious freedom. So far many had paid for their beliefs with their money, their property, all their worldly possessions. Soon their sacrifice was to be reckoned in human lives.

## THE PENTLAND RISING

On Tuesday, 13th November 1666 four covenanters who had been forced to take to the hills for safety, ventured to pay a visit to the village of Dalry in the Glenkens to get food. They were McClelland of Barscobe, Maxwell the younger of Monreith, Wallace of Auchanes and another. As they entered the Clachan they saw a party of villagers, under the escort of a guard of soldiers, threshing some corn which had been confiscated from a very old man named Grier, a resident in Dalry. He had fled without paying a fine for non-attendance at church, and so his corn crop had been seized.

Later that morning the four covenanters were having a meal at the inn when a messenger rushed in with the news that the old man, Grier, had been captured while making a secret visit to his home in the village in an attempt to obtain some desperately needed food. Now his captors were stripping him and heating the girdle to roast him on in order to make him reveal the whereabouts of certain of his fellow-outcasts. The four covenanters immediately ran to his rescue and, after blows were exchanged and swords drawn, McClelland of Barscobe shot and wounded one of the soldiers with his pistol.

Realising that their lives were now forfeit anyway, McClelland and his companions resolved at least to go down fighting and to do as much damage as they could in the process. They quickly recruited a small body of local covenanters and the next day captured a detachment of a dozen soldiers stationed in Balmaclellan. There they were fortunate in making contact with that grand old covenanter John Neilson of Corsock, in whose house the first conventicle had been held. Since then Neilson had lost his whole estate by way of fines to Turner's troops, his tenants had also been ruined and driven from their homes, and he himself had for long been hiding on the moors between Corsock and Balmaclellan. All members of this first tiny covenant armed force were greatly encouraged to have the active support of this highly respected figure.

The following day they reached Dumfries, where they made a daring raid on the lodging occupied by Sir James Turner and were delighted to find him at home. Some of the covenanters wanted to kill Turner at once, but Neilson restrained them. Instead they made their way to the town cross so that Neilson could explain the purpose of their rising: that it was a justifiable protest against the persecution of the covenanters by Turner's soldiers, and in no way treasonable. To prove this they drank the king's health and, after reaffirming their allegiance to the Covenant, they marched off back to Dalry, taking Sir James Turner as a prisoner with them.

During their homeward journey they picked up many more recruits, and on reaching Dalry they learned that the Ayrshire covenanters were ready to join them in rebellion on a larger scale. Their aim now was to march on Edinburgh, hoping to gather a larger force of supporters on the way, and then to compel the government to abolish the episcopacy and restore presbyterianism. On 21st November, only eight days after the rising began in Dalry, the covenant army, about 1000 strong, assembled at the Bridge of Doon, near Ayr. Although they were poorly armed—many had only scythe blades mounted on sticks—it was a considerable achievement to enlist such a number of men in so short a time.

Four days later they were in Lanark, where their strength was increased to about 1500—far short of the number they had hoped for. Speed was essential, however, if they were to surprise the capital, and so they decided not to wait for more recruits but to press on. In Lanark the demand for the execution of Turner was renewed more vehemently than ever, and it was all that Neilson could do to prevent his comrades from carrying it out.

As they approached the outskirts of Edinburgh they heard that the government had raised a far superior force to meet them, and realising now that their task was hopeless the covenanters decided to retire by Biggar to the safety of the south-west. Many had already dispersed when the government army, under the renowned General Sir Tam Dalziell of the Binns, caught up with them on 28th November at Rullion Green, at the foot of the Pentland Hills. The covenanters, now reduced to about 1000 in number, were quickly defeated and put to flight. Some 50 of them were killed and about 150 captured.

On 4th December the privy council issued a proclamation naming 42 land-owners and 15 displaced ministers (half of the total from Galloway) as rebels and outlaws and warning anyone against harbouring them on pain of treason. Later another order declared that all those named should be executed when arrested and that their estates were forfeited to the crown. Some of these outlaws remained for long in hiding in the hills of the south-west; others fled to exile in Ulster or Holland. Members of their families had also to seek safety in hiding in order to escape the victimisation that would undoubtedly follow because of their relationship with the rebels.

Eleven of the covenant prisoners from Rullion Green were put on trial immediately and were hanged in Edinburgh on 7th December. The heads of McCulloch of Barholm and of the two Gordon brothers from Knockbrex were cut off and sent to Kirkcudbright to be mounted on the main gate of the burgh as a warning to the covenanters of the Stewartry.

John Neilson of Corsock was in the next batch of prisoners to be sentenced to death. Before he was hanged, however, the authorities submitted him to torture with the boot in an attempt to obtain from him details of the covenants' plans for future rebellions; but, since there were no such plans, there was nothing for Neilson to reveal. Sir James Turner, to his great credit, then made every effort to have the elderly covenanter reprieved, and he might well have succeeded; but Dalgleish, the episcopal curate of Kirkpatrick Durham, intervened and gave evidence that Neilson was the ringleader of the rebels, and so he was hanged.

After the Pentland Rising the persecution of the covenanters was stepped up, and a regiment of 400 foot soldiers and 80 horsemen, under Sir William Bannatyne, was sent to Galloway and stationed mostly in the Glenkens area. They quickly ate up all the crops from the last harvest and the few cattle and sheep that remained, and thus caused great destitution to the local inhabitants. Heavy fines were imposed and imprisonment inflicted on many people merely on the suspicion that they were covenanters. Those related to men who had taken part in the rebellion were especially severely dealt with. Gordon of Knockbrex, whose two sons had been hanged in Edinburgh, was stripped of the few possessions he had left, and a relative in slightly better circumstances was fined 16,000 merks.

The atrocities committed by Sir William Bannatyne and his men were even more horrible than those of former years: where Turner had contented himself with lining his pockets, Bannatyne took a fiendish and sadistic delight in inflicting suffering on the covenanters, and the troops followed his example. The wife of David McGill of Dalry, suspected of helping her husband to escape from the soldiers, was captured and tortured by having lighted brands placed between her fingers. One of her hands was burned off and she died from her ordeal.

Sir William Bannatyne himself was personally responsible for some of the most inhuman acts committed against the covenanters. On one occasion, for example, in the parish of Balmaghie, after drinking freely in an inn, he attempted to molest the innkeeper's wife. Her husband went to her rescue and Bannatyne struck him dead on the spot. Then, according to one account of this incident, " Bannatyne and his party drunk in the house most of the Lord's Day; and when they could drink no more let what remained run upon the ground, and rifled the house of all in it. In short, it was known in this country that Bannatyne never refused to let his men rob and plunder whenever they pleased. His oppressions, murders, robberies, rapes, adulteries were so many and atrocious that the managers themselves were ashamed of them, and we shall afterwards hear that he was called to account for them."

And so the brutal and indiscriminate persecution continued until even government supporters sickened of it and began at last to think that it was time to call a halt to it.

THE SANDS OF ROUGH FIRTH AT LOW TIDE, OUT FROM ROCKCLIFFE. 'HESTAN ISLAND IN THE DISTANCE TO THE LEFT IS ASSOCIATED WITH MUSSELS, MONKS AND SMUGGLERS'

## CHAPTER XX

# THE COVENANT DEFIANT

### THE GOVERNMENT SHOWS TOLERATION

ABOUT a year after the Pentland Rising the government began to show some weakening in their attitude towards the covenanters. The reason for this change of heart is not clear. It may have been that the lords of the privy council had at last decided to display some signs of common humanity and decency in their handling of the covenanting problem; it may have resulted from the realisation that even non-conformists were entitled to some measure of personal liberty in their religious practices. More probably, however, it was simply that the government had been forced reluctantly to the conclusion that none of their oppressive measures would ever succeed in taming the wild covenanters of Galloway.

At any rate, whatever its reasons, during the next few years the government decided to change its policy to one of conciliation. The privy council made a number of important concessions and they hoped that in return the presbyterians would accept these gratefully and co-operate in an attempt to bring about better relations. As proof of its good faith the privy council was reconstituted with Lauderdale and the very moderate Tweeddale as its leading ministers. The detested Archbishop Sharp was forced to withdraw from the government, and his place was filled by the gentle Leighton (then bishop of Dunkeld, and later to be archbishop of Glasgow), who was previously known to have been opposed to the use of force. The council, however, was soon to discover that, despite all its attempts at conciliation, the covenanters were in no mood for compromise.

About the end of 1667 Sheriff Agnew and the Lords Galloway and Kenmure, although they were royalists and therefore supporters of the episcopacy, felt it their duty to complain to the government, on behalf of the sorely persecuted covenanters of Galloway, about the extortions and horrible cruelties of the occupying forces. Their representations were accepted by the privy council, and a court of enquiry, consisting of the Earl of Nithsdale, Lord Kenmure and the laird of Craigdarroch, was appointed to investigate the conduct of the two commanders of the soldiers.

Sir James Turner was faced with some 25 charges, all dealing with the various ways in which he and his troops had illegally extracted money by way of fines from the people of Galloway. The various charges against Sir William Bannatyne were even more serious, since they were all connected with outrages and atrocities for which he was personally responsible and which had often been committed against people who had not even broken the law. Although the members of the court were by no means predisposed to favouring the covenanters, they had no option but to find the two commanders guilty of the charges against them. Turner was dismissed the service. Bannatyne was fined £2400 and banished from Scotland with a warning not to return under penalty of £6000 fine.

The departure from the scene of these two arch-villains of the early persecutions was hailed with unrestrained delight by the many hundreds of covenanters in Galloway who had been made to suffer so grieviously. Their only regret was that the punishment had not come sooner and been much more severe.

The government continued its policy of conciliation by introducing, in January 1668 an Act which required all nobles, heritors and tenants to take a bond on behalf of themselves and their servants "to keep the public peace." Acceptance of this oath meant a free pardon to those already known as covenanters and even to many who had taken part in the Pentland Rising. The only exceptions were some 60 of the extremist covenanting leaders who were therefore still outlawed; many of them were in exile in Holland, and so it did not affect them anyway.

Trouble arose immediately, however, in the south-west over the terms of the bond. Government supporters claimed that what it required was simply obedience to the civil laws and acceptance of the powers of magistrates in civil affairs. This did seem quite a reasonable interpretation of the Act, and a number of Galloway covenanters, believing that the bond in no way interfered with their presbyterian principles, agreed to swear to it; others signed it with a reservation asserting their freedom and independence in religious matters.

The majority of covenanters in Galloway, however, suspected that it was a government trick and that by signing it they would be acting contrary to their religious beliefs. That spring a long list of those Galloway land-owners and tenants who refused the bond was drawn up: the list for Carsphairn and Dalry parishes, for example, contains 48 names, all of prominent people in the district; the Glenkens was still staunchly anti-government. Some of these more militant covenanters were arrested and sentenced to transportation to the colonies, but, on the whole, the action taken against them was nothing like so vicious as the persecution of previous years. In fact, many continued to live in or near their homes, going into hiding only when danger seemed imminent.

It was about this time that Bishop Leighton and Lord Tweeddale proposed an Act of Indulgence which they hoped would reconcile all ministers of religion in Scotland—presbyterian and episcopalian—and bring them once again into a united and established church. This genuine move towards reconciliation was instituted by the two most enlightened members of the privy council, and it certainly did open the door to all protestants of good will who still possessed some spirit of toleration.

Unfortunately, before the Act of Indulgence could be made law, the attempted assassination of Archbishop Sharp took place in July 1668, and once again the government had to re-introduce more stringent measures against the covenanters, but still nothing approaching the previous reign of terror. The privy council did, however, enact further legislation against conventicles and non-attendance at church. In March 1669 the baptism of children was prohibited by any other than the parish minister, the penalties for offences against his law being: A heritor was fined one-fourth of the value of his yearly rent-roll; a tenant £100 plus six months' imprisonment; and a peasant £20 with six weeks' imprisonment. Another Act against open-air services in the counties of the south-west laid down that each heritor on whose ground a conventicle was held would be liable to a fine of £50 for each offence.

By the summer of 1669 Leighton and Tweeddale's plans for the Indulgence were at last brought to fruition. They had succeeded in persuading a number of the outed presbyterian ministers to send a letter to London expressing their affection for the king and disclaiming any treasonable intentions on the part of the majority of covenanters. Other moderate members of the privy council added their support to this overture and advised the king on the need for conciliation. They were successful.

On 15th July 1669 the privy council received a letter from Charles II authorising them to appoint as many of the outed presbyterian ministers "as have lived peaceably and orderly" to their old charges if vacant, or to other charges where the patrons were agreeable. Those presbyterian ministers who were prepared to have their appointments confirmed by the bishops of their dioceses were then to be paid their full stipends and enjoy the same privileges as their episcopal brethren. Now came the big concession! It concerned those presbyterian ministers who still refused to acknowledge the episcopal hierarchy and accept the bishop's collation. They could also be appointed to charges, but were only to possess the manse and glebe and to have, instead of the official stipend, what money their congregations were prepared to give them for their maintenance. (And in view of their popularity this allowance would probably have been generous.) Finally, those elderly ministers who had behaved well and who were now too old to obtain churches were to be allowed an annual pension of 400 merks.

The only condition that was attached to this Act of Indulgence was a perfectly reasonable one. Since there was now nothing to debar peaceable presbyterian ministers from obtaining charges, there was also now no need for conventicles; and the Act ordained that all who attended such meetings would be dealt with most severely.

A final concession made by the privy council at this time was that the billeting of soldiers on private persons was to cease—a practice which had brought economic ruin to hundreds of poor families in the south-west during the previous six years—and also that all troops were to be withdrawn immediately from Galloway.

The government had at last proferred a genuine olive branch to the presbyterians of Scotland. It only remained now to see how the wild covenanters of Galloway would receive it.

The covenanters, however, would have nothing to do with it. Only four ministers in the whole of Galloway were prepared to subscribe to this Indulgence. A second Indulgence in 1672 persuaded eight more ministers in the province to change over, but several of these almost immediately regretted their decision and were heavily fined and lost half their stipends for refusing to do the bishops' bidding.

As for the rank and file of presbyterians in Galloway, they had no hesitation at all in denouncing those ministers who had accepted the Indulgence as "King's Curates," ' dumb dogs " and in various other unprintable terms. Because the indulged ministers carefully avoided topics of a controversial or political nature their sermons were as dull as ditchwater to the true Gallovidian presbyterians who much preferred the hell-fire and damnation inevitably prophesied (for episcopalians only, of course) by the non-indulged divines, at the numerous open-air services which were still being held.

## THE HIGHLAND HOST

It was the notorious "Black Act" of 13th August 1670 which, paradoxically, made conventiles even more popular than ever before with many covenanters, for it added that spice of real danger which often appeals to the young and adventurous spirits of all ages. This Act made field preaching an offence punishable by death; and anyone attending a conventicle or even failing to report such a meeting was guilty of treason and therefore also liable to capital punishment. It is only fair to remark, however, that the government did not at first invoke the death penalty for those guilty of this offence, but substituted imprisonment for life on the Bass Rock or transportation to the colonies.

The only member of the government who opposed the passage of this Bill was Lord Cassilis, who described it as a piece of truly barbaric legislation. Until after it had been safely passed the provisions of the Act had been carefully concealed from that most moderate of the high churchmen, Bishop Leighton. But when he heard of it he described it as an inhuman Act and, had he not been assured that it was not intended to enforce it rigorously, he would probably have resigned in protest.

Attendance at field services was now not only dangerous but also a deliberate act of defiance against the government, and it was perhaps just these two factors that attracted many fiery young recruits to the covenant ranks. Whether the ministers approved of it or not, they frequently found themselves attended on their journeys and at their services in the hills by a bodyguard of armed youths, all of them well versed in Old Testament history and longing to play the part of David against any Goliath whom the philistine government might choose to send.

For these young lads, accustomed to the monotonous and heart-breaking task of wresting a living from the infertile fields of impoverished crofts, the life of a covenanter became an adventure full of romance and excitement. The hills were their home and their bed the heather; the barking of the hill foxes attended their sleeping and the cry of the whaups their waking. They became tough and hardy, living off the natural resources of the land—game from the hills, fish from the river, helped out by occasional raids on the stock and crops of unsympathetic farmers of the valleys.

During their raids some of these rowdy young zealots took the chance of venting their spite on several occasions against the episcopal curates. One night three of them, disguised as women, broke into the manse of the curate at Balmaclellan, hauled him out of bed, assaulted him and stole everything of any use to them from the house. Another time three covenanters, also in disguise, burgled the home of the curate at Urr, and since they could not find the curate himself they carried off his wife, but later freed her. For these assaults the heritors of the two parishes, although in no way implicated, were fined a total of £1800.

The hundreds of hill folk of the 1670's, however, were not only young, but of all ages, male and female, and from all classes of society: some had once been important land-owners, others well-doing tenant farmers, but the majority had been penniless peasants with nothing left to lose. The one thing they had in common was that they were all homeless outlaws and dared not return to their former haunts. Families were often divided, the parents remaining peacefully at home and conforming to the law, while their sons and daughters, branded as rebels, dwelt in the hills. No communication was allowed between outlaws and their relatives at home; to harbour a rebel was just as serious an offence as to be one.

Some of the ministers were now also becoming more defiant, and even militant. that great hero of the hill folk, Alexander Peden, former minister of Old Luce, rampaged over the hills of Galloway, broadsword and pistols at his side, and, with his wild prophetic sermons, inspired his many followers with fresh zeal for the covenant. Peden was captured in 1773, removed to the Bass Rock, and the officer who arrested him was awarded £600. The two most sought after of the conventicle preachers, however, were two other Galloway ministers, John Welsh of Irongray and Gabriel Semple of Corsock, who regularly conducted services all over the hills and moors of the south-west. Their congregations always numbered several hundreds, and on one occasion they served communion in the open to about 3,000 covenanters. Although a reward of £4800 was offered for the capture of each, neither was every betrayed, and they were always too closely guarded to be surprised and caught by the militia.

The arrival in 1678 of the Highland Host, under James Graham of Claverhouse, heralded the opening of the final grim decade of persecution for the covenanters. This move was yet another attempt by the privy council to gain control over the presbyterians of Galloway. But, like so many of their earlier schemes, all it did was to inflict still more undeserved suffering, and in the end it actually strengthened rather than weakened the resistance of the covenanters.

The previous year the privy council had ordered all heritors and life-renters to sign a bond, not only for themselves but also on behalf of all who lived on their lands, not to attend conventicles or to have any dealings with the rebels. Most of the Galloway land-owners, led by Cassilis, Galloway, Ravenstone, Castle-Stewart, all the Gordons, the McDowalls of Freugh and Sheriff Agnew, protested vehemently against the injustice of such a bond and refused to sign it.

In reply to this act of defiance the privy council, in 1677, ordered a force of 6000 highlanders to be sent to teach these rebellious land-owners a lesson. Not only did the government turn this horde of uncivilised savages loose in Galloway, but it idemnified them before they went there for anything they might do. In the words of the proclamation, the highlanders were "authorised to take free quarter, to seize all horses for carrying their sick men, ammunition and other provisions, and are indemnified against all pursuits civil and criminal for anything they do, whether killing, wounding, apprehending, or imprisoning such as shall make opposition to authority."

The highlanders welcomed this open invitation to indulge in brutality and took full advantage of it in the first four months of 1678. They lived in free quarters, plundered and pillaged, killed cattle they did not need, stole and drove off all the horses they could lay their hands on, and tortured and outraged the people indiscriminately, never stopping to enquire whether they might be friend or foe. They ransacked Lochnaw and other country mansions of heirlooms, pictures and family treasures that had been accumulated over generations.

When the highlanders were sent north in the late spring—it was always their custom to return to their homes at seed-time and harvest—their departure was described in one account as follows: "One would have thought they had been at the sacking of some besieged town by their baggage and luggage. They were loaded with spoil; they carried away a great many horses and no small quantity of goods, whole webs of linen and woollen cloth, some silver plate bearing the names and arms of gentlemen. You would have seen them with loads of bedclothes, carpets, men and women's wearing clothes, pots, pants, girdirons, shoes, and other furniture where of they had pillaged the country."

The occupation of Galloway by the highlanders had two important consequences: first, many of the more moderate presbyterians, especially among those land-owners who had been victimised by the clansmen, now declared their open support for the covenant side; secondly, the covenanters began to take up arms in real earnest and formed themselves into troops of horse and foot soldiers to be used in defence of their conventicles. The departure of the highlanders had not really lessened the danger of attack, for they had been replaced by a strong force of militia, regular soldiers from other parts of Scotland, and English dragoons under their own officers. Moreover, Graham of Claverhouse still remained in charge of operations against the covenanters; and he was quite seriously regarded by the local inhabitants as having supernatural powers—some even believed he was the devil himself.

Despite the danger, however, it was on three successive days during the summer of 1678 that the greatest conventicles of covenanting times were held, in the parish of Irongray. These memorable services were attended by people from Galloway, Nithsdale and even from distant Clydesdale, and the whole proceedings demonstrated how highly efficient the covenanters' organisation had become. Three of the most eminent and respected of Galloway's noted ministers took part—John Welsh of Irongray, Samuel Arnot of Tongland and John Blackadder of Troqueer (who had been leading the covenanters in Fife for the previous eight years and had been specially invited to attend). The preparatory service was held on the Saturday at Meiklewood, about seven miles from Dumfries, and communion arranged for the following day.

Early on the Sunday morning the covenanters began to assemble on Skeoch Hill, and by the time they had all settled there was a congregation of some 3000 men, women and children. Sentries were posted on the surrounding hills, the foot soldiers in the inner ring and the horsemen farther out, ready to engage any government troops who might approach.

The communion tables, some of which remain to this day and are the only specimens of the kind in Scotland, consisted of four parallel rows of long, flat, oblong stones, each row about 20 yards in length. At one end there was a circular cairn of stones several feet high, where the officiating minister stood. The communion was served in relays to several hundred communicants at a time, and the services continued all through the day and into the evening.

It was late in the day when the only alarm was sounded, and the covenant troops quickly rushed to the point of danger. The cause of the alarm, however, proved to be no more than a small body of scouts sent out by the Earl of Nithsdale to find out what was going on. They were quickly dispersed, but it was by then too late in the day for them to call up the government militia. When the services were ended the covenant troops safely conveyed the members of the congregation to their various resting places for the night in the shelter of a near-by forest, and mounted guard over them.

The following day another conventicle was held in the parish, but several miles away from the place of the Sunday meeting, and almost as many again received communion at this service. Once more the sentries were out in strength, and, although the enemy must have known by now what was going on, they did not dare attack. The covenanters had discovered that there was safety in numbers, especially when they were well armed.

The last of these three impressive ceremonies was closed by a moving sermon from John Blackadder on the text "Let brotherly love continue."

During the following two years scores of prominent land-owners were ordered to appear before the courts because they, or more often their servants, had attended conventicles. In the majority of cases they failed to attend and consequently were outlawed; some fled to Holland, but most joined the ranks of ever-increasing bands of homeless covenanters lurking in the hills. The three noted ministers from Galloway—John Welsh, Gabriel Semple and Samuel Arnot—still continued their ministries in the hills, and even though the rewards for their capture were increased to as much as £6000 a head no one betrayed them. Glaverhouse and Grierson of Lagg were among the depute sheriffs specially appointed to enforce the laws against the covenanters with the utmost severity—a task which Grierson certainly took a fiendish delight in during the following eight years.

## BOTHWELL BRIDGE

The many hundreds of covenanters in refuge in the hills were now invariably well armed, for they could expect no mercy from the dragoons, who had orders to shoot on sight. Thus, on Sunday, 1st June, 1679, when Claverhouse and his troops attacked a conventicle at Drumclog the covenanters were able to retaliate so effectively that they won a decisive victory and the government force was put to flight.

This success inspired the covenanters of the south-west to such an extent that within a couple of weeks they had assembled a force of some 5000 well-armed men eager to join battle with the government troops. But once again that eternal curse of the covenanting cause—theological and political disputes—split their ranks wide open and removed any possibility of success.

There were two bodies of opinion, the moderates and extremists; and the gulf between them was too wide to be bridged by leaders who were so completely bigoted that any compromise was out of the question. John Welsh, former minister of Irongray, led the moderates, who were prepared to acknowledge the king's supremacy in all civil matters but demanded freedom of conscience in religion. These more tolerant covenanters even went so far as to send a deputation, headed by Welsh, to the Duke of Monmouth, who commanded the government troops, suggesting an armistice and asking that the religious question be referred to a free parliament and free general assembly. But their petition was turned down, and so the fight was on. The extremists, on the other hand, led by that firebrand Donald Cargill, demanded the total abolition of episcopacy and, what was most damaging to the covenant cause, refused to have any dealings with their more moderate brethren. In their war councils before the battle the covenanters were hopelessly divided, disagreeing violently over religion and politics alike. The extremists refused to fight under moderate officers, and vice versa; commanders were chosen for their evangelical rather than their military ability.

As a result, when the covenanters engaged the enemy at Bothwell Bridge on 22nd June the the battle was in every sense of the word a complete shambles. Some 1500 of the covenanters were immediately out-manœuvred and captured without ever striking a blow. In the rout that followed Claverhouse and his men avenged themselves for Drumclog by deliberately cutting down some 500 men of the fleeing covenanters, a large number of them Galloway men. That noted covenanting figure, the aged Alexander Gordon of Earlston, who had been a fugitive and exile for a great part of his life, was killed by the enemy while hastening to join in the battle, not realising the day had already been lost.

After Bothwell Bridge there was the customary forfeiture to the government of the lands of those who had taken part in the battle. Scores of well-known figures were listed as rebels, liable to be shot on sight; some remained in the hills, others fled to Holland. The government garrisons in Galloway were strengthened and the depute sheriffs given commissions to seize the movable goods of all who had been in the battle or attending conventicles. The courts presided over by Cornet Graham, a brother of Claverhouse, and Grierson of Lagg were notorious for their cruelty and injustice. Informers regularly committed perjury against completely innocent people just for the sake of the reward, and those whom they testified against, guilty and innocent alike, were sentenced without proper trial to imprisonment or, more frequently since the prisons were full, to transportation.

On the first anniversary of Bothwell bridge Richard and Michael Cameron, accompanied by a score of horsemen, descended from the hills and nailed their famous declaration to the Market Cross of Sanquhar. Copies were then posted at dead of night on kirk doors all over the south-west for all to read. This extremist document was hailed with approval by the great majority of the covenanters of Galloway, who had now come to realise that moderation was getting them nowhere. There can be no doubt about the treasonable nature of part of this declaration, as the following extract shows:—

"We for ourselves as the representatives of the true Presbyterian Kirk and Covenanted nation of Scotland do disown Charles Stuart that has been reigning (or rather tyrannising, as we may say) on the throne of Britain these years bygone, as having any right, title to, or interest in the said Crown of Scotland, as forfeited several years since, by his perjury and breach of covenant both to God and his Kirk and usurpation of His Crown and Royal prerogative therein, and many other breaches in matters ecclesiastical. . . . For which reason we declare that he should have been denuded of being King, Ruler or Magistrate, or of having any power to act, or to be obeyed as such. . . . We, being under the standard of the Lord Jesus Christ, do declare war with such a tyrant and usurper, and all men of his practices, as enemies to our Lord Jesus Christ and His cause and covenants."

Episcopalians in 1680, and many since then, have been tumbling over themselves in their eagerness to condemn the covenanters as out-and-out traitors and the whole of their cause as treasonable, just because of the terms of the Sanquhar Declaration. Two comments may be made in answer to such charges. In the first place some of the provisions contained in the Declaration of 1680 were actually embodied in the law of Scotland only eight years later. Secondly, while on the subject of public declarations it might be appropriate here to recall the solemn oath sworn on more than one occasion by the king, Charles II:

"I, Charles, King of Great Britain, do assure and declare, by my solemn oath, in the presence of Almighty God, my approbation of the National Covenant, and of the Solemn League and Covenant, and faithfully oblige my self to prosecute the ends thereof in my station and calling; and that I shall consent and agree to all Acts of Parliament establishing Presbyterial Government, the Confession of Faith and Catechisms in the Kingdom of Scotland, as they are approved by the General Assembly of this Kirk and Parliament of this Kingdom. And that I shall give my royal assent to the Acts of Parliament, passed or to be passed, enjoining the same in the rest of my dominions, and that I shall observe them in my own practice, and shall never make any opposition to any of these, or endeavour any change thereof."

So much for royal promises! There can be little doubt that it was this gross breach of faith on the part of the king that was fundamentally responsible for the whole of the covenant troubles in Scotland.

CHAPTER XXI

# THE KILLING TIMES

## MERCILESS PERSECUTION BY THE COURTS

FIFTH column infiltration, brain-washing and psychological warfare are generally regarded as twentieth century innovations. But this is not so, for Graham of Claverhouse was already employing these methods against the covenanters in Galloway in the 1680's. In addition to these refinements he also had available all the older means of torture perfected by the Spanish Inquisition—the thumb-screw, the boot and the rack—as well as one specially reserved for the women, the prolonged agony of death by drowning while tied to a stake in the Solway.

Claverhouse did not lack for capable assistants in his devilish work. There were his two brothers, depute sheriff David and cornet William, as well as numerous other dragoon officers, chiefly Englishmen, who were not so squeamish as to boggle at a bit of extra brutality. Few local men, however, not even those whose sympathies were episcopalian and pro-government, could be induced to participate in the inhuman persecution of their fellow-Gallovidians. The nobles and the leading land-owners, whatever their politics, refused to be associated in any way with such dirty business. But a small number of local inhabitants did achieve everlasting notoriety and shame by currying favour with Claverhouse and helping him in his merciless oppression. In the Stewartry these were Sir Robert Grierson of Lagg, undoubtedly the worst of them all, and Thomas Lidderdale of St Mary's Isle; and in the Shire Sir Godfrey McCulloch of Myretoun and that brace of sadistic toadies from Wigtown, Provost William Coltrane and Bailie Patrick Stewart.

It was the Test Act, passed in August 1681 by the first Scottish parliament to sit for nine years, that began the final stage in the covenanting struggle. The "Test" prescribed an oath originally designed to be sworn by all holders of public offices, but it was later applied to common people as well. Anyone accepting the Test agreed to acknowledge the king's authority in all matters, ecclesiastical as well as civil, and to renounce the presbyterian form of religion. In the words of the oath: "I shall never rise in arms, or enter into covenants, and there lies no obligation upon me from the National Covenant or the Solemn League and Covenant to endeavour any change or alteration in the government either in Church or State as it is now established by the laws of this kingdom."

This was completely unacceptable to all true presbyterians, whether they were covenanting extremists or not. All manner of people declined to take the Test, including many who had no deep religious convictions one way or the other. Sir John Dalrymple of Stair, who held an appointment under the government in Edinburgh, refused the Test, demitted office and, after being fined £500 and having his lands at Glenluce forfeited, had to flee to Holland. Agnew of Lochnaw was also removed from his office as Sheriff Principal, and was succeeded by Claverhouse himself. The earls of Nithsdale and Galloway and Viscount Kenmure were among the many other nobles who refused to subscribe to this oath and were punished by loss of offices, lands and emoluments.

For many years before this, many of these titled land-owners had deemed it prudent to have a foot in each camp. Their rank undoubtedly afforded them some measure of protection from persecution, but they also took great care not to commit any offence that would bring them into serious trouble with the government. At the same time, although they did not openly support the covenant cause, they appear to have secretly encouraged their servants and dependants in doing so, as Claverhouse was soon to discover. In a report from Wigtown in March 1682, Claverhouse complained bitterly about the conduct of such people: "Here in this shire I find the lairds all following the example of a considerable heritor among them (Dalrymple of Stair), which is to live regularly themselves, but have their houses constant haunts of rebels and intercommuned persons, and have their children baptized by the same and then lay the blame on their wives. But I am resolved this jest shall pass no longer here, for it is laughing and fooling the government."

Claverhouse may not have succeeded in making much impression on the nobility, but he was certainly determined to use all means at his disposal to break the resistance and spirit of the common people. The courts, presided over by his brothers and Grierson and Lidderdale, sat almost continuously. Those parishes nearest to the hills, and especially in the Glenkens area, were the most severely dealt with, and the only part of Galloway that appears to have escaped trouble was the south eastern corner, around New Abbey, Southwick and Dalbeattie.

The procedure generally followed by the courts was that all inhabitants of a parish between the ages of 16-70 years were ordered to attend at some central place on a certain day. The court, accompanied by a strong detachment of soldiers, then examined them all carefully one by one. Cornet Graham's customary greeting was, "You dog, hold up your hand and swear! . . . How many conventicles have you been at since Bothwell, who preached at them, who had their children baptized?" And so the questioning and intimidation went on hour after hour, day after day. The local curate was usually present in court and was required to give evidence about his parishioners' church attendance and conduct. In many cases this testimony, if damning, was reluctantly given, but some curates, like the notorious Colin Dalgleish of Kirkcudbright and Peter Pearson of Carsphairn, took a fiendish delight in deliberately committing perjury in order to vent their spite on those members of their congregations whom they disliked.

Witnesses and suspected persons were kept in attendance for weeks at a time and, although often completely innocent, were interrogated daily by third-degree methods until they confessed or yielded any information they might have about the covenanters or their meetings. A common trick was to have a number of informers repeatedly denounce an innocent person until he was so confused that he really did not know whether he was guilty or not; and very often, in defending himself of the trumped-up charge, he would give away secrets about others.

There was never any pretence at a trial. Guilty, suspected and innocent alike were herded together in irons and marched off to Kirkcudbright or Wigtown Tolbooth. There they were subjected to torture by thumb-screw or boot, or they had their ears cut off, to persuade them to talk. From prison these unfortunate wretches were then passed in batches to convict ships and transported to the American colonies where they were sold as slaves. A number of the more important offenders were taken to Edinburgh to be dealt with by the courts there and were usually heavily fined as well as being imprisoned on the Bass Rock, in Blackness Castle, or transported.

Another method, employed by both Claverhouse and Grierson, was to send spies to infiltrate into bands of covenanters in the hills by pretending to be presbyterian sympathisers from others parts of the country, and thus to be able to report to the government officers any information they might pick up. This, however, was not very succesful, because the hill-folk soon became suspicious of strangers in their midst and learned not to confide in any they could not wholly trust. Several government agents, whose activities had been unmasked, were beaten up (but not killed) and returned, much the worse of their treatment, to their masters.

The covenanters then adopted less crude and more cunning methods and began to out-play the government at their own game of espionage. As soon as a man was suspected of being a government spy, the covenanters fed him with false information about the time and place of conventicles, or the location of bodies of rebels, and then allowed him the opportunity to report his information to the troops. In this way the government forces were often induced to go marching off in one direction on some false trail, while the covenanters were left to meet in complete safety in some other place many miles away.

One government spy, however, enjoyed a long run of success before he was eventually found out, and he was responsible for scores of covenanters being arrested and brought before the courts. This was an elderly worthy by the name of John Gib. For many years he played the part of a travelling packman and was a familiar figure in all the up-land parishes between New Luce and Glencairn. Along with his other wares, he invariably carried a large stock of religious pamphlets and reprints of sermons by famous covenating ministers, literature specially designed to appeal to the hill-folk. Gib was clever enough first of all to build up a good reputation for himself by carrying accurately messages and news from one covenanting body to another; and, once his bona fides had been established, he became the trusted confidant of many of the outlaws. After he had informed on any of the rebels, he took great care that he himself was well away from the scene when the actual arrest was made; in this way Gib was not noticeably implicated in the business, and no suspicion fell on him. Exact details of his activities are very scarce, and all that is known for certain about him is his method of operating and that he was the most successful government spy of the 1680's. Gib eventually gave himself away and was appropriately "dealt with" (to quote an ancient account) by the hill-folk; he was probably killed, although there is no actual record of this.

But, on the whole, the government had again failed to do what they intended. Not even the dreaded courts, presided over by such monsters as Grierson of Lagg, nor all the merciless tortures and punishments they imposed could break the spirit of the covenanters. No doubt this cruel oppression had a properly chastening effect on hundreds of innocent and inoffensive creatures who were never real rebels anyway. But countless scores of genuine covenanters still roamed the hills and defied all the efforts of the government to dislodge them.

Claverhouse, however, considered it necessary to inform his masters on the privy council that he had achieved some measure of success, and he did so in a long written report in which he seems to glory in the callous methods he employed, as the following extract (in Graham's own spelling) shows:—

"In the meantyme we quartered on the rebelles, and indevoured to distroy them by eating up their provisions: but they quickly perceived the dessein, and soued their corns on untilled ground. After which we fell in search of the rebelles, played them hotly with pairtys, so that there were severall taken, many fleid the country, and all were dung from their hants; and then rifled so their houses, ruined their goods, and imprisoned their servants, that their wyfes and childring were broght to sterving; which forced them to have recours to the saif conduct, and maid them glaid to renounce their principles . . . ."

The long covenanting struggle was now drawing near its close, but there still remained the hardest ordeal of all to be faced, when "the blood of the martyrs became the seed of the church."

## THE BLOOD OF THE MARTYRS

In May, 1684, the privy council drew up a Roll of Fugitives for Galloway, and on this appear the names of 209 men and 12 women who were outlawed and homeless. They were all people of substance—heritors, life-renters, tenant-farmers or merchants from the burghs; the women belonged to the Glenkens area and were widows who were landowners or tenants in their own rights. In fact, about three-quarters of all those listed had lived in the parishes of Twynholm, Tongland and those of the Glenkens; in Wigtownshire the main covenanting areas lay in the parishes of Penninghame and Ochiltree. It must be emphasised that this roll lists only people of some means, but makes no mention of the wives and younger members of their families, who were often fugitives as well; nor does it include the hundreds of peasants and cottars who had followed their employers into voluntary exile in the hills. The covenanters were obviously then present in the remote areas in very large numbers indeed, for government reports of that time mention the fact that the rebels were careful always to move in bodies of 500-600 strong, so that they were too powerful to be attacked by any ordinary detachment of soldiers.

By the autumn of 1684 the government had greatly strengthened their garrisons in the troubled areas and issued them with new orders for the persecution of relatives of the covenanters: 'You shall turn out all the wives and children of the fugitives from their habitations if it shall appear that they have conversed with their parents or husbands. It was the duty of all to inform the military as to where the rebels could be found; failure, or suspected failure to do so was a criminal offence. The courts continued their horrible work and, since the Scottish prisons were all full up, the most common form of punishment for those who were fortunate enough to escape hanging was now transportation into life-long slavery in the West Indies. Many of these prisoners were perhaps fortunate when their rotten old convict ships foundered in the

Atlantic gales, or when they died from some epidemic contracted in the rat-infested, disease-ridden holds.

In October James Renwick, a native of Moniaive, who had taken over the leadership of the extremist covenanters after the death of the Cameron brothers at Ayrsmoss, published his Apologetical Declaration. This document hurled defiance and abuse at the king and his ministers and threatened immediate death to all informers. Most of the Galloway covenanters subscribed to this treasonable declaration, which was secretly affixed to kirk doors and market crosses.

The government retaliated immediately by introducing the Abjuration Oath which people all over the south-west were required to take in addition to the Test, thus renouncing completely the terms of Renwick's Declaration. At the same time the privy council passed an Act which empowered the military to kill covenanters anywhere and at any time: "The lords of his majesty's privy council do hereby ordain any person who owns, or will not disown, the late treasonable document (the Apologetical Declaration), whether they have arms or not, to be immediately put to death."

It was this Act which opened the period, covering the autumn of 1684 and the whole of 1685, that came to be known in the history of the covenanters as "the Killing Times". Courts were now virtually unnecessary, for anyone could be shot on the spot, or even more cruelly done to death, without any need for trial or proof of guilt. Examination of the records of those killed in this way reveals the following facts:—Some of the victims were undoubtedly fanatical covenanters, rebels, and therefore guilty according to the law; some were clearly quite harmless creatures whose only crime was that their consciences would not allow them to swear away their presbyterian beliefs by taking the Test or the Oath; others were quite obviously completely innocent.

Records have been compiled giving details of the deaths of 82 persons who were summarily killed by the troops in Galloway during 1684-85. Once again, of course, these numbers are by no means complete, since they represent only those whose deaths were witnessed and recorded. All over the more desolate parts the covenanters were being massacred by the soldiers and their bodies left to rot on the heather where they fell. No records were kept of such killings; the victims were simply regarded as "missing," for none of their relatives or friends knew how or where they had died. For many years after the killing times shepherds were continually finding on hills and moors the bleached skeletons of covenanters who had been killed in this way.

It is perhaps impossible to determine from those reports that do exist whether the victims were guilty or not; but the accounts relating the circumstances and details of their deaths certainly make gruesome reading. The few examples that can be mentioned here will show that the atrocities then committed in Galloway by the government forces are unparalleled for sheer cold blooded brutality, in the whole of Scottish history.

Claverhouse himself was responsible for some horrible deeds. In December, 1684, for example, he came upon six covenanters in the parish of Girthon and, when they appeared reluctant to take the oath, he wasted no more time with them but ordered four to be shot at once. The two survivors and friends carried the bodies of the dead men to their home village of Dalry and buried them in the graveyard there. Claverhouse, however, on hearing of this, sent soldiers to disinter the corpses and ensure that, in accordance with the law, they remained exposed for several days, one of the dead bodies being suspended from a tree.

Colonel James Douglas, commanding one of the many companies of dragoons in the area, was also the author of many atrocious murders. On one occasion, in New Galloway, he entered the house of the aged Andrew McWhan and began to interrogate him. But the old man was so weak from fever that he was unable to answer the questions or to take Oath properly. Douglas had him carried out from his bed and shot. It was this same Colonel Douglas who was later responsible for the execution, in sight of their wives and families, of six covenanters at the Caldon Woods in Glentrool. On another occasion Colonel Douglas's troops trapped five Balmaclellan men in a cave near Glencairn. The covenanters were dragged out and ordered to be shot. The mother and sister of one of the fugitives were present and interceded for him, but in vain. He was allowed to read part of Psalm 17 and from John, Chapter 16, and then, after praying, was killed. The other four were allowed no time for preparation, but were shot immediately. One of the prisoners who was not dead had to be dispatched with a sword, but before he expired he cried out, "Though every hair of my head were a man, I am willing to die all these deaths for Christ and His cause."

Even the completely innocent were not safe. William Auchinleck, a conformist who had taken the Test and the Oath, was riding home to Buittle one day when he met a detachment of dragoons near Tongland. Although his conscience should have been quite clear, he deemed it prudent to keep out of the way of the soldiers and deviated from the road slightly to avoid them. But, unknown to him, he had been spotted and followed. An hour or two later he was shot as he emerged from an inn near Carlingwark Loch. The sound of the muskets frightened the horse of a young lad who had met in with Auchinleck, and he was thrown from the saddle. Perhaps it looked to the soldiers as if the boy was trying to escape. At any rate, he too was shot on the spot.

Sir Robert Grierson of Lagg has always had the reputation of being the most foul fiend of them all, and well he deserved it. One day Lord Annandale and his troops had arrested two covenanters in the parish of Twynholm, and he had spared their lives until they should face trial at the court at Kirkcudbright. Grierson then fell in with the company and ordered the two prisoners to be shot immediately; but Annandale explained that he had already promised them a trial and refused to carry out the execution. Grierson, however, had no time for such leniency, and when the troops also refused to carry out his orders he himself threw the prisoners, tied together, to the ground and dispatched them on the spot.

A party of dragoons, under a Captain Bruce, came upon a number of covenanters at Lochenkit, near Kirkpatrick Durham, and shot four of them immediately. Two more were taken to the Bridge of Urr where Grierson of Lagg was questioning the local inhabitants. Bruce intimated that he wanted his two prisoners tried by the court, but Grierson objected to such time-wasting and demanded summary execution. Despite Bruce's protests, he marched them to Irongray and hanged them on a tree outside the church. One of the men, when asked if he wished to send a final message to his wife replied: "I will leave her and the two babes upon the Lord, and to His promise. A father to the fatherless and a judge to the widows is God in His holy habitation." The two bodies were left hanging there for some time as a warning to others.

On another occasion on the hill of Kirkconnel in the parish of Tongland, Grierson captured five covenanters, one of whom was John Bell of Whiteside, a relation of Viscount Kenmure. When Bell begged for a quarter of an hour's grace to prepare for death Grierson retorted with an oath, "What! Have you not had enough time for preparation since Bothwell Brig?" The men were shot immediately, and Grierson would not allow their bodies to be buried. A few days later, in Kirkcudbright, Viscount Kenmure upbraided Grierson for his cruelty, and especially for refusing to allow his dead relative to be decently interred. Grierson's callous reply was, "Take him if you will and salt him in your own beef barrel." Kenmure at once drew his sword and would have killed Grierson had not Claverhouse, who was present, intervened.

These are but a few of the massacres that took place during the Killing Times; most of those mentioned have been commemorated by memorials which can still be seen. They are sufficient, however, to illustrate the way in which so many covenanters accepted martyrdom during the darkest days in the history of Galloway. But there still remains to be recounted the most horrible atrocity of them all, the story of the Wigtown Martyrs.

## THE SEED OF THE CHURCH

On a lovely spring morning in May, 1685, a vast crowd assembled on the foreshore at Wigtown to witness one of the most dramatic and horrifying events of covenanting times. They had gathered to watch the public execution, by drowning, of two women who had chosen to accept this horrible death rather than renounce their religious principles. Eye-witness accounts, recorded in writing by various bodies very soon afterwards, have provided a detailed picture of that tragic scene.

While they waited for the drama to unfold, the spectators, numbering several hundred, reacted in many different ways. Some of them tried to relieve the awful tension that gripped their conscious minds by chattering nervously and excitedly with their neighbours; others stood grimfaced and silent; many knelt unashamedly in prayer.

Whatever noise there was quickly died away as soon as the prisoners, under a strong escort of soldiers, were led forward. There was then a sudden murmur from the crowd, a keening wail of commiseration from the women and muffled rumble of anger from the men, when they caught sight of the two victims—a fair young girl of eighteen and a haggard old woman of over sixty.

Gilbert Wilson was a well-doing tenant farmer at Glenvernock, in the parish of Penninghame, and both he and his wife conformed in every way to the episcopal form of religion. Their three children, however, Margaret (aged 18), Thomas (16) and Agnes (13), had left home and thrown in their lot with the covenanters. From their subsequent actions and statements it is quite clear that both Margaret and Thomas, despite their youth, had the strongest reasons for the stand they took. It was not just youthful craving for the novelty and excitement of the life that drove them to join the rebels; both held genuine religious convictions, and they acted in accordance with those. In fact they felt much the same way about the covenant cause as do many of their 'teen-age descendants of today about nuclear disarmament.

During the bitter months of January and February, 1685, the three Wilsons had been living with a band of covenanters in the hills around Glentrool. Life under such conditions had proved too much for young Agnes, and it was found necessary for the sake of her health to take her to shelter. They did not dare go home, for that would have rendered the parents liable to severe punishment for conversing with or harbouring rebels. Instead the two girls decided to make for the burgh of Wigtown, where there were friends of the family who might be willing to give food and lodging, at least to Agnes.

Unfortunately they chose the wrong person to approach. One

day towards the end of February they called at the house of Bailie Patrick Stewart, expecting that he would be willing to help them, since he was a friend of their father. Stewart, however, knowing that they were fugitives from their home, immediately betrayed them to the soldiers, and the two young girls were imprisoned in the Tolbooth.

There they were lodged in the same foul cell as Margaret McLachlan, a widow about 63 years of age, from the parish of Kirkinner. Although by no means a raving fanatic about her beliefs, she was undoubtedly a stubborn and bigoted old woman. As a staunch covenanter she had quite defiantly attended conventicles whenever possible, deliberately absented herself from the curate's services in her parish church and held private prayer-meetings in her own house, with no attempt at concealment. And for these heinous offences she was arrested and cast into Wigtown jail, there to await trial.

The local government commissioners were determined to deal drastically with these women, by way of warning to others, and in order to make the offences appear as grave as possible they concocted a list of charges, some of which were obviously quite fictitious. All three women were accused of "being present at the Battle of Bothwell Bridge, Ayrsmoss, 20 field conventicles, and 20 house conventicles." Although it is quite likely that they were all indeed guilty of attendance at conventicles, one finds it difficult to understand how Margaret and Agnes Wilson could possibly have been at Bothwell, since they would then have been only twelve and seven years old respectively; it was also highly improbable that the old woman had been there either. Nevertheless, these were the charges they had to face when, after having been in prison for over a month, they were at last led into court on 13th April.

On the bench sat five of the most vicious scoundrels in Scotland at that time—Grierson of Lagg, Sheriff David Graham, Major Windram, Captain Strachan and Provost Coltrane. The court warmed up by dealing first with another case, against a Margaret Maxwell, a servant woman, also from Kirkinner, who was accused of non-conformity. She was sentenced to be flogged through the streets of Wigtown and to be put in the jougs for three days. She survived her punishment and later was one of the witnesses who recorded evidence about the drowning of her fellow-prisoners.

The case against the aged Margaret McLachlan and Margaret and Agnes Wilson was almost as quickly disposed of. No evidence by the prosecution was required to substantiate the charges, and none was permitted by way of defence. The indictment was read out, the prisoners were pronounced guilty and were sentenced "to be tied to palisades fixed in the sand, within the flood mark of the sea, and there to stand until the flood overflowed them and drowned them." The three women were then given the chance to renounce their beliefs, and thus save their lives, by taking the Abjuration Oath, but all refused. The day of execution was fixed for exactly four weeks later, and the prisoners were returned to the cells.

During the intervening weeks several attempts were made to have the three women reprieved. Gilbert Wilson journeyed to Edinburgh and succeeded in obtaining the release of his younger daughter Agnes on a bond of £100 sterling. A number of Margaret McLachlan's friends also prepared a petition on her behalf and sent it to Edinburgh. The privy council considered these representations and, on 30th April they issued a reprieve for both women.

Now comes the mystery! What happened to this reprieve? One thing certain is that it was not even known that a reprieve had been granted, until several years after the sentences had been carried out. There are two possible explanations for the disappearance of this vital document.

First, the reprieve was quite clearly addressed to the magistrates of Edinburgh (not Wigtown) discharging them from putting the sentences to execution until an unspecified date (left blank on the form), so that the king's remission might be obtained. It is possible therefore that the reprieve was pigeon-holed in Edinburgh, in expectation of the women being eventually brought there for execution; and then, since the women never did arrive in the capital, the document would have been forgotten. A second explanation is that the reprieve, having been redirected, did in fact reach Wigtown, but that the authorities there deliberately suppressed it. And anyone who closely examined the records of Grierson and some of his fellow-persecutors, and knew the treacherous inhumanity they were capable of, might be quite prepared to accept this solution of the mystery. Whatever happened to the reprieve, it made no difference to the fate of the two women who were led out to execution on the sands at Wigtown that lovely May morning.

The stake to which Margaret McLachlan was tied had been driven in further out on the sands, where the beach shelved more steeply and the swiftly flowing Solway tide rose more rapidly. Margaret Wilson's stake was placed so close to the shore that it was quite easy for the spectators on the bank to talk to her. The intention was that the sight of her older companion drowning would perhaps break the younger girl's resistance and make her recant.

Margaret McLachlan remained indomitable in spirit to the very end, but physically, after many weeks in the "Thieve's Hole" of Wigtown jail, she was a poor, worn-out creature. Long before the icy waters had crept up to her face, the old woman had fainted from the cold and mercifully she was probably thus spared the ultimate horror of the actual drowning.

If the authorities had expected the young girl to break down on witnessing the horrible fate of the old woman, they were disappointed because, apart from some expressions of pity, Margaret Wilson remained unmoved in her resolve, and she now prepared, with the utmost composure, to meet her own death. Many members of the crowd entreated her to renounce her principles and save her life, but she steadfastly refused to do so. As the relentless waters rose steadily around her body she sang part of Psalm 25, beginning at verse 7:—

> Let not the errors of my youth,
> Nor sins remembered be:
> In mercy, for thy goodness' sake,
> O Lord, remember me.

Next she quoted extensively from the eighth chapter to the Romans and, as the waves were lapping round her neck, she reached the climax of that great passage. No words could have been more appropriate as the dying testimony, not only of Margaret Wilson, but of all the covenant martyrs who gave their lives for their faith.

> "Who shall separate us from the love of Christ? Shall tribulation, or distress or persecution, or famine, or nakedness, or peril, or sword?
> As it is written, for thy sake we are killed all the day long; we are accounted as sheep for the slaughter.
> Nay, in all these things we are more than conquerors through him that loved us.
> For I am persuaded, that neither death, nor life, nor angels, nor principalities, nor powers, nor things present, nor things to come.
> Nor height, nor depth, nor any other creature, shall be able to separate us from the love of God, which is in Christ Jesus our Lord."

And when the waters began to engulf her she was praying.

But before she could drown a soldier was ordered into the water to hold her head up and postpone her death for a minute or two to give her a last chance to speak. Several further attempts were made both by the soldiers and by sympathisers in the crowd to persuade the young girl to say something that could be interpreted as a renunciation of her covenanting principles. All their pleas, however, were stubbornly ignored. Finally Major Windram, commanding the troops, offered to administer the Abjuration Oath, ordering her to take it immediately or be returned to the waters. "I will not," she replied, quietly but most deliberately. "I am one of Christ's children. Let me go."

Thus perished the 18-year-old Margaret Wilson, whose martyrdom is often regarded as the saddest in all Scottish history.

Although there were still a few more victims to be claimed during 1685, the persecution then began to ease off very considerably. James II's Acts of toleration and indulgence, designed to help Roman Catholics in particular, extended to other non-conformists as well. Most Galloway covenanters, weary of terror and bloodshed, accepted these, but not the wild extremists of the hills, the Cameronians. They continued to regard themselves as the only "faithful remnant" of "true presbyterianism". Some of them still advocated the establishment in Britain of a republic ruled not by politicians but by some divinely inspired preacher, in much the same way as Moses led the children of Israel.

It was this lawless sect that has been blamed for most of the deeds of violence with which the covenanters have been charged. There is no doubt that the Cameronian hot-heads were often treasonable and anarchic in their ideas and utterances, but it is also true that their leader, James Renwick, deplored the use of force and usually succeeded in restraining them from violent action. Renwick, a native of Moniaive, proved to be the last of the covenant martyrs, being executed in Edinburgh in 1688.

Nevertheless, some historians insist that the covenanters were by no means guiltless as far as the killings were concerned. In fact one writer whose episcopalian sympathies are quite well known, has tried to convey the impression that behind every whin-bush in Galloway there lurked a gang of murderous covenanters waiting to shoot in the back any peace-loving soldier who was going innocently about his duty. Such an idea is, of course, ridiculous. There is nothing in government records to indicate the killing of soldiers by covenanters except on one or two rare occasions; secondly, every account of the times emphasises the care taken by the homeless outlaws to avoid the military detachments; finally there was never any suggestion of guerrilla warfare, such as this charge would imply, in Galloway.

One shameful killing for which the covenanters were definitely responsible was that of Peter Pierson the curate of Carsphairn, who was murdered in his own home. In his particular case the provocation was extremely great, for he had been responsible by his perjured testimony for causing death and untold misery to scores of his parishioners. The pro-episcopalian historian already mentioned refers vaguely to two soldiers who were murdered in their beds; but this is a common fate of soldiers in occupied territory and may not necessarily be connected with religion. A soldier on sentry duty was shot when a party of Cameronians tried to raid the government arms depot at Kirkcudbright, but Claverhouse and a detachment of troops caught up with the covenanters at Tongland and killed five of them. So that account was quickly settled. Other stories concerning unprovoked killings blamed on the covenanters are very vague and completely unsupported by either documentary historical records or memorials.

Many of us who live in this more tolerant and enlightened age would have found the covenanters of Galloway terribly difficult folk to live with, for in their bigoted and puritanical attitude to life and religion, they probably resembled the strictest close brethren sects of today. Yet, although we may not be attracted to these grim zealots or approve of their methods, we cannot help respecting them for the stand they took. Had it not been for the covenanters, episcopalianism would have triumphed in 1660, and the whole fabric of presbyterianism, created by Knox a century earlier, would have so completely disintegrated by 1688 that it might never have been possible to rebuild it.

Members of the Church of Scotland, therefore, must never forget the incalculable debt they owe to the covenanters, especially to those of Galloway who bore the greatest weight of the persecution; it is through their efforts that presbyterians of today can still enjoy complete freedom in church discipline and government. Truly, the blood of the martyrs was the seed of the Church.

ROCKCLIFFE, ON THE SOLWAY COAST, KNOWN BY SOME AS 'THE SCOTS RIVIERA' IS A PROFUSION OF GARDEN FLOWERS AND ROCK OUTCROPS

## CHAPTER XXII

# FIFTY YEARS OF DEPRESSION

### POVERTY-STRICKEN PEASANTRY

GALLOWAY touched rock-bottom economically about the end of the seventeenth and the beginning of the eighteenth centuries. For about fifty years, from 1690 to 1740, the province was by far the most depressed area in the whole of Scotland. Not only was trade at a complete standstill, but some years when the crops were poor a state of actual famine existed. The farms of Galloway were not producing sufficient to feed the local inhabitants, and because of the lack of trade there was neither the money nor the transport available to purchase and carry supplies from outside the area.

This deplorable economic situation was the direct result of the fifty years of religious troubles. In those days, of course, there was no kind of relief for depressed areas, and so Galloway was left to dree her weird and work out her own salvation.

The unhealthy state of agriculture may be guaged from the prices that farms were fetching. In 1780 farms which were formerly let for about £200 per annum were being given away free to their tenants provided they paid the public burdens on them. The valuable salmon fishing on the Dee at Tongland, which at one time brought its proprietor £700 a year, was leased for £8 in 1725 because there was no way of exporting the fish to the English markets.

Early eighteenth century travellers in Galloway all make much the same derogatory remarks about the methods of farming and the living conditions of the peasants. Cattle, sheep and horses, which were once the area's prime products, had never been so low in numbers or so poor in quality. It was quite common at that time for Galloway farmers to yoke to the old heavy Scots plough a mixed team of oxen and horses. Four was the minimum number in the team, but since the beasts were usually emaciated as many as eight might be needed. All country folk, whether tenant-farmers or merely peasants, still enjoyed the traditional right of free grazing on the laird's grassland which, by custom, had therefore come to be considered as "common pasture". In accordance with the centuries-old practice, all beasts for which there was no winter feeding were slaughtered at Martinmas. In these lean times there were few cattle that survived the winter, and any that did were so weak that they had to be lifted bodily to the fresh pastures in the spring; this operation was known as "the lifting". Because of the shortage of stock, Galloway's staple exports of wool and hides had dwindled away to nothing.

Farms were usually divided up in a most wasteful manner between several tenants, each of whom had one or more rigs of arable land on which he grew his crops. These usually consisted of bere (for the brewing of ale), coarse grey oats and white oats in about equal proportions. The yield was miserable to the extreme because there was never sufficient manure, the use of fertilisers was still unknown and, most of all, because the same land was grossly over-worked. Pasture land was never cropped—that was the tradition; and, since drainage was still not practised, no attempt was made to reclaim marshy land.

Galloway farmers at that time considered themselves very lucky if their crops yielded three seeds for every one sowed; some were even thankful for a two for one return. No wheat was grown in this area and, in 1735, there was not a single flour mill in the whole of Galloway. Even as late as 1741 locally grown grain was insufficient to supply local needs, for that year the town council of Kirkcudbright had to buy two ship-loads of oats from Wales and sell them at reduced prices to the townsfolks in order to avert famine.

The peasants' houses were miserable hovels, built of roughly dressed stone with holes for doorways and windows. Quite often there was no door at all, for timber was scarcer in Galloway in the early eighteenth century than at any period in history. (The landscape must have looked very bare at that time, since the woods had all been cut down during the religious troubles and never replanted.) The windows were without frames or glass, simply holes in the wall. Straw or turf was used to steek the window on the windward side, and the other served as an additional chimney. In many cottages the fire was still in the centre of the floor, but more recent buildings had the fire against the gable.

The roof, thatched with rushes or heather, was by far the most valuable part of the building, simply beacause it had to be supported by a timber frame. This was the cause of much trouble between landlords and tenants, because when cottars gave up tenancy of a cottage they frequently flitted the roof timbers with them to use in their new abode.

The interior of a cottage consisted of only one room in which everyone lived, ate and slept. It was normal in winter for the cow also to be accommodated inside the building, at the end away from the fire; and this arrangement suited both man and beast since each benefited from the extra warmth thus generated. Later in the century it became the practice to erect internal partitions separating the humans from the livestock. There was little furniture, perhaps only a few stools and a wooden chest. Bedsteads were still very rare at this time. The peasant and his family wrapped themselves in plaids and slept on beds of heather strewn over the earthen floor.

Food, prepared in an iron pot suspended from a triangle over an open hearth fire, was served up in a large wooden dish, a cross between a bowl and a platter. There were no individual plates, but each member of the family did have his or her own "personal" horn spoon. As soon as the bowl of food was placed before them it was a case of each man for himself and "de'il tak' the hindmost". Wooden bowls, or cogies, were used for drinking.

The peasants' food was not only in very short supply but most uninteresting as well. Grey oats, dried in the pot and then ground in a quern, formed their staple diet; and not all the gastronomic ingenuity of a Mrs Beaton, far less an eighteenth century peasant's wife, could turn such tasteless material into appetising fare. Kail yards were becoming more popular about that time, and these greens, boiled in salt and water, no doubt provided a welcome change. Few peasants could spare land for anything but grain crops, but some of the larger farmers grew peas and beans for their own consumption. Those who lived near any of the rivers could get plenty of salmon since there was seldom any restriction on taking them, except where the proprietor himself netted. The only chance a peasant had of meat was if he owned a beast that died or was killed at Martinmas; most of the carcase would then be sold, for that was their only way of getting cash, but some of the meat would be retained and salted. Eels were a popular local food at about that time. They were caught in large numbers in the autumn, salted in barrels and roasted in winter for food. One wonders how a present-day Gallovidian would react if presented with a dish of this eighteenth century delicacy!

Tobacco must be mentioned here, for it was the only luxury and extravagance that the peasants enjoyed. A local minister of that period, commenting on this habit of his parishioners, wrote: "The common people are great chewers of tobacco . . . therefore let not a traveller want an ounce or two of roll tobacco in his pocket, and for an inch or two thereof he need not fear the want of a guide either by night or day." A little later in the eighteenth century the tobacco craving was satisfied in a more genteel and sociable way in the form of snuff, and the tedium of many a weary sermon was relieved by the passing of the snuff mull. The smoking of tobacco in a well-seasoned clay was also popular, especially among the tinkers —and even among women.

The dress of the local inhabitants was very crude, even for those times. All of it was home-made, for only a few of the richer gentry could afford to buy materials from outside the area. The men wore suits of waulked plaiding, a mixture of coarse black and white wool, undyed, and with a rather mottled appearance. Strips of this same material, sewed together, provided them with hose. Shirts were also made of wool, and once put on they were not removed for months, when new they were probably very rough and "scratchy", and it must have taken some time for the wearer to "break in" a new one. One minister of Tongland in the early eighteenth century expressed his disgust at the lack of personal hygiene among his parishioners and roundly scolded them because they changed their shirts only twice a year, at Whitsun and Martinmas.

Men, women and children invariably went barefoot, except when going to church or during the coldest weather, when they wore crude, single-soled shoes. Footwear and headgear were provided by itinerant shoemakers and tailors; the latter also made up dresses and suits from the peasants' home-woven materials. Most of the lairds were so poor that they too patronised these travelling tailors and had their clothes made from the same coarse plaiding. In fact the only way one could distinguish a laird from one of his cottars was that the former wore a hat and the latter a "bunnet". The blue Kilmarnock bonnet was the favourite headgear of the Galloway peasant, and he wore it almost continuously from the moment of purchase—even in bed and in church; he only removed it for the prayers and the singing of psalms in church on Sunday, and during the strictly observed family worship in his cottage each evening.

Women's dresses were made of the same coarse plaiding as the men's and were no doubt rather shapeless affairs. At home the older women wore shawls over their heads and girls went bareheaded. Their only concession to finery was the wearing of coarse linen mutches or "toys'", as they called them then, when they went to church or to market.

## NO TRADE OR TRANSPORT

Conditions in the burghs were in no better shape, and reports to the Convention of Royal Burghs in 1692 reveal their state of dire poverty at about that time. All of the towns were saddled with a great weight of debt, for their common good funds, which depended largely on customs duties on trade, had then no source of revenue. Each of the burghs had to impose special taxes on the inhabitants in order to pay the interest on existing loans and, in addition, they were forced to borrow still more money every year to meet the deficit between current income and expenditure. All this had been brought about because trade was at a complete standstill.

Whithorn, Wigtown and Kirkcudbright had all been flourishing seaports and commercial centres for two or three centuries before the religious troubles broke out, and Stranraer and Portpatrick were capable of expansion. In 1692, however, all reported that they had no foreign trade—that included England—and no ships suitable for engaging in it. Indeed, the only vessels in Galloway at that time were a small eight-ton ship newly built in Kirkcudbright, and four herring boats in Stranraer, which were idle because there was no market for their catches. None of the burghs had any inland trade to speak of, not more than could be carried by a few pack horses from Ayr or Dumfries. Apart from a little surplus wool, Galloway had nothing to sell, and consequently no money to buy.

Kirkcudbright and Wigtown, which had formerly been the most prosperous trading burghs, were the hardest hit by the depression. Both admitted in their returns to having a considerable amount of dilapidated property, and in Kirkcudbright the town council reported that over half of the houses in the burgh were "aither waist or ruinous." Local lairds had long since given up their habit of having a "town house" in the county capital, the wealthy merchant class had disappeared, and their properties fell into disrepair and ruin, for no one had money to buy or maintain them.

In 1720 Kirkcudbright town council was still complaining about the lack of civic pride among the townspeople: first of all because of the number of tumble-down properties in the town, some even in the high street, which they said was an eye-sore to visitors; and secondly because the citizens had formed the deplorable habit of depositing "yr dung and making yr middens on the King's heigh street and at the market cross and at uther public places." It was at about this date too that Kirkcudbright had to give up using the tolbooth as a prison, because it was in such a ruined condition that the prisoners simply walked out, and the burgh could not afford to pay town officers to keep permanent guard on them.

Means of communication were almost non-existent in the early eighteenth century, but since there was nothing to transport anyway this was of little importance. There were no wheeled vehicles in Galloway of that time, not even a farm cart. All long distance travelling was done on horseback, along dusty tracks between the main towns and villages; goods were carried in creels or panniers by pack horses. Most rivers had to be forded, for there were no bridges, but ferries operated at Kirkcudbright over the Dee, and from what is now Creetown to Wigtown.

From about 1662, when the military created a line of post houses between Carlisle and Portpatrick, there was a recognised route through Galloway beginning at Devorgilla's Bridge in Dumfries, passing by Lochrutton, Haugh of Urr, Carlingwark Loch and then following roughly the line of the present road to Stranraer. This, however, was little more than a well-beaten track and useless for wheeled traffic.

As was the case in other parts of Scotland, the first proper roads and bridges in Galloway were built chiefly for military reasons. On several occasions during the 30 years following the 1715 Rebellion there were threats of combined Jacobite and French landings in the west of Scotland, and the coast of Galloway was considered a likely place for these. Between 1730-60 the first metal road through the province, from Dumfries to Portpatrick, was completed, as well as several side roads leading to Kirkcudbright and up the valleys of the Glenkens and the Cree; all of these were, in the words of the government contract, "passable for travellers, wheelcarts and carriages." The three "old" bridges over the Dee at Tongland, Grennyford (Threave) and Mossdale were all built for £1000 in 1737 by John Neilson of Corsock and Antony McKie of Netherlaw, who were the contractors appointed by the commissioners of supply. The first road link between the Stewartry and the Shire was made in 1745 with the building at a cost of £750 of a stone bridge over the Cree at Minnigaff.

It must be mentioned that the Church was responsible for the construction of several bridges in the south-west. In 1703, for example, a stone bridge was built over the Blackwater of the Dee between Craignell and Clatteringshaws, where the river was unfordable except in the driest weather; and soon after this others were erected over the rivers Bladnoch, Stinchar and Doon. Since the government refused to pay for these, the cost was met by door to door collections taken up by ministers and elders throughout the whole Synod of Galloway.

## THE LEVELLERS

All over Galloway, on fine nights during the winter of 1723, bands of men, sometimes as many as a hundred strong, could be seen creeping along behind the numerous drystane dykes that criss-crossed the land. At a word from their leader each man took up his position about two paces away from his neighbour and firmly inserted his "kent"—a stout oak stave about six futt long—at the base of the dyke. On the command "Ower wi't, boys! " every man levered with all his strength, and down went some 200 yards of carefully constructed drystane dyke. No time was wasted in jubilation, for the operation had to be repeated many more times before dawn. A well-trained band of levellers could demolish several miles of dyke in one night.

The disturbances caused by these levellers had been triggered off by the efforts of a number of Galloway land-owners to change and improve their methods of farming. The 1707 Treaty of Union had opened the English markets to Scottish beef cattle, and lairds and some of the wealthier tenant farmers were trying to cash in on this trade by the raising and fattening of stock. The most efficient way of doing this was by dividing their land into fields and enclosing them by drystane dykes. In this way they were able to control the grazing of the beasts and to look after them more economically. Moreover, those proprietors who leased part of their land soon discovered that they could get much higher rents for farms where the fields were enclosed.

For centuries, however, it had been the tradition that all cottars employed on estates and farms should have the right of free pasturage for their few beasts on the lairds' grazing lands; and to many this was an essential part of their livelihood. Now, the first areas to be enclosed were always the so-called "common pastures", and when this took place the peasants were no longer able to keep any livestock. Before there were any dykes, many were employed in looking after the stock day and night in the summer, keeping them off the cultivated land. The majority of these herds were now thrown out of work and usually out of their cottages as well, because the lairds wanted the peasants' rigs of arable land for still more grazing. As the stock-farming profits increased land-owners retained and enclosed more and more of their land for their own use by dispossessing the small tenant farmers, an easy matter since their leases were invariably on a year-to-year basis.

Writers of the period have left moving eye-witness accounts of the hardships suffered by those peasants who were rendered homeless. For example, during May, 1723, in the Kirkcudbright area alone, one laird evicted 16 families, a second 13 families, and a third 10 families; and "they were not allowed to erect any shelter or covering at the dyke sides to preserve their little ones from the injury of the cold." This was happening all over Galloway, and commentators of that time were comparing it with the persecutions of covenanting days. The fact that many of the land-owners responsible for the evictions were comparative new-comers to Galloway was another cause for complaint. In many cases the forfeited estates of covenanting land-owners had been given to episcopalians from England or other parts of Scotland, and they, or their sons, still owned them. Because of this, some of the peasants regarded the evictions as a continuation of the presbyterian-episcopalian struggle.

A popular ballad of the time, entitled "The Levellers Lines," described in detail the cause of the sufferings of the evicted peasants. A brief quotation will be sufficient to give the gist of the poem:

The lords and lairds they drive us out
  From maillings where we dwell;
The poor man says, "Where shall we go?"
  The rich says, "Go to hell!"

These words they spoke in jest and mocks,
  But by their works we know
That if they have their herds and flocks
  They care not where we go.

Against the poor they still prevail
  With all there wicked works,
And will enclose both moor and dale
  And turn corn fields to parks.

The levellers' campaign against the land-owners was planned when hundreds of peasants from all over Galloway assembled in June 1723 for their great social events of the year—the Kelton Hill Fair, held about two miles from Castle-Douglas. Tempers were running high and, before they returned home the peasants had decided on wide spread "strike action" in every parish where enclosures had been made.

Six months later they were very few dykes left standing in Galloway. Indeed the success of the operation may be gauged by the fact that during the latter part of the eighteenth century it was customary to point out certain dykes and comment on them as being the only ones in Galloway which survived the activities of the levellers. These dykes were: one on the Threave estate on the road to Rhonehouse; several on the lands of Palgowan in Minnigaff; and a march dyke on the estate of Baldoon.

In parts of the Stewartry the levellers' activities reached such alarming proportions that the troops had to be called in to restore order. Over 500 angry peasants met together in November, 1723, and, with no attempt at concealment, swept through the parishes of Kelton, Buittle, Rerrick, Kirkcudbright, Twynholm, Tongland and Balmaghie, razing every dyke they came across. Nor did they stop at dyke-breaking, but stole cattle and did other damage to property as well. The local landowners realising that the situation was now completely out of hand, sent for help; and detachments of dragoons were rushed in from Ayr, Dumfries and even Edinburgh.

There were several skirmishes between the rioters and the dragoons, but as the latter were under strict orders not to use their swords except in self-defence, little serious harm was done. Eventually, however, the two sides drew up in battle array on the braes of Culquha in the parish of Tongland, and it seemed as if a fight was imminent. The levellers, with nearly a a thousand men, many of them old soldiers, easily outnumbered the troops, but the latter were better armed. Probably everyone, except for some of the more violent agitators, was greatly relieved when a truce was agreed on; and, after some assurances had been given by the landowners as to some relaxation in the evictions the majority of the levellers dispersed quietly.

Nevertheless, several hundred of the insurgents reformed and continued their rioting and destruction in the parish of Balmaghie. They were finally defeated by the dragoons at Duchrae, and some 200 of them were taken prisoner. As they were being marched to Kirkcudbright, however, many of them were allowed to escape, only the ring-leaders being safely guarded. The chief culprits were punished by imprisonment, transportation and fines, but none of them was hanged.

It was most fortunate for all concerned in this rebellion that the commander of the dragoons, a Major O'Neill, happened to be an unusually enlightened and humane officer. Had he not restrained his men from the unnecessary shedding of blood, there might well have been a most awful massacre, followed by a really serious up-rising. As it was, this officer displayed commendable restraint in his handling of the affair and clearly had considerable sympathy for the grievences of the peasants. The answer he gave when several of the landowners complained about his leniency to the rebels not only revealed Major O'Neill's humanity but also provided an interesting comment by an unbiased observer on the condition in Galloway at that time:

" When I was sent here in command of the troops," O'Neill wrote, " my instructions were to suppress rebellious mobs, instead of which I find an oppressed, persecuted, suffering people, committing some irregularities; and I think it below the dignity of his majesty's field officers to act severely to such a people."

Many Gallovidians must have wished that there had been more dragoon officers of Major O'Neill's calibre during the covenanting struggle.

## A STATE OF LAWLESSNESS

In those days a period of economic depression was inevitably accompanied by a wave of unrest. There was no form of relief for people who were unemployed or turned out of their homes, except for some charity—not always welcome—from the church. Those peasants who were prevented from making a living off the land had three courses open to them: they could rebel, as the levellers did; they could emigrate; or they could throw in their lot with one of the band of gipsies who roamed Galloway at that time.

A large number of the dispossed persons did emigrate. The very few who had saved enough cash to pay their passages were lucky, for they could make a fresh start as free men in the New World. Most emigrants, however, had to accept "assisted passages" provided by plantation owners in Virginia and the West Indies, who were always on the look-out for cheap white labour. In return for a " free " passage the emigrant bound himself and his family to work virtually as slaves for a number of years before he was freed from his contract. A number of Galloway emigrants eventually prospered, and even became plantation owners, especially in the West Indies, the most common settlement for exiles from this area.

During the early eighteenth century Galloway was infested with gipsies, and it was no accident that Sir Walter Scott should have introduced Meg Merrilees and her tribe into his novel "Guy Mannering," which is set in the Stewartry. There were two powerful tribes of gipsies in Galloway of that time, one of them led by the redoubtable Billy Marshall and the other by the equally formidable but lesser known William Baillie. The gipsies described themselves as tinkers, makers of horn spoons, horse dealers, and retailers of sand from Loch Dee, specially suitable for sharpening scythes; but in reality they lived chiefly by stealing or by the still more profitable " protection racket." This took the form of intimidating farmers in isolated places until they were forced to pay up or have their stock stolen and their crops burned.

Scores of gipsies who were arrested, sometimes for the most trivial offences, received the severest punishment possible under the acts of parliament against sorners, vagrants and Egyptians. In Kirkcudbright the normal method of dealing with a gipsy convicted of some small offence was to have him burned on both cheeks, taken to Dumfries and whipped on the naked shoulders from one end of the bridge to the other. Then, if he returned to the Stewartry he could be arrested on sight, imprisoned for six months, flogged monthly and burned again on the cheeks. The magistrates of Dumfries imposed similar sentences on their unwanted vagrants, but reversed the banishment process geographically. All this, of course, did nothing to solve the problem of the gipsies, who were often so powerful anyway that they could defy the law with impunity.

The 1715 Jacobite Rebellion caused a brief flutter of excitement in Galloway during the autumn of that year. It had been intended at one time that the Old Pretender would land at Kirkcudbright, and the Earl of Nithsdale, Viscount Kenmure and Basil Hamilton of Baldoon mustered some 900 men in readiness. When the landing did not materialise these Jacobite forces moved into northern

England to assist in the rising there. The Galloway presbyteries, however, were solidly behind the government, many local inhabitants enlisted in the forces, and the synod called for volunteers and ordered financial help to be given to them. The minister of Urr, the Rev. John Hepburn, who had some military experience, trained and led 323 of his parishioners to Dumfries to help in the defence of that town against the expected attack of the Jacobites. When it was all over, no harm had come to Galloway, except that the estates of Nithsdale, Kenmure and Baldoon were all forfeited.

The 1745 Rebellion did not affect Galloway at all, although there were numerous rumours between 1715-45 that Bonnie Prince Charlie would land with a French army on the Solway coast. It was this threat that caused the government to send spies to survey Galloway for possible landing places, and one of these visitors made the following interesting comment in a report in 1722: "Kirkcudbright is an ancient town with the prettiest navigable river I have seen in Britain. It runs as smooth as the Medway at Chatham; and there is depth of water and room enough to hold all the fleet in England."

During the early eighteenth century crimes of violence were unusually common in the towns, and the burgh records of both Wigtown and Kirkcudbright describe numerous instances of what the latter calls "bluidy batterie and ryot." It is rather surprising to discover who many of the participants in these breaches of the peace were—magistrates, landowners, excisemen, merchants, schoolmasters. In these days it was apparently the custom for all men of any importance, except perhaps for ministers, to go armed, and they certainly did not hesitate to use their weapons in the settlement of arguments. Straightforward murder, duelling and brawls between the supporters of different factions were frequent occurrences.

After the middle of the eighteenth century, however, Galloway was free of disturbances, almost for the first time for centuries, and was at last able to settle down to increasing prosperity.

## CHAPTER XXIII

# A CENTURY OF PROGRESS

### IMPROVEMENTS IN AGRICULTURE

THE hundred years from 1750-1850 was the greatest period of economic progress in the history of the province; and it would be generally true to say that, in relation to the rest of Scotland, Galloway was more prosperous a century ago than she is at present. In the mid-nineteenth century most villages were then twice as large as there are now, each one offered plenty of jobs in a wide variety of rural trades and crafts, and in addition there were quite a number of cottage industries providing employment for many of the women.

During the hundred years under consideration the population of Galloway rose from 37,671 to 86,510—the latter being the census figure in 1851 and the highest ever recorded. (A population table is given at the end of the book.) This rapid increase in population resulted, of course, from a number of different causes which do not concern us here. But what is of importance is the fact that Galloway was then able to support its own inhabitants adequately in the parishes in which they were born, and still have a considerable surplus of agricultural produce available for export.

The tremendous improvements made in farming methods were largely responsible for the increased prosperity of Galloway, and this was accompanied by a boom in trade generally. Agriculture and commerce were both greatly stimulated by the provision of excellent sea communications—especially when the steamship arrived on the Solway—by the construction of passable roads and finally, of course, by the advent of the railway.

Ever since the earliest Stone Age pastoralists tended their herds of goats on the moors and hills the chief type of agriculture in Galloway has been stock-raising. In the early days of our story the province was renowned for its breed of horses; later, in the Middle Ages, it was "Galloway for 'oo"—a reminder of the important part always played by sheep in the economy of the province. By the middle of the eighteenth century, however, many of the more progressive farmers were developing a new variation in agriculture—the breeding and rearing of beef cattle, mainly for the ever-expanding English markets.

The first Galloway farmer to specialise in beef production was Lord Basil Hamilton, who was married to one of the Dunbars of Baldoon and looked after the lands there. In the 1690s he imported six score of cows from Ireland, which then had the best beef cattle, and used them to improve the local breed. About 1730 Galloway cattle were still horned, but soon after that breeders began to cross local cows with hornless bulls of some unknown breed from Cumberland. After prolonged breeding experiments they eventually produced animals which were without horns, hardy and so greatly increased in size that, by the early nineteenth century, carcase weights of 70-80 stone are quoted as being common and some are recorded of over 100 stone. The quality of their beef was also excellent that in the 1830s Galloways sold at Smithfield often fetched up to 1/- a stone more than the best English beef. The Rev. Samuel Smith, of Borgue, a noted authority on agricultural matters, writing in 1810, described an ideal Galloway bullock as follows:

"He is straight and broad in the back, and nearly level from the head to the rump, closely compacted between the shoulder and the ribs, and also betwixt the ribs and the loins—broad at the loins, not however with hooked bones or projecting knobs; so that when viewed above, the whole body appears beautifully rounded. He is deep in chest, short in the leg, and moderately fine in the bone—clean in the chop and in the neck. His head is of moderate size, with large rough ears, or heavy eyebrows, so that he has a calm, though determined look. His well proportioned form is clothed with a loose and mellow skin, adorned with long soft glossy hair."

Thus, by that time, the famous Galloway breed had been developed, and judges had already formulated the rules for testing its quality.

While the pastoralists were laying the foundations of the beef cattle trade, the arable farmers were also experimenting with new methods. Shell marl was first used as a fertiliser for crops as early as 1730, but it was not until 1765 that it became widely used in the Stewartry. Large deposits of marl were then discovered in Carlingwark Loch in the parish of Kelton, and Gordon of Greenlaw drained part of the loch by cutting a canal through to the Dee, about a mile away. The marl was transported by barges all up the Glenkens and carried by pack horses and carts—just coming into use—to other districts. Farmers were delighted with it; at last, they thought, they had found the ideal fertiliser, for it produced bumper crops. They were soon to discover, however, that when used to excess the marl quickly exhausted the fertility of the soil, and proprietors had to restrict its use to only three crops in succession. Later in the century, as shipping facilities to the Solway ports improved, lime imported from Cumberland proved a more satisfactory substitute.

By about the beginning of the nineteenth century Galloway farmers had discovered the excellence of bone meal as a fertiliser, specially for potatoes, a crop which was then becoming popular. In fact Galloway was one of the first districts in Scotland to produce this crop when they were introduced by William Hyland from Ireland in 1725. He grew the potatoes on his farm near Kirkcudbright and then transported them by pack horse to Edinburgh where the were so scarce and dear that they were sold by the pound, and even by the ounce.

One of the best known of all the Scottish "improvers" was William Craik of Arbigland, who lived from 1703-98 and introduced many of the new English agriculture methods to the Stewartry during the second half of the eighteenth century. He enclosed his land, drained the fields with the old-fashioned stone drains, dressed them judiciously with lime and observed a strict rotation of crops and pasture. Probably his greatest achievement, however, was the introduction of crops which could provide winter feeding for his cattle. He pioneered the use of lucerne grasses for improved hay and also the sowing of turnips, by machine, in drills. Another of Craik's mechanical innovations was the light English plough which could be drawn by only two horses and was a remarkable improvement on the old Scottish implement pulled by a team of four or more.

At the same time, in the western half of the province, the earls of Galloway and Stair were completely changing the state of agriculture in Wigtownshire. As soon as the lease of each of his farms expired, the earl of Galloway retained it for himself for a year or two. In that time he built a new farm-house and steading, erected dykes, dressed the fields with shell or lime, reclaimed unproductive land by draining or burning, and then re-let the farm, usually on a nineteen-year lease at anything up to ten times its former rent. On his estate at the Inch, near Stranraer, the earl of Stair was effecting similar improvements, and the old Statistical Account gives two instances of the consequent increase in the valuation of his farms: "One farm which, preceding 1790, was let for the sum of £7 2s 6d now rents at £195; and another was rented at £48 4s 8d and is now let at £245.

The same earl of Stair must be given credit for re-introducing the practice of afforestation to Galloway by planting out tens of thousands of trees, shrubs and hedgerows on his estate. As has been already mentioned, the south-west was almost denuded of trees in the early eighteenth century; so much so, in fact, that when the mid-steeple building was being erected in Dumfries in 1703, the nearest suitable timber that could be obtained had to be transported from the Cree valley. Another enthusiastic forestry pioneer, as well as agricultural improver, of the same period was Lord Daer, son of the earl of Selkirk, who looked after the estate of St. Mary's Isle at Kirkcudbright. There he had a permanent 20-acre nursery for seedlings which were then planted out, not only in woods but also along hedge-rows and fences. Lord Daer was responsible for another pleasant innovation, inspired perhaps by the fruit growing monks at near-by Dundrennan during the middle ages; this was the provision of an orchard at every farmhouse on his estate. This example in afforestation set by these two noblemen was soon followed by other landowners all over Galloway and must have completely transformed and greatly enhanced the beauty of the countryside.

One of the most successful experiments in land reclamation was carried out about the beginning of the nineteenth century by George Maxwell of the Munches, when he converted some 400 acres of bog on his estate on the west bank of the Urr estuary, into fertile and productive land. This area was formerly covered with water, two to three feet deep in places, mosses and rushes. First of all, wide open ditches were excavated to remove most of the surface water, and then covered-in drains, made of stones and filled in with heather and brushwood, were dug in herring-bone pattern across the ground to drain the sub-soil. The dried out growth of moss and reeds was burned and, year after year, great quantities of shells were ploughed in, until the underlying blue clay was gradually turned into rich black loam. No one seeing the field of lush green grass that now cover these 400 acres would ever imagine that this land was once a useless bog. That whole process of land reclamation on the Munches estate, which took many years to accomplish, is but one example of the ingenuity and patience of the early improvers who, with only crude tools and implements and a minimum of scientific and technical knowledge, did so much to build up the agricultural prosperity of Galloway.

About 1830 the conservative beef-raising farmers of Galloway were shocked to observe the ever-increasing numbers of Ayrshire cattle appearing on some of the farms in the province, and they viewed this sordid "commercialisation" of agriculture with the utmost distaste. One Wigtownshire writer, in 1838, declared angrily that "farmers believe that the very sight of Ayrshire cows in the neighbourhood corrupts the native breed" and that these new-fangled dairy cattle would assuredly "contaminate the Galloway breed and perhaps displace it altogether." The main talking point in farming circles at that time was undoubtedly "beef or milk," and a Stewartry observer probably summed up the whole controversy rather more shrewdly when he wrote, in 1841: "The dispute is settled in this way: those who can afford to indulge in luxuries retain the Galloway; while those to whom quantity is an object of importance—as the keepers of dairies—adopt the Ayrshire breed of cows." The rapidly increasing population everywhere had created a rising demand for milk, butter and cheese, and Galloway's naturally heavy crops of grass made dairying a profitable business. Thus, by the middle of the last century, dairy farming was well established in this area.

By that time too the rearing of blackface sheep had become the staple trade of the hill farms, some of which often carried a few score of Highland cattle as well; not Galloways, it will be noted—they were treated more considerately in those days. Many lowland farms, in addition to breeding cattle for beef or milk, bought in lambs, mostly Cheviot-Leicester crosses, for fattening on turnips in the field, as well as store cattle from Ireland. Considerably more grain, especially oats, was grown in Galloway a century ago than is the case now; in one year, for example, 11,250 quarters of grain were shipped from Palnackie alone. Details of shipping exports, given later in the chapter, will show how the excellent sea communications in operation from about 1800 onwards opened up, through Liverpool, a great new market in Lancashire for Galloway's agricultural produce. It was indeed a great day for the farmers when the first steam-ships appeared in the Solway.

## SHIPPING AND SMUGGLING

Between 1750-1850 nearly all Galloway's external trade was seaborne, and during this period almost every town and village on the coast came to have its own harbour, or at least a pier, through which the bulk of the trade passed. The following table showing the number of sailing ships registered in and belonging to Galloway ports gives some indication of the rising importance of sea communications at that time:

| | 1790 | 1801 | 1818 | 1840 |
|---|---|---|---|---|
| Kirkcudbright | 28 | 37 | 44 | 54 |
| Wigtown | 27 | 25 | 43 | 64 |
| Stranraer | 18 | 44 | 52 | 34 |
| Palnackie | — | — | — | 20 |

Some of the boats were as large as 180 tons, but the average size seems to have been about 60-70 tons. The drop in Stranraer's figures in 1840 was the result of increasing competition by steamships from other ports in the Clyde trade. In the Solway, however, sailing vessels remained popular and continued to operate until the early years of this century.

In 1835 the first steamship, appropriately named The Countess of Galloway, came into regular service to the ports of the Solway. It made two weekly trips between Liverpool and Kirkcudbright, calling at other harbours on the way. In 1840, by taking the train to Liverpool and then the steamer, it was possible for travellers to have breakfast in London one day and in Kirkcudbright the next. This first passenger vessel was quickly followed by other steamers which concentrated on freight carrying, and the speed and regularity of their sailings were a tremendous benefit to exporters of livestock and perishable agricultural produce.

Imports, mostly from Liverpool and Whitehaven but also from the Clyde, consisted of coals, lime, fertilisers, slates, timber, ironmongery, clothing and other manufactured goods of all kinds. Once again a few statistics will most quickly illustrate the volume and nature of this seaborne trade.

In 1830 Wigtown exported 5000 tons of agricultural products and imported 6500 tons of goods. Kirkcudbright's exports in one year, between 1842-43, were 5268 quarters of oats, 338 qrs. of barley, 50 qrs. of wheat, 6 qrs. of beans, 8 tons of meal, 688 tons of potatoes, 7840 stones of wool, 60 tons of turnips, 4 tons of rye-grass seed, 721 black cattle and 12,005 sheep.

Even tiny harbours like Palnackie at the mouth of the River Urr were handling an extraordinary amount of trade. In 1835, for example, Palnackie exported 11,250 qrs. of grain, 125 tons of oatmeal, 685 tons of potatoes, 7480 fat cattle and sheep; and in that same year imports through the same port were: 24,000 cubic ft. of foreign timber, 4032 tons of coal, 33,000 bushels of lime, 18,200 bushels of bone meal, 417 tons of slates, and 1408 tons of manufactured goods.

Anyone visiting Palnackie today will be forced to wonder how such a tiny harbour could ever possibly have handled these vast quantities of goods, and just how many carts would have been required to transport them to and from the port. Similar shipments were being made, in lesser amounts no doubt, through piers in many other coastal towns and villages in Galloway: Carsethorn, Kippford, Dalbeattie, Gatehouse, Creetown, Baldoon, Garlieston, Isle of Whithorn, Portwilliam, Stairhaven, Drummore, and Port Logan, and possibly several others as well. Quite a number of these tiny ports had the added benefit of operating their own shipbuildings yards.

During the early part of the nineteenth century Portpatrick enjoyed a rather unique reputation for a variety of reasons, all of which arose from its geographical position a mere 21 miles from Ireland and at the British end of the shortest crossing of the frequently stormy Irish Channel. This made it the most popular route with humans and animals. At that time all troops going to and from Ireland went via Portpatrick, being temporarily accommodated in the large barracks which once stood there. The animals that passed through the port—cattle and horses from Ireland—had one-way tickets only, but even at that they were big business for the shipowners: in 1790 they numbered 17,000, and in 1812, the peak year, the figure rose to 20,000. All these animals were then driven on the hoof through Galloway to the English markets. By 1837, however, the import figure had dropped to only 1000, for the animals, as well as the humans, had transferred their custom to the steamers which were by then plying direct to English ports.

A weekly postal service from England and Scotland to Ireland, via Portpatrick, had been inaugurated as early as 1662, and by 1790 this had become a daily service. About 1800 the "new" military road from Dumfries to Portpatrick was completed, and four years later a mail coach was in operation daily each way, serving all towns along the road, as well as carrying the Irish mail. Although Portpatrick was then handling some 15,000 postal packets every day, the post office ceased using this route in 1849. Finally, on a lighter note, in the early nineteenth century Portpatrick was the "Gretna Green" for Irish run-away marriages. Several hundred couples who had found obstacles in the way of marriage at home crossed over from Ireland to Portpatrick and had the ceremony immediately performed there by the local minister. Although the return fare on the boat was only about 5/- each, the wedding was rather a costly business, since the minimum fee was £10 for the parson and £1 for the session clerk. The Church put a stop to the practice in 1826.

In the second half of the eighteenth century smuggling was a well-organised and highly profitable occupation in this corner of Scotland, and many Gallovidians derived more financial benefit from the contraband trade than ever they did from any of their legitimate enterprises. Landowners frequently complained that their tenants neglected their farms because they were so busily engaged in smuggling.

The south-west was ideally situated, since the main "free trade" route from France and the Isle of Man led up the Irish Channel. On the Stewartry coast there are numerous creeks and caves, such as those at Port o' Warren, Heston Isle, Borgue and Ravenshall, which were all in regular use by the smugglers, despite the constant vigilance of the customs men, one of whom was the poet Robert Burns. Several of these places claim the honour of being the hide-out of Dirk Hatterick, who was immortalised by Sir Walter Scott in "' Guy Mannering." In the Shire the contraband runners seemed to have more freedom of movement, for they sometimes landed their cargoes in broad daylight at Monreith, Portwilliam or Stairhaven, loaded them on trains of 150-200 pack horses, and conveyed them inland while the preventive men looked on helplessly from a distance.

Many landowners, magistrates and professional men, if they were not actually participating in the smuggling, certainly turned a blind eye to it and were rewarded for their connivance with kegs of brandy for themselves and bolts of silk for their wives. In those days it was not uncommon for a popular minister to open the back door of his manse in the morning and to discover a generous gift of tobacco, tea and lace left there during the night by some unknown benefactor. Some ministers were even more deeply implicated in the trade, for at least one, the Rev. Mr Carson of Anwoth, was deprived of his living in 1767 because of his smuggling activities.

In Wigtownshire, where the coast was not so well provided with caves as that of the Stewartry, hiding places were often cunningly constructed underneath farm buildings. One farm had an ordinary cellar beneath the house and a second secret one below that, with entrance to it by a trap door concealed in the earthen floor of the upper one. When this particular hoard, at Clone in Wigtownshire, was discovered and raided in 1777 the customs officers found 80 chests of tea, 140 ankers of brandy, 200 bales of tobacco, and many other dutiable goods. Another successful hiding-place was a cavern excavated under the stone-floor of a grain-drying kiln where a fire was kept burning whenever customs men were in the neighbourhood. The preventive men rarely succeeded in making a haul, but when they did they were well rewarded. In the case of the seizure of contraband mentioned above the lieutenant in charge of the raiding party received-£269 14/- in prize-money, the sergeant £42 16/10, and others similar awards according to their ranks.

## FLOURISHING INDUSTRIES

It was during this period, 1750-1850, that Galloway was for the only time in its history an industrial area producing quite a variety of consumer goods.

First of all there were the cottage industries which manufactured goods not only for the local but also for the export market. Most cottars' wives were adept at the spinning wheel, some had their own hand-looms as well, and there were quite a number whose skill with the needle brought them a good income from piece-work they did for manufacturers outwith Galloway. Throughout this period practically all the local inhabitants' clothing, woollen or linen, was home-produced and home-made. Besides spinning and weaving their own woollen garments, the local women provided large quantities of thread to be used in mills in Dumfries and elsewhere. A fair amount of flax was grown locally and some was imported from Ireland and Holland. Although there were a number of lint-mills in Galloway, much of the flax was spun by women in their own homes, and all the linen clothing worn by the common folk was manufactured locally. Only the minister and the laird could afford to purchase the finer material from outside the province.

At this time too a great deal of raw cotton was spun by the cottar's wives, many of whom were also expert lace-makers. Some of this manufacturing was carried out by the local people themselves as private enterprises, but in most cases the raw materials were supplied and the work "farmed out" by factories or agents in Ayrshire. In 1838, for example, the minister of Kirkcolm stated that in almost every home in his parish young women were employed in embroidering muslin webs obtained from Ayrshire or Glasgow, and earned as much as 1/3, and sometimes more, a day at this work.

In the early 1800's many places in Galloway had factories, with machinery driven by water-power, whose products could compete with those of the steam-powered industrial areas of other parts of Britain. At the village of Sorbie in Wigtownshire there was a nationally famous damask mill which in 1800 won the highest award for this material at an exhibition in Edinburgh. This factory, which had been in existence since about 1780, was still providing employment for 100 men in 1840. Its damask products were so popular with the nobility that its fame spread, and orders poured in from all over Britain. In the same parish, at the village port of Garlieston, a well-known ropeworks produced most of the ropes required in the Solway shipping trade.

There was a flourishing woollen mill making blankets, plaidings and flannels at Kirkcowan, and at Glenluce a dye-mill and flax-mill. The distillery at Bladnoch in the 1830s was converting 16,000 bushels of barley into whisky every year and employing some 30 men. Kirkcudbright, which had once supplied footwear for the covenant army during the Bishops' War, was still noted for its leather manufactures, especially shoes and gloves, and the products of one shoe factory, employing 24 men in the 1840's were famed far beyond the boundaries of the province. Dalbeattie had a paper-making factory and, later in the century, a brick-works which turned out excellent bricks and tiles from the extensive local deposits of blue clay.

It was the cotton boom which was chiefly responsible for the rise of three towns—Newton Stewart, Castle Douglas and Gatehouse of Fleet. Newton Stewart obtained its first charter as a burgh from a son of the earl of Galloway in 1677, but was still little more than a tiny village when Sir William Douglas tried to change it to an industrial town at the end of the eighteenth century. This William Douglas was a native of Galloway who had made a fortune as a planter and privateer in the West Indies and had returned to his native heath with the ambition of making a name (and a title) for himself as a public benefactor on a big scale. He and some others invested some £20,000 in the erection of a cotton factory at Newton Stewart and changed the name of the town to Newton Douglas. But the enterprise soon failed and the town re-assumed its original name.

Sir William, however, was determined that his name would be perpetuated somewhere in Galloway, and so he purchased a large estate in the parish of Kelton, built a most ostentatious castle there at Gelston, and in 1792 obtained a charter creating the village of Carlingwark into burgh of barony with the new name of Castle Douglas. Here too Sir William established a cotton mill to provide employment for his townspeople, but once again it failed, for the same reason as in Newton Stewart—the high price of raw cotton, the lack of sufficient water power to drive machinery, and the impossibility of introducing steam-power because of the cost of coal.

Even although their careers as industrial towns had been very brief they were sufficient to establish both Newton Stewart and Castle Douglas as important centres of population in their respective counties. Before the introduction of the cotton mills about 1790 it is doubtful if the population of either town was more than about 200 people. By 1831 the population of Newton Stewart had risen to 2241 and Castle Douglas to 1848. And by the time the cotton mill had failed Castle Douglas, with its flourishing mart every Monday, had come to be recognised not only as the principal market town of the Stewartry but also as the commercial centre, where, in the words of a writer in 1840, " the shops are remarkably elegant and well furnished so as to awaken the surprise of strangers." (Indeed visitors are still making the same comment today.)

In Gatehouse of Fleet, however, the cotton industry was much more successful, probably because the founder, Murray of Cally (and also of Broughton in Wigtownshire) was sufficiently far-sighted to put the business in the hands of expert cotton manufacturers from England. Before the cotton mills came there was no village at Gatehouse, only an inn; but in 1795, a few years after the erection of the first mill, Murray obtained a charter creating Gatehouse a burgh. As soon as the cotton industry was established there was an immediate rush of workers from all round about. One English visitor in 1792 described how all kinds of people—" ploughmen, schoolmasters, tanners and apothecaries " —forsook their jobs and flocked to the mills, tempted by the excellent wages offered. (Even in those days industry was attracting people from the teaching profession.) The cotton manufacturers of Gatehouse developed a new sources of energy for their machinery—stated in 1840 to be the equivalent of 55 horse-power —by cutting a tunnel from Loch Whinyeon at a cost of £1400 and harnessing the water thus obtained to two great mill-wheels. In the 1840's the mill was producing one and a half million yards of cotton cloth annually and giving employment to 200 people. Several other smaller industries flourished in Gatehouse in the early nineteenth century—a soap factory, a brewery, a tannery, a brick works and a shipbuilding yard. Murray of Cally had cut a canal capable of taking ships of 160 tons to the sea three miles away, and the harbour at Gatehouse, in 1837, handled some 3000 tons of goods. The population of Gatehouse, which prior to 1790 was nil, had increased to 1377 by 1841.

Local granite was first used for building purposes in the province when the magnificent Cally House near Gatehouse was constructed in 1763. The work, however, had to be carried out by imported masons since none of the local builders then had the tools or the skill to cut and dress this exceptionally hard stone. Granite had still not come into regular use when the beautiful Telford-designed bridge over the Dee at Tongland was built between 1804-8; the freestone blocks used in its construction were all shipped by sea from Annan. The present Cree Bridge at Newton Stewart, the first to be built of local granite, was completed in 1813 at a cost of £6000. Once again the job was done by " foreigners," the workmen being recruited this time from the Rubislaw granite quarries at Aberdeen and the contractor, Kenneth Mathieson, from Inverness. This same north-country team were also responsible for the Ken Bridge at New Galloway and the piers at Kirkcudbright and Stranraer.

By about 1830, however, Galloway masons had learned the art of handling granite and were ready for employment in this industry when the Liverpool Dock Trustees leased the granite quarries at Kirkmabreck, at Creetown, and Craignair, near Dalbeattie. Although the number of workers fluctuated according to the demand for granite, it was common between 1830-50 for the Kirkmabreck quarry to give employment to 450 men and the Craignair one to at least 250. The Liverpool Docks, the Thames Embankment in London and many famous lighthouses all over the world were built, during the nineteenth century, of granite from Creetown or Dalbeattie.

Thus, by the mid-nineteenth century Galloway was beginning to enjoy a considerable measure of prosperity. Her coastal towns were handling vast quantities of merchandise through their harbours, the inland burghs were developing as market or industrial towns, and agriculture, her basic source of wealth, was flourishing as it had never done before.

Most significant of all, however, was the fact that Galloway's rural parishes reached their peak population in 1851, when most had about twice the population that they have today. There was full employment everywhere—men on the farms or at trades and women at their cottage industries—and virtually no emigration. Country villages were almost completely self-sufficient and self-supporting. Each village had its own complement of master-tradesmen—a tailor, shoemaker, blacksmith, mason, carpenter and joiner, etc.—all of them giving work to many more journeymen and apprentices. And apart from a few grocer's commodities such as tea and sugar, every village produced nearly all its own foodstuffs.

Gallovidians of a century ago may not have had much in the way of luxuries or amenities, but at least they were adequately clothed and fed and seemed content to stay where they were.

## THE KIRK AND THE PEOPLE

Sackcloth by the bale and stools of repentance by the dozen—that was how the Church ordered these commodities in the eighteenth century, for both were in regular use in every kirk almost every Sunday. From kirk session records it appears that these instruments of correction became popular in Galloway just about the beginning of the century. To quote only one example, a minute from the Wigtown Kirk records, dated 5th March, 1702, reads: " The session appoints Mich. Shank at desire Pat Garroch, mason, to repair the Place of Public Repentance, for qh he is to be payd by the Thesaurer. Also they appoint yr officer to buy five of six ells of sackcloth, and to cause make it in a gown . . ."

Never did the Church exercise greater control over the morals and conduct of the people than during the eighteenth century. Throughout the previous century the authority of the Church had been under continuous attack. Now that the presbyterian kirk sessions had been given almost unlimited powers they were determined to wield that power with the utmost severity.

Unfortunately the gospel preached was one not of love and forgiveness but rather of repression and retribution. The minister and elders pried into the life and behaviour of every parishioner and hauled offenders before the kirk session for the slightest misdemeanour. In those days the Church authorities were more concerned with the moral behaviour of the people than with their real spiritual welfare, and it was the sins of the flesh which were considered the most serious. In the eyes of the rulers of the kirk spiritual pride seemed to be no sin at all, but indeed the hall-mark of the "elect," who being specially chosen could indulge themselves with impunity. A counterpart of Burns's "Holy Willie" was to be found in every parish in the south-west.

Church records of the eighteenth century show that even town councils were firmly under the thumb of the parish minister and his kirk session. In Wigtown, for example, the minister frequently advised the provost and councillors on some local scandal and usually succeeded in persuading the council to pass acts against it. In January, 1702, the Wigtown kirk session decided to take steps to stamp out late-night drinking in the town, and the minister was deputed to present their complaint to the town council. The following month the minister reported to the session the success of his mission: "According to the sessions appointment he had addressed the Magistrates and Town Council for the passing of an act discharging unseasonable drinking in ale-houses after ten of the clock at night: qh act is passed by the said Magistrates and Council in the terms proposed to ym by the Session." For years after this the elders of Wigtown had a rota of duty for patrolling the streets to ensure that this church-imposed licensing law was not being violated, and their reports are recorded in the minutes of the session.

Sunday drinking was mentioned as a problem in many parishes. In those days church attendance was absolutely compulsory, and it was the custom for many members who had come from some distance to repair to the ale-houses for refreshment after the morning service; and this was quite in order. The trouble arose, however, when many of them neglected to return for the afternoon diet of worship, but instead remained drinking. According to the records this pernicious practice was particularly rife in Minnigaff in the early 1700's, but the session countered it by appointing elders to take turns to visit the pubs and round up their errant flock.

Unmarried women whose conduct was not as virtuous as it might have been received special attention from Wigtown kirk session, who reported on their activities to the town council, and as a result the offenders were usually banished from the parish.

In March 1706 "the Session, considering that there are several singing young weomen that do live privately in houses in the Toun, and that thereby hath been so much sin and leudness," appealed to the council to banish these obnoxious sirens; and the council agreed. On another occasion, however, the session were not so successful, as the following minute reveals: "The minr. represents yt he addressed the Magistrates for the extruding of Agnes Stewart and other scandalous persons, unworthy to be entertained in an incorporation; but that he met with nothing but delays. Therefore he, in the name of the Session, left the Sin and Scandal of it at their doors." No doubt the town fathers had their own good reasons for not agreeing to the minister's request.

Married women who fell from grace were not let off lightly, but had to face up to the ridicule of being publicly rebuked before the whole parish, as is shown in an extract from the session records of Twynholm dated 25th April 1703: "John McKitrick and Marjory Hallum appeared in the habit of sackcloth before the congregation this day, he for the tenth time and she for the ninth, and acknowledged their guilt of the sin of adultery with one another."

It has been suggested that such treatment only made the offenders more shameless in their behaviour, and that the oftener they appeared in the place of repentance the more brazen became their attitude to the whole business. An English historian of that time made an interesting comment on this: "It has been an old observation that wherever presbytery was established there witchcraft and adultery have been particularly rampant. The records of the stools of repentance would astonish you, where such multitudes of men and women come daily to make their show for adultery and fornication, that it has almost ceased to be a shame." And presbytery was nowhere more firmly established than in Galloway. However, the apparent prevalence of fornication in this part of the country may be accounted for by an extract from the Minnigaff kirk session records: "November 1695—It is enacted yt persons driving goods on ye Sabbath shall be caused pay two pounds Scots, toties quoties, and shall be censured as fornicators besides." It seems rather a severe condemnation for pushing a barrow-load of peats on the Sunday, but it may explain quite a lot!

From the time of Knox the Church of Scotland had been

particularly vicious in its attitude towards witchcraft. (It should be mentioned perhaps that the episcopalians in Scotland had a comparatively clean record in this respect; but perhaps this was simply because they were too busy hunting covenanters to be bothered with witches.) The last witch to be burned in Galloway was Elspeth McEwen from Cubbox in the Glenkens. She was condemned by her minister and kirk session, imprisoned for two years in Kirkcudbright tolbooth and tortured to make her confess. In the end her condition became so wretched that she begged her tormentors to end her life. Her last request was considerately granted, and she was burned to death at Kirkcudbright in 1698. Witch-hunting continued well into the 1700s, but the victims were no longer killed, only banished from their parishes. The session records of both Kirkcudbright and Twynholm contain several examples of the ridiculous evidence offered by ministers and elders by way of proof against women accused of witchcraft.

It would be wrong, however, to leave the impression that the role of the Church was solely a disciplinary one. All of the session records reveal countless instances of relief given in cash and kind to the poor people and orphans of each parish. It is also interesting to note that even as early as 1700 churches in Galloway were giving help to unfortunate creatures furth of Scotland, for in December of that year Minnigaff records announce that " a collection is ordered to be made for the slaves in Algiers."

By the nineteenth century, with the rise of a more moderate race of churchmen, the kirk adopted a much more tolerant attitude towards the shortcomings of its members. Presbytery meetings became less formal and indeed often convivial affairs, and after that many a minister was glad he had brought his "man" along with him. Accounts still in existence show that in the first half of the nineteenth century whisky and brandy were large items in the grocers' bills of many ministers.

With its long tradition of religious independence it is not surprising that Galloway should have produced the leader of one of the many sects which broke away from the Church of Scotland. This was the Rev. John Macmillan, the well-loved but contumacious minister of Balmaghie. In 1703, along with the ministers of Carsphairn and Buittle he attacked the leaders of the Church for their alleged corruption and mismanagement and objected to the Church swearing allegiance to the monarch. After a bitter controversy with the presbytery and the synod, Macmillan was deposed from his parish and another incumbent appointed in his place. Macmillan, however, refused to move, and for the next fifteen years, backed by the moral and sometimes physical support of his faithful parishioners, he continued to occupy the manse, work the glebe and hold the services in the church while the "official" minister had to suffer all manner of abuse and conduct worship for a handful of folk in a barn.

Later Macmillan became the leader of the Cameronians, that "suffering remnant" of covenanters who had refused to re-unite with the parent church and had adopted for themselves the high sounding title of the "Anti-Popish, Anti-Prelatic, Anti-Erastian, Anti-Sectarian, true Presbyterian Church of Scotland." Although their official designation was Reformed Presbyterian, they were then nick-named "Macmillanites." This sect attracted a considerable following in Galloway and Nithsdale and as late as the last quarter of the nineteenth century they still had a place of worship and a small flourishing congregation in Castle Douglas.

No account of the religious bodies in Galloway in the eighteenth century would be complete without mention of the Buchanites, surely the most fantastic sect that ever practised in Scotland. Their leader was a Mrs Elspeth Buchan, born in 1738, the daughter of an innkeeper near Portsoy in Banffshire. Mrs Buchan, who claimed to have "divine vision and revelations" and to be "clothed with the sun, and the moon under her feet," gathered her first followers at Irvine in Ayrshire. Soon she had a band of over fifty enthusiastic disciples, who referred to her, at her own request, as "Friend Mother in the Lord."

About 1784 they all moved to a farm near Thornhill, where Mrs Buchan suddenly announced that the day of judgment was at hand, when she and her faithful adherents would be resurrected bodily into heaven. In order to make the ascent easier they built a great wooden platform, and on the appointed day they all mounted on this, Friend Mother in a white gown at the top. For a time nothing happened, but then came a gust of wind and down fell the tower with all its sadly disillusioned occupants. Many of her followers deserted after this physical and spiritual disaster—which their leader explained away as the result of their lack of faith—but Mrs Buchan and the remainder moved to Crocketford.

They were in fact the founders of the village of Crocketford, where they bought land, built cottages and settled down to work and worship quietly and diligently. These Buchanites were the first to introduce to Galloway the two-handed spinning wheel, and they quickly established the reputation of being able to produce finer linen yarn than any other spinners in the country.

Mrs Buchan died at Crocketford on 29 March, 1791, but before she departed she had already informed her followers that she would rise from the dead in six days, and if not then in either ten or 50 years exactly after her death. Accordingly her body was not buried, but kept above ground in its coffin in order to be ready for resurrection. There was no sign of life after either the six days or the ten years, but as the fiftieth anniversary approached the last of her disciples, Andrew Innes, was still alive and watching faithfully and expectantly over his Friend Mother's remains. Poor Andrew must have been a sadly disappointed man when again nothing happened on 29 March, 1841, but his faith was so profound that when he himself died four years later their two coffins were interred in the same grave behind his house at Crocketford. His coffin was laid above his leader's, so that if she should rise again he would be bound to do so too.

In this brief account of life in Galloway no mention has been made of scales of wages or the cost of goods. If this is done, it must be done thoroughly, relating one to the other, or not at all. Nevertheless there is one interesting comparison which might be made since it illustrates the respective positions of the minister and the schoolmaster in society over a century ago. In 1840 the minimum stipend was £150 per annum, but some Galloway ministers received as much as £292 at Kirkcowan, and £299 at Kells. Ministers, of course, also had the use of the glebe and often other perquisites as well. Schoolmasters, on the other hand, were much less fortunate, their salaries (including fees) ranging from £20-£30 per annum (the most common rate of pay) to £100 at Wigtown school, and £137 at Castle Douglas.

From the ministers' point of view, however, there was one drawback, and this arose from the fact that they were dependent for at least part of their income on the heritors of the parish, and occasionally they were slow to pay up. We find, for example, the minister of Stranraer complaining in 1839 that not only was he on the minimum stipend, but that the portion of his stipend payable by the burgh magistrates as heritors—£24 10s 8d annually —was four years in arrears. Although school teachers received much smaller salaries by comparison, there were a number of emoluments that came their way for extra service to the community as precentors, session clerks and registrars.

The standard of living of Gallovidians about a century ago was probably very much higher than that of the people of the industrial areas. Writers of that time, coming from outwith the district, give the impression that there was little to be seen in the way of poverty and they frequently comment on the well-fed and well-dressed appearance of the local inhabitants. The diet of Gallovidians a hundred years ago might by present standards be regarded as monotonous, since oatmeal in the form of porridge or oatcakes was their staple food. But in addition to this there was apparently no great shortage of milk or butter, and certainly not of cheese; and at least one contemporary writer describes their normal dinner as being of barley broth, with beef or mutton and potatoes. Perhaps he was fortunate where he dined. Nevertheless, their diet, if wholesome rather than appetising, does seem to have been adequate.

The only people who did not enjoy such good living conditions were the Irish who crossed over into Galloway in their thousands throughout the nineteenth century. Some settled down as farm servants, but the majority were largely itinerant, seeking what seasonal work might be available and living in considerable poverty when unemployed. After the 1841 census a Wigtownshire minister estimated that one person in every five in his parish was Irish, or born of Irish parents who were immigrants. About that same time the minister of Stranraer, also commenting on the great influx of Irish people, complained that their accent was tainting and even driving out the local dialect. Was this the beginning of the so-called "Wigtownshire-Irish" accent?

A century ago, long before sport had become highly organised and commercialised, Gallovidians enjoyed a number of simple games and entertainments. For example, every village and town had its quoiting ground which resounded on fine summer evenings to the cheers of the spectators and the shouts of the players as they fought out a battle against some neighbouring team. There were a number of local quoiting leagues in Galloway then, and and great rivalry existed between certain villages. The people of the coastal towns and villages enjoyed all the excitement of their annual summer regattas in which they displayed their skill and strength in sailing and rowing. This was a sport for everyone, not just for the few who could afford expensive yachts. The competitors were all working-class people, and the vessels their ordinary work-a-day boats all specially cleaned, painted and gaily bedecked for the occasion.

In the winter, when weather permitted, the most popular sport was curling, that most democratic of all games in which all rank is abandoned and laird and servant hurl abuse or approbation at each other without fear or favour. It was about this time that skating was beginning to be popular, especially with people of the middle and upper classes, who regarded it as an elegant and healthy exercise and one in which even ladies were becoming daring enough to participate. Cards, dominoes, draughts and chess were popular indoor games in the winter evenings, although as the Victorian era progressed cards came to be frowned on in the more strict presbyterian homes.

## SOME FAMOUS GALLOVIDIANS

During recent centuries Galloway cannot boast of having produced many figures who gained international or even national reputations. There are, however, perhaps half a dozen—five men and one woman—who in a variety of different ways made their mark in history and whose deeds have become known beyond the province. They therefore deserve to be mentioned here.

Galloway's chief attraction for American tourists is the birthplace of Paul Jones, the founder of the United States navy, at Arbigland on the Solway coast near Kirkbean. John Paul, which was his real name, was born there in 1747, the son of a gardener. At the age of twelve he enlisted as an apprentice in a British merchant ship and made his first voyage from Whitehaven in Cumberland. His intrepid seamanship and firm discipline gained him rapid promotion and by the age of 21 John Paul was already a captain. He adopted the surname of Jones from an American family who showed him great kindness during his frequent visits there. Paul Jones soon came to sympathise with the colonists' aspirations for independence and began to regard America as his home.

In 1775 he was appointed a lieutenant in the American navy and was largely responsible during the following decade for successfully modelling and training it on the lines of the British navy. In 1778 he paid his last visit to Galloway when, after bombarding Whitehaven, he sailed his American ship The Ranger into Kirkcudbright Bay and landed his men at St Mary's Isle with the intention of kidnapping the earl of Selkirk. But since the earl was not at home the Americans had to content themselves with carrying off his silver plate; this, however, was later returned by Paul Jones with a long letter of apology. After the American War of Independence had finished Paul Jones sought further excitement and honours by becoming a famous admiral of the Russian navy. When he died in France in 1792 the revolutionary national assembly there went into mourning in honour of a man whom they regarded as a hero because of his naval exploits against Britain.

Anyone studying an atlas of the Arctic coast to the north of Canada will find there a number of familiar Wigtownshire names: Agnew River, Cape Carrick Moore, Cape Dalrymple Hay, Port Logan, Cape MacDowall, Andrew Ross Land. These names were all put on the map by a renowned sailor and Arctic explorer, Rear Admiral Sir John Ross, a son of the minister of Inch, near Stranraer. Between 1818-1833, along with his nephew Commander James Clark Ross, he made a number of voyages in search of the north-west passage, charting a vast area of the Arctic Ocean to the north of Canada and, the most important achievement of all, establishing for the first time the true position of the North Magnetic Pole.

It has already been mentioned that Sir Walter Scott chose Galloway as the setting for " Guy Mannering," but two of his other novels, " Old Mortality,' 'and " The Heart of Midlothian " were also inspired by the lives and actions of a couple of humble Gallovidians who might never otherwise have been remembered. Although Scott never actually visited Galloway, he was supplied with a great deal of information about the province by Joseph Train, a customs officer, who spent most of his life here and died in Castle-Douglas in 1852. Train's abiding passion was antiquarian and historical research, and anything he thought might interest Scott was sent on to Abbotsford.

Old Mortality was the nick-name given to Robert Paterson, a stone engraver, who belonged to Balmaclellan, where he is commemorated by a monument in the churchyard. For a great part of his long lifetime, from 1712-1800, Paterson was a familiar figure, along with his white horse, all over the uplands of Galloway, Ayrshire and Dumfriesshire. His self-imposed mission in life was to look after the tombstones of the covenanters who had been slain during the killing times. He repaired and recarved the inscriptions and often, when no memorial existed, he himself erected and engraved a suitable stone. Because of his preoccupation with these sermons in stone, however, Old Mortality sadly neglected his family in Balmaclellan, and his wife had to keep a little school there to support herself and her children.

In 1738 Isobel Walker, of the parish of Kirkpatrick-Irongray, was condemned to death in Dumfries for the concealment of the birth and the murder of her baby. If her sister Helen had been prepared to commit perjury by saying that Isobel had informed her of the birth, then Isobel's life would have been saved, for it was the concealment that was the capital charge. But Helen's strong presbyterian conscience would not allow her to tell a lie even for such a cause, and so Isobel was sentenced to death. Helen, now full of remorse, immediately set off for London on foot, the journey taking her 14 days. There she presented a petition on behalf of her sister to the Duke of Argyll, who was so moved by the circumstances of the case that he was able to use his influence to obtain a reprieve. On leaving prison Isobel married her seducer and they lived happily in Whitehaven for the rest of their lives. Helen remained a single, hard-working and highly respected woman in her home parish until her death in 1791.

It was this sad case which, transferred to the Forth, provided Scott with the moving plot of " The Heart of Midlothian." Isobel

Walker was, of course, the original Effie Deans, and Helen the prototype of her more famous sister, Jeanie Deans. Sir Walter, by way of gratitude for such a wonderful story, and also no doubt from genuine admiration, then erected at his own expense a magnificent tombstone, with a somewhat verbose inscription composed by himself, over the grave of Helen Walker in the kirkyard at Irongray.

Alexander Murray, probably the greatest linguist that Scotland has ever produced, was the son of a hill shepherd who lived near the Palnure Burn, between Minnigaff and New Galloway. Murray was unfortunately very short sighted and consequently no use as a shepherd, and so his parents agreed to his desire for education. When he entered Edinburgh University at the age of 19, after being almost completely self-taught, Murray already had a sound knowledge of Greek, Latin, French, German, Hebrew and Arabic. At university, besides taking the normal course in divinity, he went on to master other European languages and several more oriental ones as well. From 1806-12, while he was minister of the parish of Urr, it was a regular occurrence for the Foreign Office in London to seek his aid in translating and answering communications from eastern powers. He was then appointed professor of oriental languages at Edinburgh, but he unfortunately died the following year, aged only 38, just as he seemed on the threshold of a brilliant academic career. Murray's Monument, erected on a hill not far from his birthplace, in 1834, commemorates Galloway's most learned son.

The Rev. Samuel Rutherford Crockett was undoubtedly Galloway's most distinguished literary figure. Born in the parish of Balmaghie in 1859 and educated at school in Castle-Douglas, Crockett was destined for the ministry; with such Christian names no other vocation seemed appropriate. But he much preferred writing to preaching and by the turn of the century he was established as a popular and successful romantic novelist. Several of his best stories, such as " The Raiders," and " Men of the Moss Hags " have local settings and themes, and did much to put Galloway on the English literary map. Crockett died in France in 1914 and is buried in Balmaghie churchyard; there is an elegant memorial to him in the nearby village of Laurieston.

# CHAPTER XXIV
# IN CONCLUSION

## GALLOWAY UP TO THE PRESENT DAY

This account of the Story of Galloway need not be continued in any great detail beyond the middle of the nineteenth century — for two reasons. In the first place, the Third Statistical Account, a vast mine of accurate information on all that has happened in every town and parish since about 1840, is readily available for serious historians. Another reason for not detailing specific events is that what has happened in Galloway since about 1850 has been brought about by external circumstances and influences, an experience shared by most other rural areas of Scotland. For example, the advent of the railway around 1860 and the introduction of the motor vehicle in the early years of this century had a profound effect on the economy and social life of Galloway.

Diffusionism, or the diffusion of culture and civilisation, has been blamed by many writers of the present century (for example Lewis Grassic Gibbon in "Sunset Song" and other works) for the collapse of the rural way of life in Scotland. Certainly the spread of civilisation brought many changes, not all of which have been beneficial. For the past century Galloway has no longer been "round the corner", a remote rural backwater, cut off from the main stream of civilisation and living in a golden age of rustic romanticism such as portrayed in the "kailyard' novels of S.R.Crockett. The people of Galloway have lost control of their own destiny; instead they have had to face up to, and indeed submit to the harsh realities of external economic and political pressures.

The first effect of these external pressures became apparent with the start of rural depopulation and the drift to the towns which began soon after the 1851 census, coincident with the arrival of the railway. The rapid increase in rural depopulation was not, at first, due so much to the mechanisation of agriculture as to the decline of village crafts and trades and the explosive expansion of the burghs — notably Dumfries and Stranraer at each extremity of the province, and Castle Douglas, on the main railway line, in the centre. With the advent of public transport — first the railway and then the bus services — the burghs became the main centres of trade and commerce;

and during the first half of the present century butchers, bakers and grocers had travelling vans carrying their goods to even the remotest glens of Galloway. To give only one example of the consequences of this rural depopulation, during the period 1851-1961 the total population of the Stewartry decreased by 33 per cent while the population of the burgh of Castle Douglas increased by 63 per cent, and this pattern was repeated throughout the whole area. The total population of Galloway was reduced from its maximum of 86,510 in 1851 to only 53,183 in 1985.

Villages thus declined from being self-contained economic units to being mere dormitories for a small number of people continuing to work in forestry, council jobs or in businesses in the expanding towns. The last thirty years has seen the closure of many rural schools and churches, places which used to serve as the focal points of a community's existence. Again in recent years many of the village houses have been bought up — at prices far beyond the means of potential local purchasers — as holiday cottages or by retired people from outwith the area. Welcome as some of these in-comers may be, they make little contribution to the development of the local economy.

The expansioin of the burghs was accompanied by the establishment and rapid growth of important live stock marts and many prosperous concerns in the manufacturing, retail and distributive trades. But since the second world war many of these have also succumbed to external financial pressures, and many locally owned family businesses in the towns have been forced to sell out to national multiple stores. More recently still, many of the local inhabitants do their shopping by mail-order or indulge in bulk-buying in super-markets or super-stores outwith the province.

Many local industries connected with agriculture, which were established in most of the towns in Galloway around the 1860s, continued to flourish and give employment to hundreds of workmen until about 1940. Various types of farm machinery — including milking machines, harvesters and threshing machines — were invented and manufactured in local foundries; and animal feeding stuffs and fertilisers were produced and retailed from mills situated in most of the towns. Nowadays, however, these farm services are chiefly provided by national (or international) combines, and only a very small number of local workmen are required to retail and distribute the goods.

Within the last few years the relentless march of civilisation has left its unwelcome imprint on Galloway in two other different respects. First there is the effect of the so-called "acid rain" on the lochs and forests. This wind borne, killing invader from industrial areas far outwith the province seems already to have been responsible for completely wiping out the trout population of some of the hill lochs, and, more serious still, its eventual effect on the forests and other wild life is giving grave cause for alarm. The re-forestation of Galloway during the past half century was of immense benefit locally; it engendered a great deal of employment, and the forests are still a priceless asset, both as a national investment and as a scenic attraction. Now the sulphurous fires of industry, totally alien to the area, threaten the future existence of these valuable and picturesque forests.

If proof were needed that Galloway is no longer "round the corner" from the mainstream of British trade and commerce, one has only to travel along or live near the A75 road from Dumfries to Stranraer. In recent years this has become the main thoroughfare between Britain and Northern Ireland and, as a result, the once peaceful towns and villages on the A75 are now assailed day and night by the continual noise and vibration from vast lorries. The A75 was not built to take such traffic, and a great deal more money will have to be forthcoming for the road improvements and by-passes required to reduce the menace to life and property posed by these juggernauts of civilisation.

So far, the story of Galloway during the past hundred years seems to give little cause for rejoicing, especially if one compares it with the account of happier times in the previous chapter, "A Century of Progress". Yet the outlook is not, perhaps, entirely bleak, for there are two industries which continue to thrive and which may provide some hope for the future; these are agriculture and tourism.

Despite all the vicissitudes to which agriculture has been subjected — by our own governments and more recently by the Common Market — this traditional industry has survived and prospered in varying degrees during the last hundred years. It has always been and still is the mainstay of Galloway's economic existence, giving a good livelihood not only to the farmers and farm workers but also to a host of dependent trades in the towns around. Perhaps one of the reasons for the continued success of farming lies in its diversification: sheep farming, dairy production and beef cattle. Dairying is still the basic type of farming in the lowlands of both the Stewartry and the Shire, and creameries all over the area process thousands of gallons of milk every day. Galloway Cheddar cheese is renowned and can be bought all over Britain. In the uplands the farmer still runs his

Blackface sheep in the traditional manner and derives a tidy income from his crops of lambs and wool. Hundreds of thousands of Galloway sheep are slaughtered every year and exported to the English markets. Finally there is the province's own strain of beef cattle — the Galloways — which have for years provided hardy breeding stock not only for the high lands of Britain but also for the hills of Italy, the pampas of the Argentine and the great prairies of North America. Castle Douglas auction mart is the show place and sale ring for some of the finest of Britain's Ayrshire dairy stock and for the pick of the Galloway breed. Over the years, by means of these sales, millions of pounds have poured happily into the pockets of Galloway farmers from, literally, all over the world.

Records show that over the past 180 years Galloway has had a special fascination for a particular type of visitor: one who is selective, who visits an area for a particular reason and not just for the "illuminations" or the fairground atmosphere of a popular resort. As early as 1800 tourists were making their way to the famous fish ponds at Port Logan where tame cod and other fish came to the surface at the familiar sound of the attendant's voice and were fed with titbits from her hand; this attraction existed for well over a century and a half, with only the fish and the attendants, of course, being replaced from time to time. In the Victorian years the solitude of the hills and the lochs, the keen air of the bleak moorlands, the medicinal waters of Lochenbreck Spa and other wells, the sub-tropical climate and the magnificent scenery of the coastline to be viewed at leisure during carriage drives — all of these attracted a wide variety of people. Moreover, the proximity of the province to England and the ease of access once the railway was built also contributed to Galloway's popularity with tourists from south of the Border.

Writers and artists found inspiration in the area. Early literary visitors included Wordsworth, Southey, George Borrow and R.L.Stevenson, and this century John Buchan and Dorothy Sayers spent holidays here and used the Galloway landscape as an essential background for several of their adventure tales. The "Kirkcudbright School" of artists became renowned in the world of art and exercised considerable influence on painting in the earlier years of the present century.

It is only since the last war, however, with the increase in car traffic, that tourism has become really big business for Galloway. Local authorities and private property owners who have developed caravan sites have fortunately not allowed them to become overpopulated or commercialised, and the tourist, if he wishes it, is still assured of a relaxing and restful holiday in lovely quiet surroundings. The area abounds in excellent hotels, and there are hundreds of houses all over the province which provide accommodation for bed and breakfast guests.

The reason for Galloway's popularity is perhaps the remarkable variety of the scenery and of the activities it offers to holiday makers. There can be few corners of Britain where one can find such a diversity of seascape and landscape within so small a space: for example, it is only some twenty miles from the sub-tropical vegetation of the Wigtownshire coast warmed by the Gulf-Stream to the bleak windswept 2,500 feet heights of the Galloway hills and lochs; and, in between, are the evergreen forests, the tree-lined river valleys and the lush pastures of the dairy farms. Apart from these scenic attractions, the activities available are equally varied and cater for many different types of tourist: yachting and water ski-ing on the Solway and Loch Ryan, wild fowling, hill walking, river and loch fishing, sea angling, golf on a number of courses including two of championship standard at Southerness and Stranraer, antiquarian visits to innumerable ancient abbeys and castles, ornithology on the lochs and seacoast, botanical studies among the sub-tropical trees, shrubs and plants which flourish around Port Logan and Portpatrick, or painting and craft courses at Kirkcudbright.

Tourism is thus Galloway's most important growth industry, ensuring a livelihood or, at least, a welcome source of additional income to the ever-increasing number of local families who cater for the visitors.

Although nothing can now be done to restore the rural prosperity and economic self-sufficiency that Galloway once enjoyed in the mid 1800s, its inhabitants may possibly be able to look forward to the coming century with rather more confidence. Depopulation is clearly slowing down and may soon be stabilised, if not reversed. Provided that agriculture is permitted (by government and EEC regulations) to flourish and that tourism continues to expand, the economic future of the province may well be assured; but, whatever that future holds for them, the inhabitants of Galloway will always be able to enjoy the privilege of dwelling in one of the most historic and beautiful corners of Scotland.

## POPULATION OF GALLOWAY

| | 1755 | 1801 | 1821 | 1841 | 1851 | 1871 |
|---|---|---|---|---|---|---|
| Kirkcudbrightshire | 21,205 | 29,211 | 38,903 | 41,119 | 43,121 | 41,859 |
| Wigtownshire | 16,466 | 22,918 | 33,240 | 39,195 | 43,389 | 38,830 |
| GALLOWAY | 37,671 | 52,129 | 72,143 | 80,215 | 86,510 | 80689 |

| | 1901 | 1921 | 1951 | 1961 | 1971 | 1985 |
|---|---|---|---|---|---|---|
| Kirkcudbrightshire | 39,383 | 37,155 | 30,725 | 28,877 | 27,450 | 23,033 |
| Wigtownshire | 32,685 | 30,783 | 31,620 | 29,107 | 27,335 | 30,150 |
| GALLOWAY | 72,068 | 67,938 | 62,345 | 57,984 | 54,785 | 53,183 |

*NOTES: The figures for 1755 are an estimate based on Dr Webster's census.*
*The figures for 1985 are approximate and based on District Council Returns.*
*Other figures are from government and census returns.*